## The World Bank Group

### WORKING FOR A WORLD FREE OF POVERTY

The World Bank Group consists of five institutions – the International Bank for Reconstruction and Development (IBRD), the International Finance Corporation (IFC), the International Development Association (IDA), the Multilateral Investment Guarantee Agency (MIGA), and the International Centre for the Settlement of Investment Disputes (ICSID). Its mission is to fight poverty for lasting results and to help people help themselves and their environment by providing resources, sharing knowledge, building capacity, and forging partnerships in the public and private sectors.

## The Independent Evaluation Group

### IMPROVING THE WORLD BANK GROUP'S DEVELOPMENT RESULTS THROUGH EXCELLENCE IN EVALUATION

The Independent Evaluation Group (IEG) is an independent unit within the World Bank Group. It reports directly to the Board of Executive Directors, which oversees IEG's work through its Committee on Development Effectiveness. IEG is charged with evaluating the activities of the World Bank (the International Bank for Reconstruction and Development and the International Development Association), the work of the International Finance Corporation in private sector development, and the guarantee projects and services of the Multilateral Investment Guarantee Agency.

The goals of evaluation are to learn from experience, to provide an objective basis for assessing the results of the Bank Group's work, and to provide accountability in the achievement of its objectives. It also improves Bank Group work by identifying and disseminating the lessons learned from experience and by framing recommendations drawn from evaluation findings.

# Youth Employment Programs

IEG WORLD BANK | IFC | MIGA

INDEPENDENT EVALUATION GROUP

# Youth Employment Programs

## An Evaluation of World Bank and International Finance Corporation Support

# Contents

# Abbreviations

| | |
|---|---|
| A2F | Access to Finance |
| AAA | Analytic and advisory activity |
| AFR | Africa Region |
| AGI | Adolescent Girls Initiative |
| ALMP | Active Labor Market Programs |
| APL | Adaptable Program Loan |
| CET | Center for Employment Training |
| CGA | Country Gender Assessment |
| DANIDA | Danish International Development Agency |
| DOTS | Development Outcome Tracking System |
| DPL | Development policy loan |
| DPO | Development policy operation |
| EAP | East Asia and Pacific |
| ECA | Europe and Central Asia |
| ECD | Early child development |
| EPEM | Entrenamiento para el Empleo, Honduras |
| EPL | Employment protection legislation |
| ESW | Economic and sector work |
| EU | European Union |
| e4e | e4e Initiative for Arab Youth |
| FPD | Finance and Private Sector Development |
| FY | Fiscal year |
| GATE | Growing America through Entrepreneurship |
| GBI | Grassroots Business Initiative |
| GDP | Gross domestic product |
| GEM | Gender Entrepreneurship Market |
| GMI | Guaranteed Minimum Income Program |
| GPYE | Global Partnership for Youth Employment |
| HDN | Human Development Network |
| IBRD | International Bank for Reconstruction and Development |
| ICR | Implementation Completion and Results Report |
| IDA | International Development Association |
| IDB | Islamic Development Bank |
| IEG | Independent Evaluation Group |
| IFC | International Finance Corporation |
| ILO | International Labour Organization |
| IMF | International Monetary Fund |
| ISO | International Organization for Standardization |
| KILM | Key Indicators of the Labor Market |

| | |
|---|---|
| LAC | Latin America and the Caribbean |
| LIC | Low-income country |
| LIL | Learning and Innovation Loan |
| MBA | Master of Business Administration |
| MENA | Middle East and North Africa |
| NEET | Not in education, employment, or training |
| NGO | Nongovernmental organization |
| OECD | Organisation for Economic Co-operation and Development |
| PAD | Project Appraisal Document |
| PCR | Project Completion Report (IFC) |
| PDO | Project development objective |
| PPAR | Project Performance Assessment Report |
| PREM | Poverty Reduction and Economic Management |
| PSAL | Programmatic Structural Adjustment Loan |
| SAR | South Asia Region |
| SBA | Sustainable Business Advisory |
| SDN | Sustainable Development Network |
| SIL | Specific investment loan |
| SIYB | Start and Improve Your Business |
| SME | Small and medium enterprise |
| SPL | Social Protection and Labor Strategy |
| STEP | Skills toward Employment and Productivity |
| TAL | Technical Assistance Loan |
| TEVET | Technical Education, Vocational and Entrepreneurship Training |
| TEVETA | TEVET Authority |
| TVET | Technical and vocational education and training |
| UCW | Understanding Children's Work |
| WDI | *World Development Indicators* |
| WDR | *World Development Report* |
| XPSR | Extended Project Supervision Report (IFC) |
| YEN | Youth Employment Network |

# Acknowledgments

This evaluation is a product of the Independent Evaluation Group (IEG). The report was prepared by Pia Schneider with contributions from a team of evaluators and analysts. Management oversight was provided by Vinod Thomas, Cheryl Gray, and Monika Huppi during the approach paper phase, and thereafter by Caroline Heider and Mark Sundberg. Maria Margarita Sanchez was responsible for all administrative aspects of the evaluation. William Hurlbut provided editorial support.

The Bank's project portfolio and country studies were identified by Alemayehu Ambel and Ursula Martinez. Susan Caceres, Toneema Haq, Ursula Martinez, and Pia Schneider reviewed documents for the World Bank projects. Xue Li conducted all quantitative analysis for the World Bank projects. Izlem Yenice and Geeta Batra conducted the analysis of the International Finance Corporation (IFC) portfolio and wrote the IFC chapter.

The 18 country studies were conducted by Mauricio Carizzosa (Brazil, Colombia, Turkey, and a field visit to Dominican Republic), Susan Caceres (Romania), Basil Kavalsky (Ghana, Liberia, and South Africa), Xubei Luo (China), Victoria Monchuk (Burkina Faso and Nigeria), Pia Schneider (Rwanda), and Hjalte Sederlof (Armenia, Bangladesh, Dominican Republic, Indonesia, Morocco, and Tunisia). Field visits were conducted to Dominican Republic, Ghana, Liberia, Rwanda, and Tunisia. Izlem Yenice provided private sector input to all country studies. The country studies were coordinated by Susan Caceres and Victoria Monchuk and peer-reviewed by John Eriksson. Issue notes based on the country studies were prepared by Susan Caceres and Victor Macias.

Michelle Riboud prepared a background note on the taxonomy for youth employment programs. John Middleton prepared a note on skills building. Hong Tan prepared a note on private sector development and youth employment.

Basil Kavalsky identified and reviewed 21 pieces of economic and sector work related to youth employment. Xue Li and Pia Schneider conducted the literature review and systematic review of 38 impact evaluations on youth employment programs. Amy Knaup supported this literature review. The literature review is available as a separate IEG publication.

Key informant interviews with Bank management were conducted by Victor Macias, Michelle Riboud, Pia Schneider, and Hjalte Sederlof; and with IFC management by Geeta Batra and Izlem Yenice. Victor Macias conducted and analyzed a staff survey with task team leaders of youth employment projects.

The evaluation greatly benefited from financial support from the Norwegian Agency for Development Cooperation (NORAD). Norwegian funds helped support consultants' time and travel for conducting the Tunisia country study and several background notes. The Norwegian support greatly enhanced the quality and depth of the data collection and evaluation analysis.

IEG management and colleagues provided helpful guidance and comments, including Martha Ainsworth, Marvin Taylor-Dormond, and Stoyan Tenev, among others. Many World Bank and IFC managers and staff provided useful comments and support during the evaluation. The team is grateful for the support received by the representatives of the governments of the Dominican Republic, Ghana, Liberia, Rwanda, and Tunisia, where field-based country studies were conducted. We also thank the Bank and IFC offices in these countries for mission support, as well as donors who offered their time for interviews. The team is grateful for comments received by Bruce Ross-Larson.

Peer reviewers are Gordon Betcherman (University of Ottawa and former Sector Manager, Human Development Economics, ECA Region, World Bank), Gary Fields (Cornell University), Louise Fox (Lead Economist, Poverty Reduction and Economic Management, Africa Region, World Bank), and Peter Orazem (Iowa State University). The many thoughtful and thorough comments from peer reviewers improved the report and are much appreciated.

# Overview

## World Bank and IFC Support for Youth Employment Programs, 2001–2011

### Highlights Overview

Youth employment issues are a major concern for many countries because they have negative effects on the welfare of young people, and may also adversely affect economic performance and social stability. This is the first IEG evaluation of the World Bank Group's support to countries trying to address youth employment issues.

The World Bank lending portfolio for youth employment is relatively small, although components of programs appear in 57 countries. Most projects include interventions in skills development and school-to-work transition. Half of the projects include interventions to foster job creation and work opportunities for youth.

IFC has a broad approach to job creation. Between FY01 and FY11 youth employment has not been specifically targeted, except in the Middle East and North Africa region and in a small number of other interventions. IFC invested $500 million to 50 investment operations and 18 advisory services to education.

Although youth employment is addressed in the education, social protection, and labor strategies, it is not recognized as an issue in most country strategies—even where youth unemployment is serious. Youth employment is a multisectoral issue, but few youth employment projects are implemented by multisectoral teams.

Evidence on what works in youth employment is scarce. Known factors that contribute to success are a comprehensive approach including participation of the private sector, monitoring and follow up of individual participants, and complementary interventions, such as combined training with job search and placement assistance, rather than isolated interventions. In high-unemployment environments, wage subsidies, skills training, and job search support are of little impact; and demand-side interventions are needed. Strong diagnostics are important to design interventions for youth in low-income areas. The Bank's few impact evaluations on youth employment examine short-term effects, find limited positive results, and do not calculate the cost-effectiveness of interventions.

The evaluation makes two recommendations: (i) apply an evidence-based approach to youth employment operations, and (ii) at the country level, take a strategic approach to youth employment by addressing the issue comprehensively, working across World Bank Group teams, with governments and other donors. There is a critical need to strengthen evidence-based feedback loops to the strategic planning process.

# Youth Employment Challenges

In general, a growing economy and a stable macroeconomic and political environment, access to energy and infrastructure, and a conducive business and labor market environment are basic requirements for investment and job creation for all age groups. However, in some cases, this may not be sufficient to tackle issues related to youth employment.

Even where growth is positive, the labor market position of youth differs from adults. Youth are more likely to be among the working poor than adults. They are at higher risk of unemployment, underemployment, or working in jobs with low earnings. The early work situation of young people has welfare consequences for their future. This report is the first Independent Evaluation Group (IEG) evaluation of the World Bank Group's support to clients seeking to address youth employment issues.

In 2011, the International Labour Organization (ILO) estimated that 12.6 percent of youth in the global labor force are unemployed—about 74.6 million youth. Youth unemployment rates are everywhere considerably higher than adult rates. In several middle-income countries, half of the youth workforce is unemployed. Some youth face persistent barriers to employment, among them women, ethnic groups, the less educated, and youth with disabilities.

Low-income youth cannot afford to be economically idle. They work informally under poor conditions and as unpaid laborers, and they constitute a disproportionately large share of the working poor. Slow agricultural productivity growth and access to land and credit are the main constraints for young workers in rural areas.

Addressing youth employment issues is a major concern for many countries. It negatively affects the welfare of young people and potentially the rest of the economy as well. Unemployed youth do not get a chance to build professional skills. As a result, they are more at risk for higher adult unemployment, career downgrades and lower wages later in life, and a loss in lifetime earnings.

The reasons for higher youth-to-adult unemployment rates include labor demand and supply factors, as well as constraints in the labor and credit markets. Their relative importance in a dynamic growth context varies across countries. Recognizing these differences is important for governments in designing youth employment programs tailored to the most affected youth groups, and to incorporating in program design specific interventions to address the underlying causes of youth unemployment and underemployment.

This evaluation was done to better understand the contributions of the World Bank and IFC to these efforts, their effectiveness, and what can be learned from the experience to support decision makers in finding new solutions. The evaluation addresses three questions:

- What is the nature of the World Bank Group's support to countries tackling youth employment and how should this be evaluated?

- What is the evidence that the Bank Group supports priority country needs?
- What is the evidence regarding the effectiveness of that support?

## What Are the Bank and IFC Doing in Youth Employment?

The World Bank and IFC provide support for youth employment programs through lending, investment, and analytical work. Evaluating the World Bank's and IFC's assistance to youth employment is challenging because employment outcomes are the result of a1ctions across many sectors. Interventions that affect youth employment are often not "tagged" as youth interventions.

Youth employment outcomes are determined by the demand and supply of labor and the functioning of markets and government institutions. The Bank's MILES (Macroeconomics, Investment climate, Labor market, Education, and Social protection) framework is used to examine youth employment, focusing primarily on the "I, L, and E," that is an *Investment climate* to foster job creation and work opportunities, *Labor market* institutions and the school-to-work transition, and *Education* and skills aspects. *Macroeconomic* growth policies (M) are crucially related to business cycles and affect all age groups, not just the young. Unemployed youth in higher-income countries can get access to *Social protection* (S), such as unemployment benefits, but in countries where the Bank Group operates, they usually do not have this option.

This evaluation covers fiscal years 2001–2011 and draws from a number of sources, including a systematic review of relevant interventions, key informant interviews, a review of 90 closed and ongoing Bank projects, a review of 21 pieces of Bank nonlending sector work, and 18 country studies, 5 of which involved country visits. All IFC advisory services and investment operations with components focused on job creation and skills development were included in the analysis. IFC has not categorized employment data by age.

The identified Bank lending portfolio for youth employment is small. Between FY01 and FY11, the World Bank lent $2.85 billion to support youth employment programs through 90 operations in 57 countries. New lending peaked in 2007, coinciding with the lowest youth unemployment rate during the decade and the publication of *World Development Report 2007: Development and the Next Generation*. Bank lending peaked again in 2009 and 2010 during the global economic crisis. Most Bank lending for youth employment is managed by the Human Development Network (73 percent). Africa had more than one-third of the projects, but the Europe and Central Asia Region received the most lending, with 31 percent of total lending for youth employment.

The top 10 borrowers for youth employment are countries with ongoing reform programs. They received 70 percent of youth employment lending. The remaining 30 percent of lending was split among 47 countries. Fragile states implemented 12 of the 90 operations, and 6 percent of total youth employment lending.

Bank teams prepared 34 pieces of economic and sector work, and carried out 25 technical assistance activities related to "improving labor market outcomes." There are also a small but growing number of impact evaluations of youth employment interventions. This IEG evaluation reviewed 21 economic and sector work products with a youth employment focus, and all impact evaluations of Bank projects. The Bank spent $4.4 million on 18 of these reports.

Most Bank projects include interventions in skills development (82 percent) and school-to-work transition (79 percent). Fifty-four percent include interventions to foster job creation and work opportunities for youth. However, projects are not designed comprehensively, meaning that interventions from the three categories are not complementing each other. Similarly, the 18 country studies identified a number of areas where the Bank Group contributed; however, the studies suggest a comprehensive approach was missing on a country level.

While IFC has taken a broad approach to job creation, it has supported youth through investment and advisory services in education, and 10 youth employment projects. Between FY01 and FY11, IFC invested in 50 education sector projects, committing around $500 million through loan, equity, and guarantee facilities. More than half (68 percent) were in tertiary education, and 6 projects included components for technical and vocational training. Since FY06, 100 advisory service projects had objectives linked to job creation. However, in all cases the employment data have not been categorized by age group.

## What Is the Evidence that the Bank Group Supports Priority Country Needs in Youth Employment?

Although the Bank Group does not have a youth employment strategy, corporate thinking on youth employment issues is conveyed in the sector strategies on education, social protection, and labor. It is also highlighted in several World Development Reports, as well as regional Bank reports and analytical frameworks.

In addition, the Bank Group is participating in relevant international initiatives, including the Youth Employment Network, the Adolescent Girls Initiatives, and the Global Agenda Council on Youth Employment at the World Economic Forum.

IFC has a broad approach for employment creation. It is based on the premise that investments result in private sector development, higher growth, and greater employment opportunities. Youth employment has not been identified as a priority in IFC strategies, except for the Middle East and North Africa (the FY12–14 strategy).

Most country strategies only briefly mention youth employment with limited or no follow-up. In addition, country strategy indicators rarely collect age-specific labor market outcome data. Fragmentation across ministries and government levels are additional challenges to multisectoral programs. Similarly, within the Bank, few youth employment project teams include staff from other relevant sectors. No collaboration between the Bank and IFC was reported, except a few efforts including planned joint work on the e4e Initiative for Arab Youth in the Middle East and North Africa.

## What Is the Evidence on the Effectiveness of Bank Group Support to Youth Employment?

The international literature on youth employment programs suggests a comprehensive approach works best. A "comprehensive approach" is a multipronged strategy that includes complementary interventions aimed at removing key constraints to youth employment across multiple elements of the youth employment spectrum, namely: influencing the job creation and work opportunities for youth (both demand for youth by firms and self-employment), labor markets characteristics, and labor supply (skills and labor attributes). In a comprehensive approach, Bank-supported interventions are underpinned by solid analysis within the given country context.

The IEG systematic review of 38 impact evaluations found factors that increase the probability of success include participation of the private sector, personal monitoring and follow up of individual participants, and a combination of complementary interventions, such as training with job search and placement assistance, rather than isolated interventions. Programs that combine smoothing the transition from school to work with work-based skills development appear to be most effective for youth employment and earnings in countries with a formal sector.

In rural low-income areas, where most youth are active in agriculture and non-farm employment or self-employment, stimulating the market environment for growth of farms and rural agribusinesses is essential for youth employment.

There is little evidence of the impact on youth employment-targeted interventions in labor-abundant, low-income countries with weak institutions, such as those found in Sub-Saharan Africa and parts of South Asia. Circumstantial evidence suggests they are less likely to be effective, and interventions targeting formal employment may be regressive.

The paucity of project data limits the ability to make any statements on the impact of Bank Group support on labor market outcomes. The majority of Bank projects (55 percent) provide no information on youth as a beneficiary group. The rest mainly report input and output indicators. The seven impact evaluations of six Bank projects cannot be generalized. Rather, they focus on specific interventions, such as vouchers for formal vocational training in

Kenya, entrepreneurship training for university students in Tunisia, rural entrepreneurship training in Colombia and Uganda, and short-term remedial skills building in Chile, Colombia, and the Dominican Republic. Results are mixed.

## Bank Group Support to Creating Work Opportunities for Youth

Bank Group support for most youth employment is characterized by data deficiencies. Business environment and labor market reform has been linked to investment and employment growth, but the impact on youth employment from Bank Group support is unknown. The Bank supported small-scale reforms targeted to youth-intensive industries including increasing exports, private spending on research and development, and attracting foreign investors in information technology. No information was collected on the youth employment effects from Bank-supported labor market reforms.

Entrepreneurship training has demonstrated positive impacts for rural entrepreneurs in Uganda and Colombia, negligible effects elsewhere, and limited effects on business performance.

The IFC Grassroots Business Initiative and the Russian internship program were designed to link businesses with youth. However, these projects were challenging to design and implement, and were spun-off. IFC supported equity type financing for young entrepreneurs combined with structured mentoring. The IFC Business Edge Program helps build business skills for unemployed youth and young entrepreneurs (for instance in Yemen).

Temporary wage subsidies paid to employers to hire youth can have a positive employment impact—but mainly if this work provides youth with higher-level skills. However, several countries, including Colombia, Sweden, and the United Kingdom report low uptake among employers. The youth employment impact of Bank-supported wage subsidies in middle-income countries is unknown.

The Bank supported public works programs for all age groups, including youth—although the post-program employment effect is unknown. Impact evaluations in Argentina and Colombia report short-term positive earnings effects, but provide no information on post-program employment. Various Bank analytical products recommend that these costly public works programs be self-targeted through low-wage payments to workers in rural areas.

## Bank Group Support to School-to-Work Transition Interventions

Little is known from Bank support, but international evidence suggests adding school-to-work interventions to skills building interventions increases the employment effect of skills building. The Bank-supported job search assistance in 40 percent of projects, but few report information on placement rates. Although 70 percent of Bank projects support "improving information on the labor market," little is known about how accessible and helpful job information is to job seekers and employers.

The Bank Group supports three main types of technical skills building: formal technical education and vocational education training (TVET), short-term skills training targeted to unemployed youth, and remedial skills training targeted to disadvantaged youth.

The few tracer studies find positive employment and earning effects of Bank and IFC-supported reforms in TVET. The TVET voucher program in Kenya suggests a higher training uptake if vouchers are unrestricted. Dropout rates for students are also lower in private sector training. Bank-supported TVET programs emphasize accreditation; however, potential for manipulation of the accreditation process can devalue its credibility as an instrument for accountability.

Non-formal, short-term skill training has a mixed effect around the world, with women often faring better than men. Bank impact evaluations find no impact for youth in Chile and the Dominican Republic, whereas in Colombia formality and earnings increased. The Bank also supports the transport and residential expenses of trainees, which is helpful for youth from lower-income groups.

## Recommendations

The following two main recommendations are offered to guide the Bank Group's future work in youth employment in client countries where youth employment is a concern to the government or the World Bank/IFC:

**Apply an evidence-based approach to youth employment operations.**

- Improve knowledge about youth employment by supporting government collection of labor market outcome data for youth in relevant surveys.

- Monitor the employment situation by age groups by providing statistics for inclusion in country strategies and Country Economic Memorandums.

- Ensure that World Bank and IFC youth employment interventions are informed by relevant analytical work or due diligence on their strategic relevance that also addresses likely costs of possible interventions.

- Monitor or evaluate age-specific employment and earning outcomes in Bank operations, IFC investments, and Bank analytic and advisory activities and IFC Advisory Services designed to address youth employment issues. This would include measures on gender and socioeconomic groups.

**At the country level, take a strategic approach to youth employment by addressing the issue comprehensively, working across teams.**

- Help countries address youth employment issues comprehensively, from the demand and supply side. This requires greater cross-sectoral collaboration within the World Bank Group and with other donors as appropriate.

- Help countries design interventions targeted to low-income youth. Examples for the private sector could include closing the gap between skills demanded by the private sector and those acquired through the educational system.

# Management Response

## Introduction

World Bank Group Management welcomes this Independent Evaluation Group (IEG) review of Bank support to youth employment programs and thanks IEG staff for the close dialogue with management and staff during its preparation. Given the heightened scrutiny of these issues by global policymakers, this evaluation will help focus our efforts and work more effectively to deliver services demanded by World Bank Group clients to address these concerns.

Policymakers around the world have become increasingly concerned by the events of the Arab Spring as well as the unsustainably high rates of youth unemployment and disaffection in Europe and elsewhere. The report correctly notes the growing populations of "NEETS" (the English term for "not in education, employment, or training"). There is a common fear that the growing pool of young people, without established roots or place, and without voice, will express their frustration in violence and rebellion. They certainly can, in certain circumstances, if other social, political, and economic institutions are weak or absent. But this is not the most important reason for concern. As the report notes, youth unemployment matters for welfare, for equity, for productivity and growth, for personal and collective identity, and for social cohesion. The costs of prolonged unemployment in youth, or delayed entry into work, are potentially enormous in terms of lifetime earnings and well-being.

Management provided detailed comments to IEG on the first draft and it is pleased most of its suggestions were incorporated in the final draft. The first section of this note sets out comments from World Bank Management; the second section provides comments from International Finance Corporation (IFC) Management. Following this text is the draft Management Action Record (Annex 1).

## World Bank Management Comments

Any review of programs that assist young people to enter the labor market is complicated by a number of factors. First, the broad scope of possible constraints and interventions relating to youth employment necessitate complex and coordinated responses. Second, many Bank activities that are likely to affect youth employment may not have this as a specific objective, and may therefore not be included in this evaluation due to difficulties of disentangling their specific impact on youth. Finally, relatively few Bank interventions that have reached the stage at which results are measurable since the volume of lending linked to youth interventions increased substantially only in 2009-10 after the 2007 World Development Report (WDR) on Development and the Next Generation. The report recognizes these constraints (in particular that the paucity of data limits the ability to assess the impact of Bank support to youth employment programs) and attempts to distill recommendations. However, due to these constraints, the IEG report cannot go into great detail about what works, what does not, and what interventions should be prioritized in different contexts.

The IEG report recognizes that a "growing economy and a stable macroeconomic and political environment are fundamental conditions for job creation and employment for all age groups," and that interventions specifically targeted at youth are less likely to be effective if these conditions are not in place. It then proceeds to reviewing only activities that are specifically targeted at youth. While the constraints that lead to this approach are understandable, the report only focuses on a part, and possibly a relatively small part, of the Bank activities that affect youth employment. Conversely, it should be recognized that employment is but one indicator of successful transition to adulthood and active, productive citizenship. Employment programs may have other impacts that enhance development and growth such as attitudes toward the future, behavioral skills, networks and business skills that were not measured under this evaluation.

*Ongoing Bank operations.* Lessons from a number of projects currently under way or in the pipeline will address some of the concerns raised by this review and will provide a more complete picture of the status of World Bank support to youth employment programs in the near future. For example, the Liberia Youth Employment and Skills project is targeting employment in the informal sector, by supporting small businesses and stimulating demand for skills among these employers. Similarly, the Kenya Youth Empowerment Program, which is supported both by the Bank and by a grant from the Rapid Social Response Fund, is providing both skills training and six-month internships. Employers are directly involved in determining the type of skills and knowledge offered by the program as well as the work experience available to participants. This program expects to recruit and train 10,000 young people by 2015.

*Ongoing Bank evaluation work.* Similarly, the Bank is implementing a number of impact evaluations that will soon begin to bear fruit and enable the filling in some of the knowledge gaps discussed by the IEG review. For example IEG refers to a voucher program in Kenya, which is supported by the Spanish Impact Evaluation Active Labor Market Program (ALMP) cluster. This project has yielded important evidence on the provision of training and apprenticeships; in addition, the cluster is also supporting seven other important evaluations.[1] Mid-line or end-line results from most of these evaluations are generally positive, both in terms of employment and incomes, and also in terms of other outcomes such as health, childbearing, and self-reported measures such as confidence and self-efficacy. A number of evaluations under the Adolescent Girls' Initiative, which is beginning to yield positive results, should shed light on how low-income young women in informal sectors are benefiting.

*Monitoring youth outcomes.* As the IEG report notes, it is important to monitor the situation of young people and the impact of programs on young people separately from the situation of the broader working-age population. Indeed, and this will clearly be of greater concern in some countries than others. Between 2010 and 2025, the population of people between 15 and 34 will increase globally, but the vast majority (about 95 percent) of the increase will occur in sub-Saharan Africa; China will see a large decline in its population of young people. The need to monitor outcomes separately by age group will be a function of the circumstances and demands of each country. The World Bank has a responsibility to provide assistance in monitoring youth outcomes in response to specific requests and where youth employment is considered a significant problem or where youth are explicitly targeted by programs. However, as the report notes, few countries have data with sufficient detail to permit disaggregation by age groups, or sufficient frequency to look at short-run changes in labor market outcomes. In these cases countries and Bank teams should be encouraged to look at international sources of monitoring data such as the International Labour Organization's (ILO's) Key Indicators of the Labor Market (KILM).

**Collaboration across sectors.** The Bank agrees with IEG that to better assist client countries with the most effective interventions to address the constraints facing young people in their entry to the labor market, whether from the demand or supply side, will require greater cross-sectoral collaboration within the whole World Bank Group, as well as with other partners and donors. Successful transition to work often requires that young people master and integrate a broad set of competencies that are conventionally the domain of different sectors within the World Bank Group, such as basic and technical vocational skills. In many areas the World Bank Group is already engaged across sectors, for instance across Social Protection and Education in skills development and measurement, across Social Protection, the Consultative Group to Assist the Poorest (CGAP) and Financial and Private Sector Development (FPD) on access to finance and the development of financial literacy, and Social Protection and Poverty Reduction and Economic Management (PREM) on the Adolescent Girls' Initiative. The Bank also manages the Global Partnership for Youth Employment (GPYE) with four external partners[2] as well as the Youth Employment Inventory (YEI).[3] However, cross-sectoral collaboration should reflect the goals to be achieved and the constraints identified as binding on young people's productive employment. Although a comprehensive approach is to be recommended generally, it must be recognized that in some circumstances a more targeted approach via a focused investment project may be needed to overcome a particular bottleneck.

**Future directions for Bank research and operations.** Experience accumulated during the period under review by this report suggests that some interventions are more likely than others to bear fruit, depending on contexts and constraints. For example, the vast majority of interventions on youth employment have focused on the supply side, assuming that the binding constraint is that the workers do not have the right skills. This may be true in some regions, but in other regions, other constraints may bind, such as inadequate labor demand, or problems in the labor market itself, such as overly restrictive rules on hiring and firing as well as problems with information and matching. The ongoing Youth Employment Inventory (YEI) will provide considerable insight into successful programs across contexts and participants. Experience also suggests some areas for fruitful research, and areas in which our clients are asking for more guidance. These include the design of comprehensive programs, cost-effectiveness, scale and sustainability, and the impact of programs on different groups and in different contexts – such as the poor and non-poor, and urban and rural populations.

*Specific recommendations.* Bank management is in broad agreement with IEG's recommendations for the Bank. With regard to the regular collection and reporting of age-disaggregated statistics, management will work with the Development Data Group (DECDG) to ensure that, to the extent possible, data are made available for public download on the Development Data Platform. This database already includes both the employment-to-population ratio and the unemployment rate for 15-24-year-olds. In addition, for countries for which labor market statistics are regularly collected and reported, and in which youth employment is regarded as a central concern of national policy, management will advocate the publication of age-disaggregated statistics on employment and activity. With regard to the design of evidence-based policy, management will continue to collaborate with partners and clients to collect, synthesize and utilize experiences from Bank operations and evaluations, and to assist with the integration of this evidence into project design. Finally, with regard to the design of comprehensive and cross-sectoral programs to enhance youth employment, Management will continue to assist with the design of appropriate interventions on the basis of diagnosis and dialogue as well as on the evidence and experience accumulated from other cases. At least two regions with youth employment concerns, the Middle East and North Africa (MENA) and Africa, are completing reports on youth and jobs. MENA's upcoming jobs report "Bread, Freedom and Dignity: Jobs in the Middle East and North Africa", focuses on youth. Africa is completing a flagship report on youth employment in FY13.

## IFC Management Comments

IFC management welcomes this report. We appreciate that the report recognizes that IFC has a broad approach for employment creation. Since inception, IFC has been supporting financially, economically and sustainably viable private sector enterprises that result in private sector development, higher growth, and provide direct, indirect and induced employment. IFC's advisory services help create an environment conducive to private sector development, provide entrepreneurial training, and enhance job opportunities through technical advice on access to finance, sustainable business, and private-public partnerships. In addition to this broad approach, as the report shows, IFC has undertaken youth employment targeted interventions in both investments and advisory services, including 50 education investment projects with total IFC commitments of $500 million. In advisory services, the report lists 110 projects since FY11 with objectives linked to job creation and 18 projects aimed specifically at youth employment.

IFC's engagement in skills development and education for youth focuses on the post-secondary level. The goal is to develop youth skills that are relevant to employer needs, and to facilitate the engagement of youth with companies for training and employment opportunities. IFC work in this area falls under the following programs and activities:

a. *Technical Vocational Education and Training Programs and Tertiary Education Projects*—IFC's work program in the education sector targets youth and employability, whether directly, as evidenced by 90 percent of our investments in higher education; or indirectly, mainly through investments in secondary education.

b. *e4e Initiative for Arab Youth (e4e)*—This program was launched in 2010-2011 in partnership with the Islamic Development Bank (IDB) to help restructure education systems and strengthen linkages with employers to ensure better employment opportunities for youth.

c. *Entrepreneurship and Employee Skills Building Advisory Work*—IFC has two key products in this area: Business Edge and Small and Medium Enterprise (SME) Toolkit. IFC has also a specialized program called Farmer and SME Training (FAST).

In FY2012, IFC updated its strategy for education with the objective of prioritizing efforts to increase impact in the sector. The new strategy explicitly states that IFC will continue to focus on improving access to high quality and affordable education, especially at the levels that directly lead to youth employment. IFC's strategy is aligned with the World Bank Group's Education Strategy 2020 as it supports private providers that can step in to fill gaps in education systems. The thrust of IFC's education strategy is defined by three main strategic directions: (i) *financing education service providers with a focus on quality and scalable business models,* especially those directly linked to employability; (ii) bringing together key stakeholders involved in strengthening education systems, and continuing to *build thought leadership* by sharing knowledge about successful business models and by contributing to create enabling environments for private education in partnership with the World Bank; (iii) *testing innovative business models,* both in service delivery and in other subsectors of the education market, to push the frontier of the sector and find solutions to the challenges of access, quality and relevance.

IFC also recognizes that SMEs are a very important component of employment and job creation in most developing countries. They account for over 80 percent of net job creation and 67 percent of employment in developing countries. Extending finance to a broader group of companies and SMEs is associated with greater growth and poverty reduction and leads to a more inclusive business environment. Thus, providing finance and advice to help the SME sector is an important part of IFC's activities that provide youth employment.

# Management Action Record

| IEG Findings and Conclusions | IEG Recommendations |
| --- | --- |
| **The paucity of data limits the ability to assess the impact of Bank Group support to youth employment.** | **In client countries where youth employment is a concern to the government or the World Bank/IFC:** |
| • The International Finance Corporation (IFC) does not disaggregate employment data by age groups, and the majority of Bank projects provide no information on youth as a beneficiary group. If reported, outcome indicators are generally not disaggregated by age.<br>• Few projects or analytic products include tracer studies to track the subsequent employment history of youth.<br>• Bank and IFC operations do not identify whether youth employment interventions reached low-income youth. Only one (Uganda) impact evaluation conducts quantile analysis.<br>• Diagnostic work on youth employment is insufficient. Analytical work does not identify how the recommended interventions should be formulated, nor does it include a discussion related to cost and fiscal impacts. | **Apply an evidence-based approach to youth employment programs.**<br><br>• Improve knowledge about youth employment by supporting government collection of labor market outcome data for youth in relevant surveys.<br>• Monitor the employment situation by age groups by providing statistics for inclusion in country strategies and Country Economic Memorandums.<br>• Ensure that World Bank and IFC youth employment interventions are informed by relevant analytical work or due diligence on strategic relevance which also addresses likely costs of possible interventions.<br>• Monitor or evaluate age-specific employment and earning outcomes in Bank operations, IFC investments, and Analytic and Advisory Activities (AAA)/Advisory Services designed to address issues of youth employment. This would include measures on gender and socioeconomic groups. |

| Acceptance by Management | Management Response |
|---|---|
| **World Bank: Agree** | **World Bank:** World Bank management recognizes the importance of monitoring the situation of young people and the impact of programs on young people separately from the situation of the broader working-age population. However, the need to monitor outcomes separately by age group will be a function of the circumstances and demands of each country. Few countries have data with sufficient detail to permit disaggregation by age groups, or sufficient frequency to look at short-run changes in labor market outcomes.<br><br>Where labor market data are being collected, World Bank management will explore ways to strengthen the collaboration with clients and encourage the collection and dissemination of age-disaggregated statistics, or the use of the ILO KILM. In these countries, World Bank management plans to monitor age-disaggregated statistics on labor market performance and use them to inform country strategies and Country Economic Memorandum (CEMs) as appropriate. Additionally, management will work with the Development Data Group (DECDG) to ensure that to the extent possible youth employment data are made available for public download on the Development Data Platform. This database already includes both the employment-to-population ratio and the unemployment rate for 15-24-year-olds. Management will also advocate for the publication of age-disaggregated statistics on employment and activity in countries where these kinds of data are collected and available.<br><br>Finally, World Bank management is committed to ensure that youth employment interventions are informed by relevant analytical work, and that teams developing these operations receive guidance as needed to ensure that youth employment outcomes are included in the results framework and are properly measured. |
| **IFC: Agree** | **IFC:** The items that relate to IFC are in the third and fourth bullets. Regarding the third bullet, IFC will sharpen its due diligence and at entry assessments on its youth employment targeted Investment Services and Advisory Services interventions, drawing from the knowledge base developed by the World Bank Group, and based on lessons emerging from IFC's ongoing jobs study. Early results of case studies show that IFC's impact on employment is significantly larger than originally anticipated.<br><br>IFC will continue to inform the strategic relevance of investments and advisory services in education by leveraging the knowledge base developed by the World Bank Group on education systems, in particular concerning the role of the private sector. IFC is tracking the impact on youth and women in its e4e Initiative for Arab Youth investments in the MENA region as well as in its Business Edge Programs associated with the e4e Initiative for Arab Youth across the region. |

| IEG Findings and Conclusions | IEG Recommendations |
|---|---|
| **Most country strategies do not identify youth employment as a strategic issue. A combination of complementary interventions works best, and implementation benefits from multisector teams.**<br><br>• A comprehensive approach to youth employment is more effective than isolated interventions, and a positive growth environment helps the interventions to succeed.<br>• Subgroups of youth are always worse off. These include the low-income youth without the necessary skills and connections to find work or access credit and land. | **At the country level, take a strategic approach to youth employment by addressing the issue comprehensively, working across teams.**<br><br>• Help countries address youth employment issues comprehensively, from the demand and the supply side. This requires greater cross-sectoral collaboration within the World Bank Group and with other donors as appropriate.<br>• Help countries design interventions targeted to low-income youth. Examples for the private sector could include closing the gap between skills demanded by the private sector and those acquired through the educational system. |

| Acceptance by Management | Management Response |
|---|---|
| | Regarding the fourth bullet, by definition, IFC's investments in higher education (over 2/3 of the portfolio) will target the employability of youth. IFC will continue to measure 'access to education' as a main proxy of impact. In addition, IFC will pilot measurements of the direct impact of education investments on employability and quality and explore opportunities to conduct impact evaluations in a select number of projects aimed at addressing youth employment issues. |
| | Monitoring impacts of all youth employment targeted projects will require further analysis with respect to costs and benefits. Tracking age-related job creation in every project could prove very burdensome on our clients. At the same time, as we are learning from our ongoing jobs study, measuring job creation at the firm level provides only a partial picture since the bulk of the jobs provided are outside the firms through indirect and induced employment.[4] As we continue to learn from the jobs study and from our ongoing youth employment initiatives, and if the benefits will outweigh the costs, IFC could consider monitoring impact on youth employment at the firm level for future youth employment targeted projects. |
| **World Bank: Agree** | **World Bank:** The Bank agrees that to better assist client countries with the most effective interventions to address the constraints facing young people in their entry to the labor market, whether from the demand or the supply side, will require greater cross-sectoral collaboration within the whole World Bank Group, as well as with other partners and donors. Although a comprehensive approach is to be recommended generally, it must be recognized that in some circumstances a more targeted approach via a focused investment project may be needed to overcome a particular bottleneck. |
| | In client countries where youth employment is a concern, management plans to continue to engage with partners, including IFC, as appropriate to identify and address the binding constraints facing young people and to provide analytical support to help client countries design interventions aimed at alleviating these constraints and facilitating the labor market entry of youth. In these cases, management plans to advocate for the inclusion of low-income youth among the target groups of youth-employment interventions, including when this requires a focused investment project. At least two regions, MENA and Africa (AFR), are preparing regional studies on youth and jobs, which we expect will facilitate the dialogue with partners and foster cross-sectoral collaboration on youth employment issues. |
| **IFC: Agree** | **IFC:** Regarding the first bullet, on the demand side, IFC will continue to contribute to World Bank Group objectives in this regard through its financing and advisory support for private sector investments that provide direct, indirect and induced employment opportunities to the underserved, including youth and women. |

| IEG Findings and Conclusions | IEG Recommendations |
| --- | --- |
| | |

| Acceptance by Management | Management Response |
|---|---|
| | On the supply side, IFC will continue to provide investment and advisory services products aimed at developing employable and entrepreneurship skills among youth, in particular through support for Technical and Vocational Education and Training (TVET), secondary and tertiary education, and entrepreneurship training such as Business Edge.<br><br>Regarding the second bullet, in countries where youth employment is a concern to the government and/or the World Bank and IFC, IFC will explore opportunities to work with the World Bank to map and strengthen regulatory frameworks and leverage analytical work to identify gaps in education systems, in particular concerning skills provision, where the private sector can step in. |

## Notes

1. For example, the Dominican Republic, Programa Juventud y Empleo (PJE); Malawi, Impact Evaluation of Technical and Vocational Skills Training for Orphaned, Vulnerable and Affected Youth; Tunisia: Turning Theses into Enterprises; and Uganda, The Northern Uganda Social Action Fund (NUSAF) Youth Opportunities Program (YOP).
2. See www.gpye.org for more information.
3. The YEI is a joint effort of the Bank, the Youth Employment Network, the ILO, and the German Ministry for Economic Cooperation and Development (BMZ). This consortium is assembling a database of youth employment interventions around the world, gathering the evidence of what works, and promoting both learning and the use of evidence in program design and planning. The YEI database currently contains over 500 programs, more than 100 of which have integral impact evaluations.
4. The report's Table E.1 illustrates how tracking jobs data by project could be misleading. First, the data are on jobs provided by IFC clients, not by IFC. Second, the job count is based on firm level staff count per year without adjustments for seasonality and business cycles such as construction firms that are in between projects at the time the jobs data are collected. Third, the data do not include indirect and induced jobs, as well as investments in the financial sector, which represent the bulk of jobs IFC clients provide.

# Report to the Board from the Committee on Development Effectiveness

The Committee on Development Effectiveness (CODE) met to discuss the IEG Evaluation on *World Bank and IFC Support for Youth Employment Programs* (CODE 2012-0030).

## Summary[1]

The Committee welcomed the IEG evaluation and broadly supported IEG's major recommendations for the World Bank Group's work in youth and employment programs in client countries. The Committee agreed that although the evaluation was only able to look at a small portfolio of work—with a focus on the investment climate, labor market, and education—it was valuable in highlighting the urgency of youth employment issues. Members appreciated that Bank and IFC management welcomed the evaluation and its findings, and they agreed with the broad conclusions of the review. Members also viewed the discussion as a good primer for the forthcoming meeting on the 2013 World Development Report (WDR) on Jobs.

Members underscored the need for the World Bank Group to improve its analytical capacity on youth employment, develop diagnostic tools and strengthen evidence-based approaches. Members also agreed that the Bank and IFC should be more strategic in comprehensively addressing youth employment issues. A number of members urged management to undertake a more systematic approach to data collection, including data disaggregated by age and by gender, that is, youth versus the broader working population.

Several members observed that despite the depth of youth employment problems, over the past decade there had been little country demand for operations. It was noted that while it was not a priority issue for clients in the past, given competing development demands, events in the Middle East have since brought the issue to the forefront. Accordingly, it will be important for the Bank to modify its approach to client engagement to ensure that youth unemployment receives more attention and is mainstreamed appropriately in Country Assistance and Poverty Reduction Strategies. It was further noted, however, that the magnitude of the problem is so large—including with respect to statistical capacities in client countries—that the Bank Group will not be able to address it singlehandedly. The quest to find appropriate solutions and remedies is thus a challenge not just for the World Bank Group but for the entire global community. In this sense, a number of members emphasized that the World Bank Group could play a catalytic role, spur collective action and coordinate partnerships on a global level—vis-à-vis donors, trust funds, multilateral organizations, and in particular national governments (over and above existing alliances with the United Nations [UN] and the International Labour Organization [ILO]). This is especially relevant since youth employment issues are so complex, varying greatly from region-to-region, country-to-country and across sectors.

A few members commented on the broader challenges with respect to the World Bank Group's work on "the frontiers of development," noting gender as an example in addition to youth employment, and the challenges in developing targeted approaches given the complexity of cross-cutting issues. A few members wondered how the World Bank Group's risk tolerance level is tied into these issues. It was noted, again, that these would be key items for the discussion of the WDR 2013.

## Recommendations and Next Steps

The Committee broadly supported the main recommendations of the evaluation to help guide the World Bank Group's future work on youth employment. IEG's evaluation will be made publicly available, together with comments from Bank and IFC Management (revised if needed), and the summary of the CODE Green Sheet. The Management Action Record (MAR) would be finalized 90 days after the CODE discussion to take into account the Committee's discussion and incorporate additional specificities on the steps to be undertaken.

## Issues Discussed

**Evaluation Recommendations.** Bank Management noted that while it is in broad agreement with IEG's findings, due to timing the report did not reflect some important work on new, large lending operations and ongoing operational research and evaluations that hopefully will provide important evidence going forward. IFC management also remarked that IFC has developed an evaluation strategy, and among the focus areas are jobs and poverty. Through the jobs study, IFC is also trying to get a better handle on job effects; while IFC is collecting more evidence to inform its strategy and operations, it will take time.

A member questioned whether there was a compelling case for the evaluation. IEG noted that at the Joint CODE-Board Committee meeting on May 11, 2011, members proposed advancing the work on youth employment, emphasizing the value of making the evaluation forward looking given the broad importance of the issues globally and the developments in the MENA region at the time. The majority of members welcomed the evaluation, found it timely, and sensed that it was important not only for what it conveys, but for what it cannot convey given the paucity of data.

A few members commented that the evaluation's recommendations seemed self-evident; they could and should be embedded in all aspects of the World Bank Group's work. Several members and non-members underscored that the evaluation also indicated that the World Bank Group needed to be more ambitious in dealing with results and impact. A few members added that the evaluation could have focused more on the lack of a World Bank Group strategy for addressing youth employment issues.

A few members and non-members remarked that the causes, risks and consequences (such as increased violence and adverse effects on long-term economic competitiveness) of the lack of youth employment opportunities, could have been better addressed. A few members felt that the evaluation was too narrowly focused on the economic side of youth unemployment; one member added that this may be relevant in developed countries and some middle- income countries, but is not appropriate for many lower-income countries or middle-income countries (MICs) with violence problems. To these comments, IEG noted that the evaluation concentrated on what the Bank and IFC have been doing, which has been focused on the economic side. A non-member wondered whether high youth unemployment is more of a symptom of the extensive development challenges faced by certain countries; in this respect, what are the risks if the institutions focus on what may be a symptom, rather than concentrating on the broader causes?

**Implementation of Recommendations.** In response to a member's query about how the Board will be updated on the implementation of agreed recommendations, Legal (LEG) informed that the status implementation of the recommendations by management is tracked as part of the MAR annual update.


*Hassan Ahmed Taha,* Acting Chair

# Chapter 1
Why Focus on Youth Employment?

A growing economy and a stable macroeconomic and political environment are fundamental conditions for job creation and employment for all age groups. This is the primary requirement for increasing employment overall, and youth employment as a consequence. Yet even where growth is positive, youth differ from adults in the labor, asset, and credit markets. One difference is that employers have imperfect information about the skills and productivity of young applicants, and youth are uncertain about the type of employer and job they want (Begg and Blanchflower 2000). As a result, youth have a higher job turnover rate than adults and take longer to find work. Another difference is that youth are more likely to be among the working poor than adults. In addition, they are at higher risk of unemployment, underemployment, or working in jobs with low earnings. The early work situation of young people has welfare consequences for their future. Addressing youth employment issues is a major concern for governments everywhere, and is all the more challenging where stable economic policies are not in place and institutions are weak. This report is the first Independent Evaluation Group (IEG) evaluation of the World Bank Group's support to clients seeking to address youth employment problems.

## The Nature of the Youth Employment Problem

Youth unemployment rates are everywhere considerably higher than adult rates, but the nature of the problem varies widely by country context. In 2011, the International Labour Organization (ILO) estimated that 12.6 percent of youth in the global labor force are unemployed, corresponding to about 74.6 million youth. The global youth to adult unemployment ratio is 2.8. But these ratios vary substantially across time and across countries. In Southeast Asia, for example, the ratio has increased most over the past decade (table 1.1).

Lack of growth and job creation contribute to higher youth unemployment in all countries. As the economy shrinks with the business cycle, youth—often the least educated—are the first to be let go, most without a social safety system to protect them against the financial risk related to unemployment.

| Table 1.1 | Youth Employment Indicators, by Percent, and Region | | | | | |
|---|---|---|---|---|---|---|
| | Youth labor force participation rate | | Youth unemployment rate | | Youth-to-adult employment ratio | |
| | 1998 | 2010 | 1998 | 2010 | 1998 | 2010 |
| World | 53.8 | 48.8 | 12.5 | 12.7 | 2.7 | 2.8 |
| Developed economies and European Union | 52.6 | 47.5 | 14.3 | 17.9 | 2.4 | 2.4 |
| Central and Southeastern Europe, and Commonwealth of Independent States | 43.3 | 42.0 | 22.6 | 19.4 | 2.3 | 2.5 |
| East Asia | 68.5 | 60.3 | 9.4 | 8.8 | 2.7 | 2.7 |
| Southeast Asia and Pacific | 53.9 | 52.5 | 12.2 | 13.6 | 4.8 | 4.9 |
| South Asia | 48.9 | 41.3 | 9.0 | 9.9 | 3.8 | 4.5 |
| Latin America and Caribbean | 55.6 | 52.8 | 15.6 | 14.4 | 2.6 | 2.7 |
| Middle East | 32.5 | 30.3 | 24.0 | 25.5 | 3.9 | 4.1 |
| North Africa | 36.4 | 33.6 | 26.6 | 23.8 | 3.5 | 3.8 |
| Sub-Saharan Africa | 53.7 | 53.6 | 13.8 | 12.5 | 2.0 | 2.0 |

*Source:* ILO 2011a.

*Note:* The ILO defines youth as an age group of between 15 to 24 years. An unemployed person is not employed, but actively looking for work. Labor force participation rate is the percentage of the working age population who are employed or unemployed and looking for work. The youth unemployment rate is the percentage of the labor force ages 15–24 without work, but available for work.

In several middle-income countries, half of the youth workforce is now unemployed. In the Organisation for Economic Co-operation and Development (OECD) countries, the recent economic crisis has increased youth unemployment to more than 40 percent (for example, in Spain and Greece).

Only in Africa, which already has the largest youth bulge, will the youth cohort continue to grow. Almost half (42 percent) of the population in Sub-Saharan Africa is under the age of 14 years. Between 2010 and 2020, the number of youth living in the region is expected to increase by 42.5 million (Bloom 2011; Proctor 2012). In most countries, wage employment is not growing fast enough to absorb these youth, and they will continue to work in the informal sector (Fox and Sohnesen 2012).

Some countries have voluntary unemployment among higher-income youth who have higher reservation than market wages, and benefit from family support while waiting for a "better job" (Rama 1999). When working conditions and pay vary across jobs and sectors, the labor market can become segmented (Fields 2007). Access to social networks and better jobs is generally restricted to more privileged members of society who have connections and can afford to wait for a better job. Thus, youth may prefer to remain unemployed and queue for better jobs, often in the public sector (appendix A, box A.1). Several countries (Tunisia and Sri Lanka among them) had a large public sector that absorbed the increments of tertiary graduates, but can no longer do so.

By contrast, low-income youth have to work early in menial jobs in the informal sector without the possibility of moving to higher-productivity work and earnings. Eighty-seven percent of the world's youth live in low-income countries including in Sub-Saharan Africa and Asia. Both regions report low unemployment rates and high labor force participation (table 1.1) because poor youth cannot afford to be economically idle. Many of these youth start out as support labor in family businesses (such as informal household enterprises) or farms, or work in low-productivity jobs in the informal (unregistered) sector (Fox and Sohnesen 2012). They often work under poor conditions as unpaid laborers and make up a disproportionately large share of the working poor (World Bank 2008–09). Their chances to transition to paid formal sector employment are slim.

Rural agriculture is the main employment source for youth in Africa and Asia. In 2009, the agriculture sector provided 59 percent of the total employment share in Sub-Saharan Africa and 54 percent in South Asia. Slow agricultural productivity growth and access to land and credit are the main constraints for young workers, with many working on small-scale farms (Proctor and Lucchesi 2012).

| Table 1.2 | Overview on the Nature of Youth Employment Problems in Different Contexts |
|---|---|
| Nature of Problem | Context |
| Youth unemployment high (or rising) for all young workers | • Economic crisis, structural reforms and lack of job creation in all countries<br>• Youth cohort growth is larger than job growth (for example, in Sub-Saharan Africa) |
| High youth unemployment for highly-educated young workers | • Voluntary unemployment among higher-income youth in middle- and low-income countries (for example, in Sri Lanka and the Middle East and North Africa [MENA] region) |
| Large number of casual, low-productivity, low-paid jobs held by youth | • In middle- and low-income countries with a small formal sector<br>• Rural areas (farm and off-farm)<br>• Children in workforce and low school enrollment |
| High youth unemployment concentrated in subgroups of youth population (minorities, poor) | • Regional disparities in all countries<br>• Discrimination against subgroups |

*Source:* IEG.

*Note:* See appendix A, table A.1 for policy directions.

The few youth who work in non-farm household enterprises are financially constrained, but have an opportunity for upward mobility. Although the share of non-farm, self-employment in the informal sector is increasing, youth under the age of 25 are the least likely to own a household enterprise. Their main constraint is access to start-up capital. However, panel data suggest that self-employment increases the probability for upward mobility (Fox and Sohnesen 2012).

Children in the workforce are lost opportunities. Low-income countries have low secondary school enrollment rates, and a large share of the children between 10 and 14 years are in the labor force mainly in agricultural employment (Fasih 2008). Poor children who are out of school cannot acquire the necessary skills for a job with higher earnings.

Subgroups of youth face persistent barriers to employment. The European Union, Croatia, the former Yugoslav Republic of Macedonia, and Turkey report the highest unemployment rates among the least-educated people, including minorities such as the Roma (box 1.1), and the disabled (Bell and Blanchflower 2010). Young women are worse off in some areas. Whereas Bangladesh[1] and other countries report increasing school enrollment and labor participation rates for females, better education has had limited impact on low labor force participation rates for young women in the Middle East (12.9 percent) and North Africa (19.5 percent), where young women report the highest unemployment rates (39.4 percent in Middle East, and 34.1 percent in North Africa) (Chamlou and others 2011).

The socioeconomic context is important in addressing the youth employment challenge. Where economic policies are stable and market institutions well developed, youth-targeted interventions are likely to have greater impact. Where there is a large youth bulge, little formal employment, and a large low-wage or informal economy, lifetime poverty traps are a threat and youth-targeted interventions may be less effective.

| Box 1.1 | Roma Youth in Europe |
| --- | --- |

In Central and Eastern Europe, less than 20 percent of working age Roma have completed secondary school. The Roma have significantly higher unemployment rates than non-Roma across all age cohorts and all education categories (Roma Education Fund 2007). Lack of education and skills and employment discrimination account for this low employment rate. Employers in the Czech Republic report that with diminishing manual work, fewer unskilled workers, among them Roma, are needed. Indeed, most jobs required functional knowledge of the Czech language and literacy skills to be able to adapt to new production methods. Employers also described a generational divide among Roma, with older Roma workers being more skilled and motivated than younger Roma (World Bank 2008).

*Sources:* Roma Education Fund 2007; World Bank 2008b.

## Consequences

Early unemployment is stressful and can leave scars. Unemployed youth do not get a chance to build professional skills. As a result, they are more at risk for higher adult unemployment, career downgrades and lower wages later in life, and a loss in lifetime earnings (Kahn 2010). In the United Kingdom, Gregg and Tominey (2005) found a large and significant wage penalty of 13 to 21 percent up to 26 years later as a result of early unemployment. Such long-term evidence for developing countries is scarce. However, other evidence points to similar problems: Low-skilled youth who are not in education, employment, or training (NEET)—around 70 percent of youth in Egypt and Pakistan (World Bank 2012)—are more likely to remain in this situation. Surveys from 60 developing countries show that young people take an average of 1.4 years to find stable employment after school (World Bank 2007). Many youth are discouraged and some migrate to find work. Joblessness has negative externalities on social cohesion, which may affect conflicts and poverty.

The agriculture sector remains a significant employer of young workers in Asia and Africa, yet many youth are migrating to find higher earnings. Young people are the key to the future of agriculture. However, given the low earnings and growing disinterest of youth in agriculture, the lack of capacity of other rural sectors to absorb youth, particularly in Asia and Africa, contributes to migration, joblessness, disillusionment, and the associated risks of instability (Lochner and Moretti 2004).

The youth dividend, that is the added productivity to economic growth when youth cohorts enter the workforce, cannot materialize without creating higher productivity jobs for youth. Increasing youth cohorts add to the challenges for youth in search of decent livelihoods and employment, and for governments in providing education and accelerating job growth to accommodate these youth (appendix A, box A.3).

Youth unemployment is costly. Related costs include direct costs to the government, depending on the extent of support programs, such as unemployment insurance, public works programs, and costs related to the economic loss of investment in education, forgone earnings, savings, and aggregated demand (ILO 2010). Instead of contributing to society, unemployed youth create a direct cost estimated at $40–50 billion annually for the Middle East and North Africa (IFC 2011a), reflecting about 3 percent of the region's gross domestic product (GDP) in 2010 (GDP in constant US$ for all MENA countries, World Development Indicators). Youth unemployment is now an important component in the misery index (Dao and Loungani 2010), the sum of inflation and unemployment, as governments have tamed inflation (figure 1.1).

## Figure 1.1 Youth Unemployment in the Misery Index, by Region, 2010

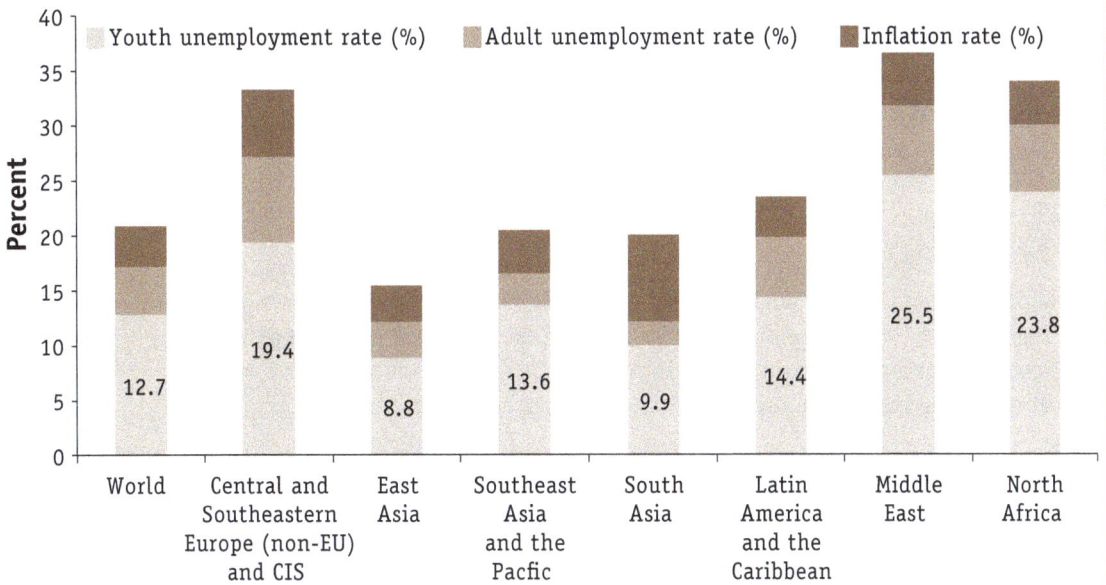

Legend: Youth unemployment rate (%) · Adult unemployment rate (%) · Inflation rate (%)

Bar values: World 12.7; Central and Southeastern Europe (non-EU) and CIS 19.4; East Asia 8.8; Southeast Asia and the Pacfic 13.6; South Asia 9.9; Latin America and the Caribbean 14.4; Middle East 25.5; North Africa 23.8

*Sources:* ILO 2011b; IMF 2001.
*Note:* The median inflation rate for each region is based on the median of Bank countries in the region. Africa is excluded, as unemployment is not an appropriate indicator.

## Objective of this Evaluation

This is the first IEG evaluation of the World Bank Group's involvement in youth employment or labor markets. The objective of this evaluation is to address three questions, which are the topics of the next three chapters:

- What is the nature of the Bank Group's support to countries tackling youth employment problems and how should they be evaluated?
- What is the evidence that the Bank Group supports priority country needs in youth employment issues?
- What is the evidence regarding the effectiveness of that support?

The evaluation seeks to understand the factors that affect the success of different interventions and offers lessons for informing future Bank Group lending.

## Note

1. The total fertility rate declined from 6.9 to 2.3 children from 1971-2009, and girls' school enrollment increased from 1.1 million to 4 million between 1991 and 2005. Labor force participation doubled.

# References

Begg, David, Stanley Fischer, and Rudiger Dornbusch. 2000. "Economics." New York: The McGraw-Hill Companies.

Bell, David, and David Blanchflower. 2010. Youth Unemployment: "Déjà vu? " IZA DP No. 4705. Forschungsinstitut zur Zukunft der Arbeit: Bonn, Germany.

Bloom, David E., 2011, "7 Billion and Counting," *Science,* Vol. 33, No. 6042, pp. 562–69.

Chamlou, Nadereh, Silvia Muzi, and Hanane Ahmed. 2011. "The determinants of female labor force participation in the Middle East and North Africa Region: The role of education and social norms in Amman, Cairo and Sana'a." Paper presented at the Economist Forum, April 18, 2011. Washington, DC: World Bank.

Dao, Mai Chi, and Prakash Loungani. 2010. "The Tragedy of Unemployment." *Finance and Development* 47(4):22-25.

Fasih, Tazeen. 2008. "Linking Education Policy to Labor Market Outcomes." Washington, DC: World Bank.

Fields, Gary. 2007. Labor Market Policy in Developing Countries: A Selective Review of the Literature and Needs for the Future. Cornell University and IZA.

Fox, Louise, and Thomas Pave Sohnesen. 2012. Household Enterprise in Sub-Saharan Africa – Why They Matter for Growth, Jobs and Poverty Reduction. The World Bank.

Fox, Louise, and Ana Maria Oviedo. 2008. "Institutions and Labor Market Outcomes in Sub-Saharan Africa." Policy Research Working Paper 4721. The World Bank.

Gregg, Paul, and Emma Tominey. 2005. "The wage scar from male youth unemployment." *Labour Economics* 12:487–509.

International Finance Corporation. 2011a. "Education for Employment (e4e): Realizing Arab Youth Potential—Executive Summary." www.e4earabyouth.com

International Labour Organization. 2011a. Estimates and projections of labor market indicators. http://www.ilo.org/empelm/projects/WCMS_114246/lang--en/index.htm

———. Global Employment Trends for Youth. 2011b. Update.

———. 2010. Global Employment Trends for Youth. Special issue on the impact of the global economic crisis on youth. Geneva.

International Monetary Fund (IMF). 2011. World Economic Outlook Database. September 2011.

Kahn, Lisa. 2010. "The long-term labor market consequences of graduating from college in a bad economy." *Labour Economics* 17:303–316.

Lochner, Lance J., and Enrico Moretti. 2004. "The Effect of Education on Crime: Evidence from Prison Inmates, Arrests, and Self-Reports." *American Economic Review* 94(1): 155–89.

Proctor, Felicity, and Valerio Lucchesi. 2012. Small-scale farming and youth in an era of rapid rural change. IIED. London. http://pubs.iied.org/

Rama, Martin. 1999. "The Sri Lanka Unemployment Problem Revisited." South Asia Region. Washington, DC: World Bank.

Roma Education Fund. 2007. Country Assessment Roman Education Fund's Strategic Direction: Advancing Education of Roma in Romania. Bucharest.

World Bank. 2012. *World Development Report 2013 on Jobs: Preliminary Findings and Emerging Messages*. March 15.

———. 2008–09. "ADI Africa Development Indicators 2008/09. Youth and Employment in Africa: The Potential, the Problem, the Promise." Washington, DC: World Bank.

———. 2008. Czech Republic Improving Employment Chances of the Roma. Human Development Sector Unit Europe and Central Asia. Washington, D.C.

———. 2007. *World Development Report 2007: Development and the Next Generation*. Washington, DC.

# Chapter 2

What Are the World Bank and IFC
Doing in Youth Employment?

- The Bank lending portfolio for youth employment is small and young. IFC has not specifically targeted youth employment programs.

- Higher youth-to-adult unemployment rates are determined by demand and supply factors, as well as by labor, asset, and credit market constraints. These factors vary across countries and regions. Being aware of which factors drive youth employment issues is important for governments in designing youth employment programs tailored to those youth who are most adversely affected.

- Broad policy interventions, such as promoting macroeconomic growth and foreign investment are necessary to promote employment, but they are not enough to address the situation of youth. As youth are worse off than adults, specific interventions for youth are needed. Accordingly, the evaluation focuses on the investment climate, labor market, and skill building.

The World Bank and IFC provide support for youth employment through lending, investment, and analytical work. Evaluating the World Bank's assistance to youth employment programs is challenging because employment outcomes are the result of actions across many sectors. The interventions that affect youth employment may not be "tagged" as youth interventions. Moreover, most Bank projects that can be easily categorized as targeting youth employment are relatively recent and have not closed yet. IFC has a broad approach for job creation. Many Bank Group activities in youth employment are analytic and advisory in nature, but often aim to affect policy just as financial support does.

These constraints on the evaluation have led to a methodological approach that focuses on a subset of activities using a framework developed by the World Bank. It also means that a later evaluation on a more mature portfolio may result in different findings. Nonetheless, the findings are timely and important as governments look for new approaches to improve the situation for youth.

## The Evaluation Applies the Bank's MILES Framework

Youth employment outcomes are determined by the demand and supply of labor and the functioning of markets and government institutions (Gustman and Steinmeier 1988; Ryan 2001). Box 2.1 presents the Bank's MILES framework for analyzing the labor market adapted to youth employment.

### DETERMINANTS OF YOUTH EMPLOYMENT

The labor demand-side factors that affect youth employment are economic growth, structural changes in the economy, and employers' preferences.

The strength and openness of the economy and its capacity to increase overall labor demand, are determined by factors such as access to energy, infrastructure, and logistics. These in turn affect the work opportunities for youth. The type of work opportunities that will be available—whether they provide regular wages, stable employment, and productive informal and farm employment, or expose youth to low and uncertain earnings—largely depends on the stage of economic development (Ryan 2001). As structural changes in the economy occur, such as shifts from agriculture to industry and manufacturing, the resulting changes in demand for skills will affect youth employment. Employer preferences for experienced workers typically put youth more at risk. In addition, the young self-employed are constrained by limited access to capital, networks, and land needed to start a business. In addition, they are also sometimes constrained by societal norms.

The labor supply-side factors that affect youth employment are education, growing youth cohorts, and individual attributes. The ability of youth to find work is affected by the skills learned compared to the changing needs of the labor market, and whether education has a signaling effect for employers. Specific individual attributes and behaviors, including gender, women's preference for raising children, health, socioeconomic background, access to networks, and preference for public sector jobs will also affect employment. Finally, the size of the youth cohort entering the labor market compared to the number of jobs available and the flexibility of wages to adjust, affect employment opportunities (Biagi and Lucifora 2008; World Bank 2007).

Institutional factors matter, including information, regulations, wage levels, access to land, and credit. Youth have less access to information and networks than adults do, which increases the time it takes them to find a job, obtain credit, or access land. Insufficient information about young workers' potential performance increases the uncertainty for firms in hiring an untested young person. Strict labor market regulations and contracts generally protect workers who already have a job and put youth at a disadvantage. The young self-employed have accumulated less human and physical capital, which makes them a higher risk for banks or informal lenders, and affects their access to credit (Begg and others 2000). Land tenure policies, access to credit, and markets are barriers for young farmers and household enterprises in Africa and Asia (Proctor and Lucchesi 2012).

As these factors are influenced by overall development efforts—including Bank Group support to countries' macroeconomic framework, infrastructure, energy, and to the public and private sectors—a full picture of the Bank Group's effects on the general labor demand and related impact on youth employment outcomes presents a considerable challenge. It would only be possible to get a full picture if the impact of these interventions on youth employment could be identified, but they cannot. Thus, the evaluation focused on the "I, L, and E" of the MILES framework (box 2.1).

The evaluation adapts the World Bank's MILES framework to look at youth employment. The Bank uses MILES in designing labor market strategies by identifying key constraints for job creation within five components (Holzmann 2007):

- **M**acroeconomics: Economic growth and net job creation.
- **I**nvestment climate: Incentives for employers to invest and create jobs.
- **L**abor market: Regulations affecting job search, hiring process and cost.
- **E**ducation: Individual education, socioeconomics, and demographics.
- **S**ocial Protection: Security against loss of earnings, unemployment insurance.

The determinants of youth employment are embedded in MILES and help to define the nature of the youth employment problem in a country (see figure, below).

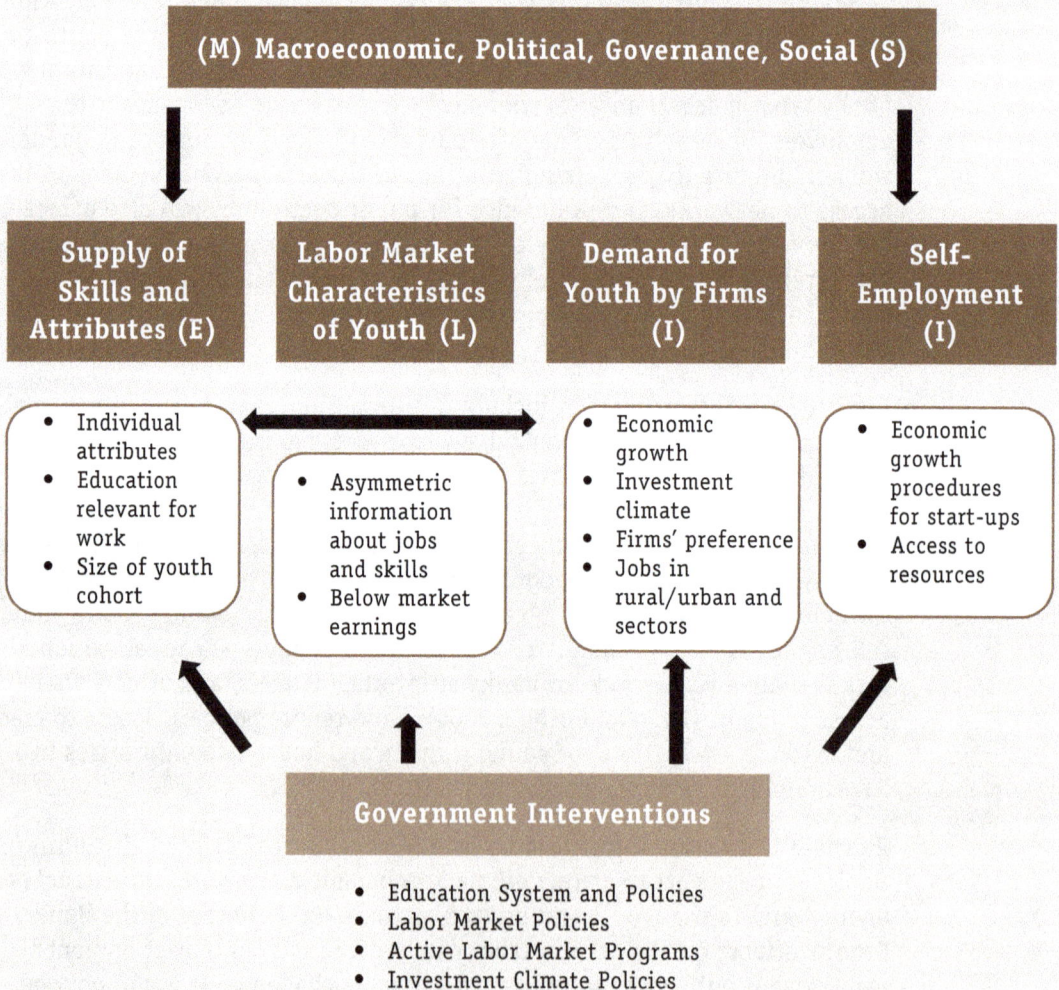

**(M) Macroeconomic, Political, Governance, Social (S)**

| Supply of Skills and Attributes (E) | Labor Market Characteristics of Youth (L) | Demand for Youth by Firms (I) | Self-Employment (I) |
|---|---|---|---|

- Individual attributes
- Education relevant for work
- Size of youth cohort

- Asymmetric information about jobs and skills
- Below market earnings

- Economic growth
- Investment climate
- Firms' preference
- Jobs in rural/urban and sectors

- Economic growth procedures for start-ups
- Access to resources

**Government Interventions**

- Education System and Policies
- Labor Market Policies
- Active Labor Market Programs
- Investment Climate Policies

*Source:* Authors, adapted from Holzmann (2007).

Broad policy interventions, such as supporting macroeconomic growth, trade, and foreign investment are necessary to promote overall employment, as well as a stable political and macroeconomic environment, access to energy and infrastructure, and a conducive business and labor market environment are all basic requirements for investment and job creation, and affect all age groups. However, in some cases, this may not be sufficient to tackle youth employment. Government interventions with a "youth lens" may be needed.

Governments design youth employment interventions to address imperfect information, externalities, and market regulations that may negatively affect development outcomes. For instance, education interventions address information failure in education management, which negatively affects quality and the registration and accreditation of providers (Robalino and others 2010). With more education, girls from lower-income groups delay their marriage age, which helps decrease fertility rates. Labor and credit market constraints limit access to jobs, credit, and markets for lower-income groups (Begg and others 2000).

The country context is an important driver for policy directions. As emphasized in chapter 1, differences in country context (table 1.2) imply differences in policy effectiveness. Governments use three main strategic directions—policies to increase the demand for young workers, labor market reforms, and education reforms—to address youth employment. Appendix A, table A.1 categorizes youth employment problems and the related determinants by country context. It suggests the main strategic directions to address these issues. In each youth employment context, policies to improve the business environment and foster trade, entrepreneurship, and growth are crucial to increase net job creation and labor demand. They may need to be accompanied by education policies to address a skill mismatch, and increase the human capital level and employability of youth, especially in countries with growing youth cohorts and structural changes in the economy. Reforms in labor regulation may be needed in middle-income countries to increase flexibility in contracting and pay, and to reduce segmentation and discrimination.

Youth-specific strategic directions and their interventions (table 4.1) align with the "I, L, and E" of the Bank's MILES framework (box 2.1). MILES classifies labor market regulations under (L); however, because they influence the demand by firms for workers, for the purpose of this evaluation, regulations are classified under (I). Macroeconomic growth policies (M) are closely tied to business cycles and affect all age groups. Similarly, investments in infrastructure and energy are necessary for firms to create jobs for all age groups, and not just for youth. Unemployed youth in higher-income countries can get access to unemployment benefits (S), but in most Bank client countries this is not an option. Public works programs can play a temporary safety net role for low-income groups. Social safety nets and aspects of social insurance were assessed in earlier IEG evaluations on social safety nets and on the Bank Group response to the financial crisis.

Demand-side interventions aim at expanding work opportunities for youth (I). Related reforms are generally targeted to the entire workforce and not just youth. However, they may have a youth effect by changing the way firms do business in youth-intensive industries. Such reforms aim to improve the business environment, open the economy to trade, foster investment and growth, increase productivity in agriculture, and create jobs with increased earnings power. Interventions to foster self-employment and entrepreneurship target young entrepreneurs who lack the knowledge, finance, and experience to become self-employed. These interventions support the self-employed with training and access to capital. Interventions for young farmers provide training, access to land, credit, and markets (Proctor and Lucchesi 2012). Interventions to relax rigid labor market regulations aim to allow employers more flexibility in hiring and firing, including young workers, and to reduce regulatory and union protection of "insiders." Wage subsidies and public works programs are part of Active Labor Market Programs (ALMP). Both offer work and income for a finite period, which provides immediate relief for the most disadvantaged and a temporary safety net function.

School-to-work interventions (L) aim to reduce the time of search, facilitate a better job-skills match, and reduce the costs of job search for both workers and employers, if enough jobs are available. However, its applicability to developing countries with a large informal and agriculture sector is limited. Also, improved matching for youth might displace adults where the number of jobs is finite. Some governments (for example, the Philippines and Tunisia) facilitate overseas employment for youth in search of work if there are not enough jobs.

On the supply-side, education interventions (E) include reforms in the formal education system and skills building. Reforms in the formal education system aim to improve the quality and relevance of skills acquired. In countries with a private sector, there is increasing private sector participation in decisions on learning and work-based training. Remedial and short-term training programs are part of ALMP and help unemployed youth re-engage into the workplace. Key interventions in low-income areas are increasing the low primary and secondary school enrollment rates, and improving the quality of learning to equip children with basic skills for future learning and the workforce. The performance of Bank support to education projects is analyzed in the recent IEG Education Sector Review (IEG 2011g). Supply-side interventions are less effective where there is already an oversupply of skills, but they can be targeted to subgroups to improve their employability.

## The Bank's Lending and Analytic and Advisory Activities Portfolio for Youth Employment is Small and Young

The identified Bank lending portfolio for youth employment is small. Direct youth employment lending accounts for a small portion—0.9 percent—of total commitments by the International Bank for Reconstruction and Development (IBRD) and International Development Association (IDA). Between FY01 and FY11, the Bank loaned $2.85 billion to youth employment programs through 90 operations in 57 countries (appendixes B and D). Of the 90 operations, 36 are closed (40 percent) and 54 are ongoing. Fragile states implemented 12 of the 90 operations and about 6 percent of total youth employment lending (appendix D, box D.1 and table D.5). The portfolio includes 15 development policy operations and 75 investment loans. Most of Bank support for youth employment projects is in Africa, and most lending went to Europe and Central Asia (appendix D, tables D.2 and D.3, and figure D.3).

Spending on youth employment increased over time. The level of new commitments to youth employment was low in the first half of the decade despite high global youth unemployment rates. Bank lending peaked in 2007, which coincides with the lowest youth unemployment rate during the decade and the publication of the *World Development Report 2007: Development and the Next Generation,* and again in 2009 and 2010 during the global economic crisis (figure 2.1).

The World Bank has undertaken analysis and promoted knowledge sharing to encourage youth employment and skills building. Between 2001 and 2011, World Bank teams prepared 34 pieces of economic and sector work (ESW) and carried out 25 technical assistance activities related to "improving labor market outcomes." Most of this work (85 percent) was done after 2006. For the purpose of this evaluation, 21 ESW products with a youth employment focus were reviewed, all of them published since 2005[1] (appendix B). The Bank spent $4.4 million on 18 of these reports.[2] Ten of the 21 countries with ESW had a youth employment project.

The small but growing number of impact evaluations of Bank projects highlights the need for more evidence on what works in low-income areas, as well as for cost-effectiveness analysis of interventions. Most of the international evaluation evidence on youth employment is from countries in Latin America and in the OECD. Short-term skills building and vouchers are most frequently evaluated. The seven Bank impact evaluations of projects included in this portfolio review reflect the international trend but add much-needed information on Africa. These impact evaluations examine short-term effects, so the persistence of any positive effects over time is uncertain. Only one of the impact evaluations included a cost and cost-benefit analysis of the intervention (Attanasio and others 2011).

## What Is the Bank Doing in the Three ILE Intervention Categories?

The Bank most often supports skills building and school-to-work transition activities. Using the MILES framework (box 2.1), the portfolio review found that most Bank youth employment projects include interventions in skills development (82 percent) and school–to–work transition (79 percent). Fifty-four

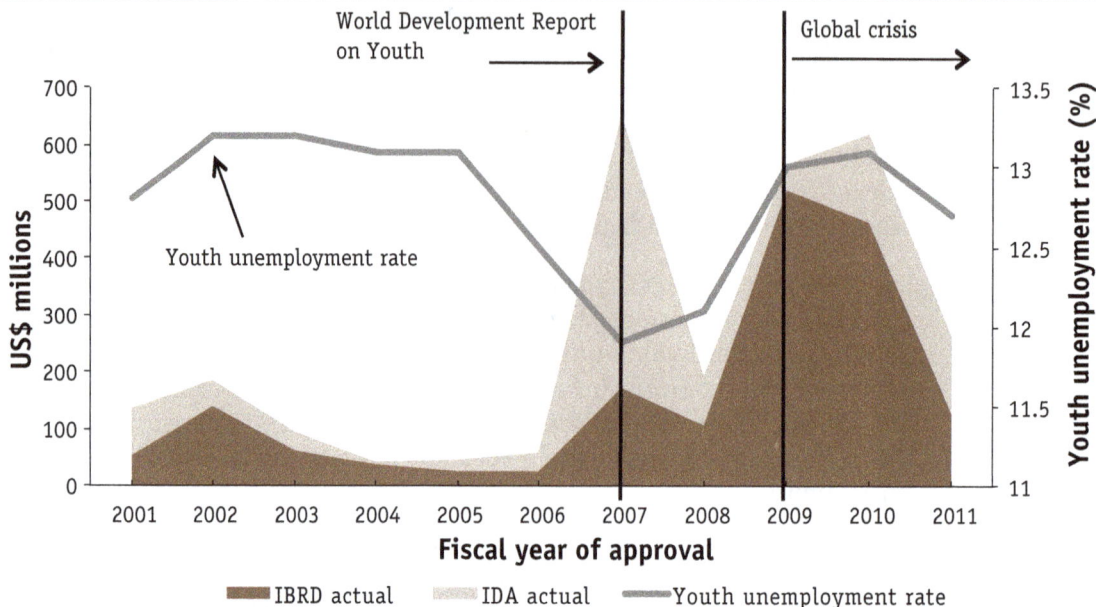

**Figure 2.1**     Actual World Bank Support to Youth Employment, 2001–2011 (US$ millions)

*Sources:* IEG project portfolio. ILO 2012.
*Note:* Appendix A describes identification of Bank support to youth employment.

percent include interventions to foster job creation and work opportunities for youth. This share is lower because other Bank operations provide support to foster job creation and investment climate reforms, and not just youth employment projects. The distribution of project objectives and interventions by sector and region is presented in appendix D, tables D.7–D.14.

Bank projects most often include interventions to improve "information on the labor market," and "quality of formal vocational education" (figure 2.2). Interventions in the area of labor market information generally consist of setting up a government management information system to report labor data and building monitoring and evaluation capacity. Interventions related to formal vocational education with recognition of skills and work-based TVET are gaining new traction amid shortages in skilled employees. Less than 30 percent of operations support job-creation interventions, such as entrepreneurship training or business startups, access to credit, and public works programs. Public works programs for youth are most prominent in fragile settings where they rank second (appendix D and box 3.2).

Bank lending and nonlending equally target young women and men, or rural low-income groups, but little is known about how women, rural and low-income youth in informal sectors are benefiting from this support. Project interventions were fairly equally targeted to women and men and to rural low-income areas. However, the monitoring framework used in the 90 projects

## Figure 2.2    Top 12 Youth Employment Interventions in 90 Bank Projects

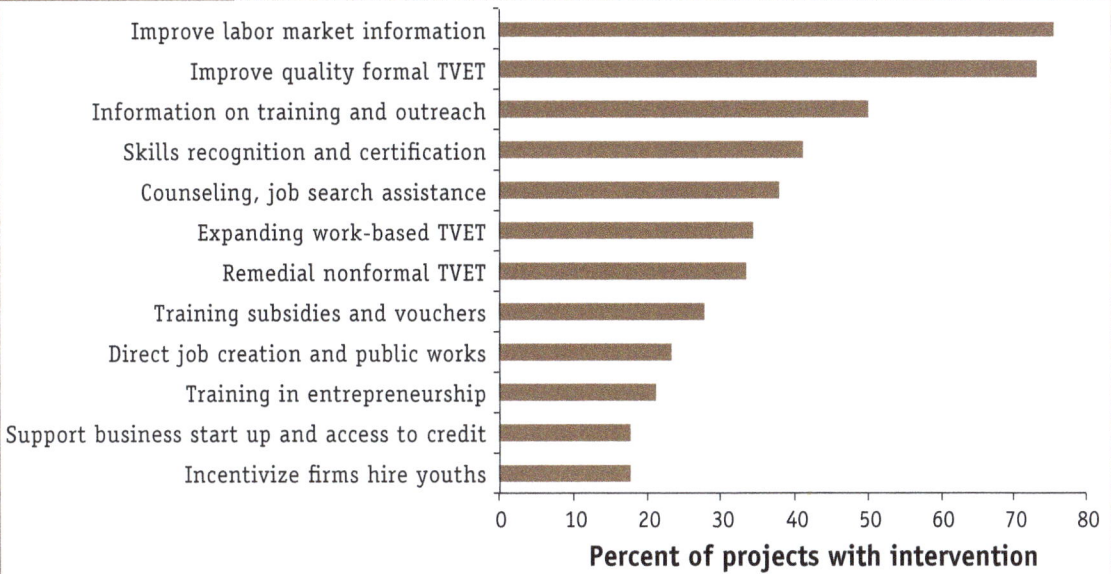

A horizontal bar chart titled "Top 12 Youth Employment Interventions in 90 Bank Projects." The x-axis is labeled "Percent of projects with intervention" ranging from 0 to 80. The interventions and approximate values are:

- Improve labor market information: ~76
- Improve quality formal TVET: ~73
- Information on training and outreach: ~50
- Skills recognition and certification: ~41
- Counseling, job search assistance: ~38
- Expanding work-based TVET: ~34
- Remedial nonformal TVET: ~33
- Training subsidies and vouchers: ~28
- Direct job creation and public works: ~23
- Training in entrepreneurship: ~21
- Support business start up and access to credit: ~18
- Incentivize firms hire youths: ~18

*Source:* IEG portfolio review based on World Bank data.
*Note:* TVET=technical and vocational education and training.

is weak in identifying benefits by gender, socioeconomic groups, geographic areas, and the informal sector. Similarly, the Bank's analytical work examines employment for young women, but rarely provides gender-specific recommendations. Employment and earnings issues could be systematically discussed and policy options identified for young women, youth in rural areas and the informal sector, and low-income youth.

## IFC Has a Broad Approach to Employment Creation

At IFC, few specific youth employment programs or projects have been developed. Except in the education sector, youth have not been specifically targeted as beneficiaries. Job creation and increasing job opportunities for all age groups has been a focus for IFC. Investment and advisory operations have supported projects that have created overall jobs, including those for youth. For example, in 2010 IFC clients directly employed 2.4 million individuals, which included "youth-friendly" sectors such as agribusiness, information technology, and services. Since FY06, approximately 100 advisory service projects have had objectives that were linked to job creation. However, youth employment has not been a specific objective, with the recent exception of special initiatives in a few countries. Appendix E provides a detailed discussion of IFC support as relevant to youth employment.

IFC has supported 10 advisory services projects, worth $6 million (reflecting 0.5 percent of the total IFC portfolio), with a youth employment objective.

Six of these programs were under the Grassroots Business Initiative (GBI).[3] They intended to support the grassroots level through investing in social enterprises, or grassroots business organizations. IFC supported structured mentoring, training, and internship opportunities for Russia's disadvantaged youth and financial literacy training for South African youth. However, IFC has discontinued or spun-off these initiatives. Two other projects included equity-type financing for young Indian entrepreneurs and business training for the youth in Yemen.

IFC is supporting education sector investments and related advisory services. Between FY01 and FY11, IFC invested in 50 education sector projects, committing around $500 million through loan, equity, and guarantee facilities.[4] More than half (68 percent) were in tertiary education, and six projects included components for technical and vocational training (TVET; see regional distribution in appendix E, figure E.3). IFC has also supported educational institutions through capacity building. Although there have been few such interventions, IFC provided 18 advisory services projects, mostly in Africa, totaling $12 million.

IFC has recently begun some youth employment initiatives. In collaboration with the Islamic Development Bank, IFC undertook a study on the role of the private sector in job creation in the Middle East and North Africa (IFC 2011a). Based on the findings, IFC initiated the e4e Initiative for Arab Youth, a program that seeks to develop a private sector education agenda to address the mismatch between employer needs and skills developed through the education system in the Arab world. The project focuses on the role that the private sector can play in addressing the skill mismatch problem, and will guide the first joint Bank-IFC strategy in the region. In addition, IFC participates in the Global Agenda Council on Youth Employment at the World Economic Forum.

## Paucity of Data on Youth Employment Limits Analysis

The paucity of project data severely constrains the ability to assess Bank and IFC support on labor market outcomes. The majority of Bank projects (55 percent) in the portfolio (appendix B, table B.3) provide no information on youth as a beneficiary group. The remaining projects mainly report on *input indicators*—such as enrollment capacity in diploma and vocational training courses and the number of technical and vocational education and training (TVET) programs—and *output indicators*—such as the number of students enrolled and the number of beneficiaries subsidized.

If reported, *outcome indicators* (unemployment rate, employment rate, labor force participation rate, employment rate within one year of graduation) are generally not disaggregated by age. Rather, they are presented for the entire population and not specifically for the project beneficiary population and a comparison group. Project indicators do not identify earnings, the socioeconomic background, sector, and geographic area of beneficiaries.

Of the three projects with a gender emphasis in the objective, only one collected the relevant indicator. Few projects or analytic products include tracer studies to track the subsequent employment history of the youth who participated in training. IFC does not disaggregate employment data by age groups, even for the Middle East and North Africa, where youth employment is a priority, and placement rates or wages are generally not tracked (box 2.2). Appendix B provides detailed information on data and methodology.

Data limitations prevent the assessment of most standard labor market outcomes in Bank and IFC projects. The paucity of project data does not allow for analysis of other relevant outcome variables of youth employment programs including:

- outflow into employment in the formal or informal sector;
- shift from informal to formal work;
- the type and the quality of employment with benefits;
- unemployment spells;
- productivity and earnings;

| Box 2.2 | Methodology: How Do We Know What the World Bank Group Is Doing? |
| --- | --- |

This evaluation examines the Bank Group's support to youth employment during FY01–FY11. It draws on analysis of 90 closed and ongoing Bank operations relevant to youth employment approved since FY01, as well as a review of 21 pieces of economic and sector work (ESW) and 18 country studies. In addition, the evaluation conducted a systematic review of 38 impact evaluations of youth employment programs (7 of which were on Bank-supported projects), 9 Project Performance Assessment Reports (PPARs), semi-structured key informant interviews with Bank Group management and chief economists, and an electronic survey of Bank task team leaders of youth employment projects. IFC does not identify youth as a beneficiary group. Therefore, the evaluation draws from the jobs data of 853 clients, 159 advisory services projects with jobs objectives, and an analysis of 50 investment and 18 advisory services operations in education.

The evaluation is limited by the portfolio selection, methodology, and data. First, many Bank Group operations have an indirect effect on youth employment (for example, through infrastructure and labor market operations). These operations were not included in the Bank portfolio review, as their effect on youth employment cannot be disentangled from their overall effect on the working population. Second, only 17 of the 36 closed projects have a project objective related to skills building or youth employment, and an Implementation Completion Report (ICR) reviewed by IEG. Thus, a full assessment of project outcomes against their objectives using data from ICR reviews is impossible. Third, standard labor market outcomes (employment and earnings) have been examined where available. The absence of other outcomes and distributional data does not allow for analysis of other relevant outcome variables, distributional effects, and medium- and longer-term impacts. Further detail on the data and methodology of the evaluation can be found in appendix B.

*Source:* IEG.

- the substitution effect of better skilled individuals at the expense of less qualified youth;
- general equilibrium effect with more skilled workers in the labor market causing the employment of all individuals to increase;
- the poverty and crime impact of unemployment;
- social cohesion effects; and
- cost-effectiveness and the fiscal impact of youth employment interventions.

This evaluation should be seen as only a selective assessment of the World Bank Group's engagement in youth employment issues. The next two sections will focus on two questions:

- What is the evidence that the Bank and IFC support priority country needs in youth employment?
- What is the evidence regarding the effectiveness of this support?

## Notes

1. With the exception of one Tunisia report from 2004.

2. Data are not available for Sri Lanka, Tanzania, and Zambia.

3. These projects sought to provide: (i) opportunities to youth through the targeting and scaling up of existing youth enterprise development initiatives; (ii) capacity building grants, and; (iii) loan guarantees and technical assistance to financial institutions and business development services providers who, in turn, support business training and mentoring to informal/young rural micro entrepreneurs.

4. Since the first education investment in 1987, to date IFC invested in 73 education sector projects, committing over $600million through loan, equity and guarantee facilities.

## References

Attanasio, Orazio, Adriana Kugler, and Costas Meghir. 2011. "Subsidizing Vocational Training for Disadvantaged Youth in Colombia: Evidence from a Randomized Trial." *American Economic Journal: Applied Economics* 3(3): 188–220.

Begg, David, Stanley Fischer, and Rudiger Dornbusch. 2000. "Economics." New York: The McGraw-Hill Companies.

Biagi, Federico, and Claudio Lucifora. 2008. "Demographic and education effects on unemployment in Europe." *Labour Economics* 15:1076–1101.

Gustman, Alan, and Thomas Steinmeier. 1988. "A model for analyzing youth labor market policies." *Journal of Labor Economics* 6(3): 376–396.

Holzmann, Robert. 2007. MILES: Identifying Binding Constraints to Job Creation and Productivity Growth. An Introduction. Washington, DC: World Bank.

Independent Evaluation Group. 2011. "World Bank Support to Education since 2001: A Portfolio Note." Washington, DC: World Bank.

International Finance Corporation. 2011. "Education for Employment (e4e): Realizing Arab Youth Potential—Executive Summary." www.e4earabyouth.com

International Labour Organization. (ILO). 2012. "Global Employment Trends for Youth." http://www.ilo.org/global/publications/books/global-employment-trends/WCMS_171571/lang--en/index.htm

Proctor, Felicity, and Valerio Lucchesi. 2012. Small-scale farming and youth in an era of rapid rural change. IIED. London. http://pubs.iied.org/

Robalino, David, Rita Almeida, Jere Behrman. 2010. "Skills Development Strategies to Improve Employability and Productivity." Unpublished report.

Ryan, P. 2001. "The School to Work Transition: A Cross-National Perspective." *Journal of Economic Literature* 39(1): 34–92.

World Bank. 2007. *World Development Report 2007: Development and the next generation*. Washington, DC.

# Chapter 3

What Is the Evidence that the World Bank and IFC Support Priority Country Needs in Youth Employment?

- Youth employment is addressed in the Bank's education and social protection and labor strategies, but it is not recognized as an issue in most Bank country strategies, even in countries where youth employment is a problem.

- The top 10 Bank borrowers received 70 percent of youth employment lending in the past decade; among them are four IDA countries. The remaining 30 percent of lending was split among 47 countries. Most Bank operations have two to six interventions, but they are not designed comprehensively.

- A "comprehensive approach" is a multipronged strategy that includes complementary interventions aimed at removing key constraints to youth employment across multiple elements, namely: influencing the job creation and work opportunities for youth, market characteristics, and labor supply.

- Few youth employment projects are implemented by a multisectoral team.

To assess the relevance of Bank Group engagement, one must ask to what extent youth employment interventions have been analyzed and prioritized in strategy documents. Even more important, is there a strategic engagement in youth employment in the implementation of country programs?

## Youth Employment in Sector Strategic Documents

Although the Bank Group does not have a strategy focused on youth employment, several sector strategies cover aspects of this issue. The corporate thinking on youth employment is set out in the sector strategies on education and social protection and labor. It is also emphasized in the 2007 World Development Report and appears in analytical frameworks. The Bank's new Social Protection and Labor (SPL) Strategy, 2012–2022, "Building Resilience and Opportunity," emphasizes promoting opportunity, productivity, and growth through human capital building and access to jobs. The SPL strategy focuses on engaging individuals, especially youth, and improving the functioning of labor markets to include them by using incentives and ALMPs to link individuals to jobs, and facilitate transitions between jobs. Youth transiting from school to work are an important target group for ALMPs, which in addition to training can include counseling, job search assistance, intermediation services, skills certification, and wage subsidies (World Bank 2012).

The Education Strategy 2020 "Learning for All" states that better knowledge and skills are expected to influence individual productivity and ability to adapt to new technologies and opportunities. The strategy addresses youth employment by ensuring that those youth who leave school have the necessary skills for productive employment. It also highlights the need to target young school dropouts early. Learning opportunities, such as work-skills training through remedial, second-chance, and job training programs are needed to help them find employment. The strategy calls for the engagement of non-state players in meeting a range of educational needs, especially through technical and vocational education and training. It also recommends that governments focus on quality assurance and reducing inequality to leverage the growth of private institutions in tertiary education and TVET.

Youth employment has not been identified as a priority in IFC strategies, except in the Middle East and North Africa. Creating jobs and opportunities for jobs, regardless of gender and age, have been a focus of IFC. The facility for technical assistance to support private sector development has a mandate to "stimulate private sector growth and reduce the high unemployment, especially among the young and female entrants into the labor markets" (IFC 2006). IFC's recent strategy (FY12–14) for the region pays special attention to addressing the needs of youth by aiming to support: employment-generating investments; access to finance for student borrowers; and improved quality of post-secondary education to meet the needs of the private sector and provide jobs for youth. Youth are the main beneficiaries of IFC's investments in education. In the future, IFC is looking to increase access in underserved areas, reach lower-income households, and improve employment opportunities (IFC 2012).

The *World Development Report 2007: Development and the Next Generation* (World Bank 2007) highlighted that young people make up nearly half of the unemployed worldwide. Decisions about continuing education and starting to work have the biggest long-term impact on how human capital is developed and deployed. To support youth in their development, the report presents three strategic policies: expanding opportunities, improving capabilities, and offering second chances for those who have fallen behind due to difficult circumstances or poor choices. (Appendix C, box C.1; World Development Reports).

Two frameworks developed by the Bank apply to the youth employment context. The MILES framework (box 2.1) applies to the entire labor market (Holzmann 2007), whereas the Skills towards Employment and Productivity (STEP) framework is a sequenced combination of education, training, and labor market activities for effective skills building. STEP consists of five interlinked components:

1. Get children off to the right start through early child development (ECD).
2. Ensure that all students learn.
3. Build job-relevant skills that employers demand.
4. Encourage entrepreneurship and innovation.
5. Match the supply of skills with demand through better functioning labor markets, labor mobility, and job searches while strengthening income protection (World Bank 2010).

## Youth Employment is Not a Strategic Issue in the Bank's Country Strategies

Youth employment lending is concentrated in 10 countries that received 70 percent of lending (figure 3.1). Among the top 10 borrowers for youth employment are four IDA countries (Ghana, India, Kenya, and Nigeria). Support to youth employment was mainly to middle-income countries with large lending programs. These countries have programs in vocational training, school-to-work transition, and the investment climate to address youth employment issues. The remaining 30 percent of youth employment lending was split among 47 countries (appendix D, table D.2).

Bank lending was not targeted to the countries with the largest youth employment problems. The lending portfolio analysis found no correlation between the actual lending amount for youth employment and selected youth employment indicators in countries. This may reflect the lending priority of countries for other needs. IDA countries might borrow less for youth employment because their borrowing is constrained, so they instead focus on addressing poverty, weak administration, and low educational attainment. Also, countries receive support from other donors.

Youth employment program design and context matter, and careful diagnostics are needed. Limited evidence exists from cross-country

| Figure 3.1 | Top 10 Youth Employment Borrowers (US$ millions) |

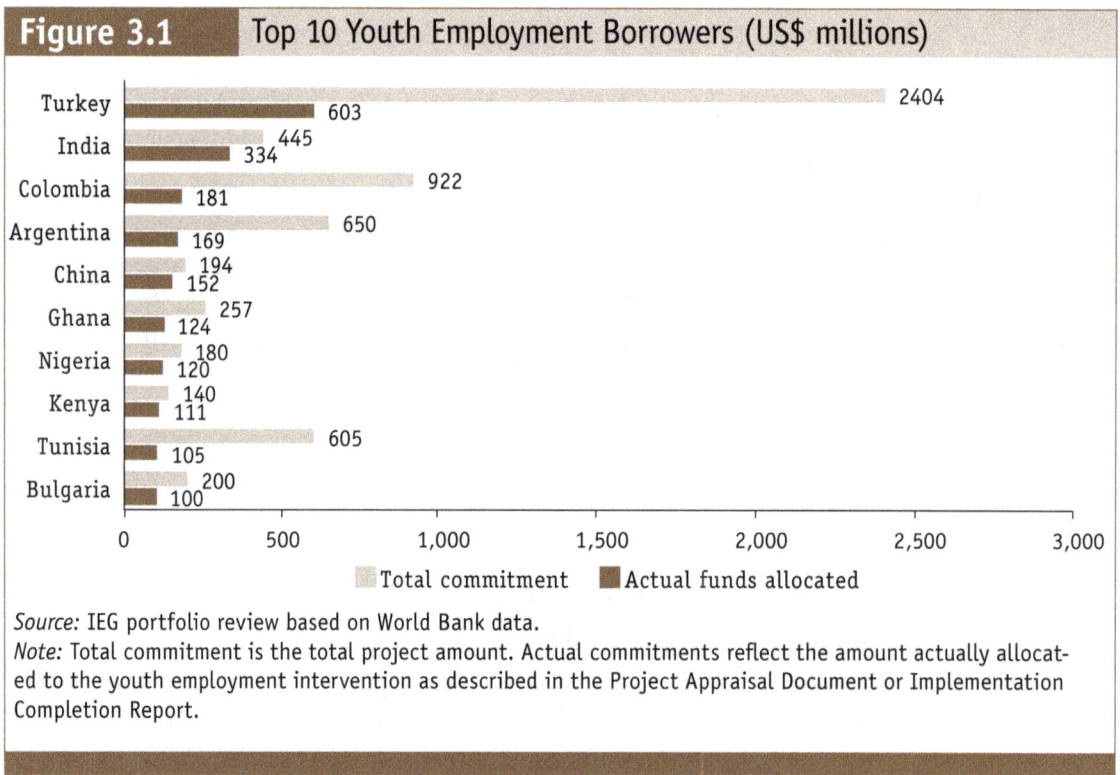

Source: IEG portfolio review based on World Bank data.
Note: Total commitment is the total project amount. Actual commitments reflect the amount actually allocated to the youth employment intervention as described in the Project Appraisal Document or Implementation Completion Report.

evaluations on what works best to promote youth employment. In 2007, Betcherman and others analyzed the effectiveness of interventions collected in an inventory of 289 youth employment interventions in 84 countries. Only 73 interventions (25 percent) were properly evaluated, most of them from OECD countries, Eastern Europe, and Latin America. Program success was determined not by the type of intervention but by its design and appropriateness to tackle the problem identified. Recommendations highlight the need for a careful diagnostic of the youth employment problem, and the need for interventions to be closely monitored and evaluated.

A "comprehensive approach" is a multipronged strategy that includes complementary interventions aimed at removing key constraints to youth employment across multiple elements, namely: influencing the job creation and work opportunities for youth (both demand for youth by firms and self-employment), labor and credit market characteristics, and labor supply (box 3.1).

Most country strategies (Country Assistance Strategies and Country Partnership Strategies) do not identify youth employment as a strategic issue. All 18 country programs examined for this study have either high youth unemployment rates, large youth cohorts, or high inactivity rates (appendix B, table B.7). In 5 of these countries, the Bank's country strategies presented youth employment as a strategic issue with specific actions (lending, nonlending, donor coordination) for implementation (World Bank 2009a (Dominican Republic); World Bank 2009b (Morocco); World Bank 2009c (Nigeria); World Bank 2009d (Tunisia); and World Bank 2008 (Turkey). However, the issue only recently became prominent, and none of the strategies focuses on youth in agriculture and rural non-farm sectors. Most country strategies only briefly mention youth employment with limited or no follow-up. Strategy indicators rarely collect age-specific labor market outcome data.

---

**Box 3.1**      A Comprehensive Approach in Youth Employment Programs

A combination of complementary interventions and a positive growth environment are needed. The IEG systematic review of 38 impact program evaluations from 19 countries and 4 regions finds that a positive growth environment helps to ensure the success of the interventions. In low- or no-growth environments in which there are no jobs, wage subsidies, skills training, and job search will not have much of an impact on jobs.

Factors that increase the probability of success include participation of the private sector, personal monitoring and follow up of individual participants, and a combination of complementary interventions, such as training with job search and placement assistance, rather than isolated interventions. Programs that combine smoothing the transition from school to work with work-based skills development appear to be most effective for youth employment and earnings. Counseling and job search assistance is the only type of intervention that most often appears to provide positive labor outcomes. However, its applicability to developing countries with a large informal sector is limited. Almost all other interventions work in some cases, but not every case.

*Source:* IEG analysis.

---

A comprehensive approach is missing in the Bank's youth employment projects (box 3.2). Most Bank projects (69 percent) include two to six interventions. However, the projects are not designed comprehensively, and interventions from the three categories are not complementary. Rarely did projects support youth in the rural economy. A comprehensive approach also requires that Bank-supported interventions be underpinned by solid analysis within the given country context.

## Challenges in Multisector Collaboration

Fragmented collaboration across ministries and levels of governments are challenges to multisector programs. Youth employment programs are often spread across different government agencies and ministries and central and local government levels, which creates an additional burden on collaboration. In some countries, responsibilities for youth employment reside in the Ministry of Labor and Ministry of Youth. Often several ministries share the responsibility. For example, in Burkina Faso, six ministries (Commerce,

---

| Box 3.2 | What the Bank is Supporting: Findings from 18 Countries |
|---------|--------------------------------------------------------|

IEG identified a number of areas where the World Bank Group is engaged. World Bank activities vary across countries:

- In Armenia, the Bank helped promote a better business environment to improve the investment climate and encourage the hiring of young workers. It also made the TVET system more responsive to employers' needs.

- The Bank and IFC support the investment climate in Rwanda to encourage employers to hire young workers, and a TVET project to build skills.

- In Burkina Faso, the Bank has helped to improve the TVET system with more labor market relevant curricula and training and private sector participation.

- In Tunisia, the analytical work contributed to knowledge and public discussion on youth employment.

- In other countries, experience was gained by promoting specific initiatives such as: supporting a comprehensive skills development strategy in Ghana: investing in secondary education to produce more employable graduates in Indonesia and Macedonia; and revising terms and conditions of employment contracts in Macedonia, Turkey, and Tunisia to allow for more flexibility in hiring youth.

- IFC has supported tertiary education and TVET for young working adults from middle- and low-income backgrounds in Brazil, Chile, and Colombia.

These findings illustrate that in most countries the Bank and IFC did not take a comprehensive approach addressing both supply and demand factors in a complementary way and underpinned by diagnostic work. Furthermore, the employment and earnings effects of these interventions were not tracked.

*Source:* IEG country program analysis.

Agriculture, Health, Education, Social Service, and Justice) operate specialized training centers (World Bank 2006).

Collaboration across sector teams within the Bank and with IFC is limited in youth employment operations. Education sector staff participated in about 40 percent of the preparation and 33 percent of the supervision of the 15 projects managed by other sectors with a skills-building component. However, staff from the Social Protection and Finance and Private Sector Development units worked less often in multisector teams (figure 3.2). The four Social Development Network projects with interventions in education, school-to-work transition, and investment climate did not include any sector specialists. Similarly, the four Development Policy Operations (DPOs) with skills building that were led by Finance and Private Sector Development had no education staff on the team.

There were few cross-collaboration efforts between the Bank and IFC. Joint teams prepared a student loan program in Colombia, an impact evaluation of IFC's Kenya Risk Shared Facilities project that did not materialize, and the e4e Initiative for Arab Youth.[1] The two institutions also collaborated in preparing the new Education Strategy 2020 "Learning for All." Weak cross-sector collaboration was confirmed in the IEG matrix evaluation (IEG 2012).

The Bank is participating in international initiatives, albeit small in scope, relevant to youth employment. Millennium Development Goal 1,

**Figure 3.2** Participation of Sector Specialists in Relevant Components Managed by Other Sectors

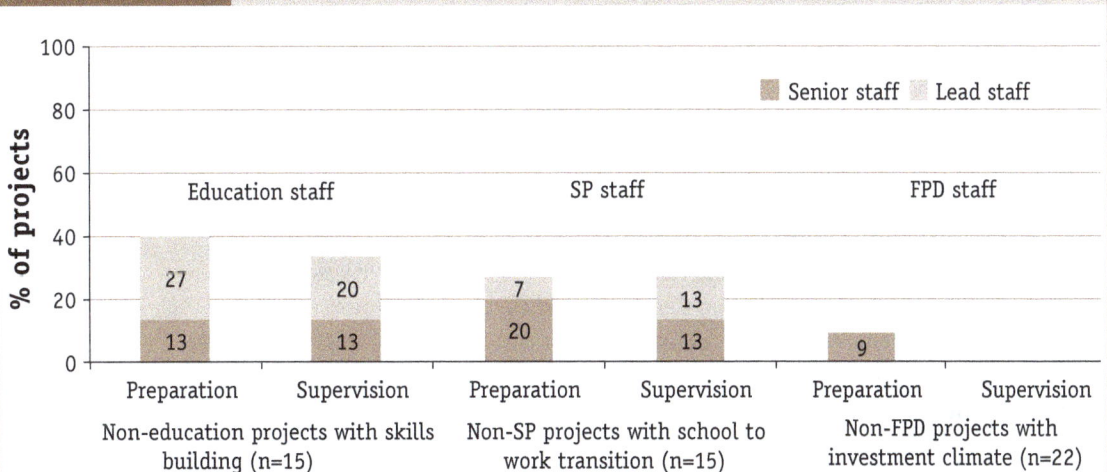

Source: IEG review of Implementation Completion Reports.
Note: n=number of projects in the sample with relevant component. Total n > the number of closed projects because a project can have more than one component. FPD=Finance and Private Sector Development; SP=Social Protection.

"Eradicating Poverty and Hunger," has been expanded to include Target 1B, which focuses on "employment and decent work for all, including women and young people." However, the relevant youth employment indicators are not being tracked. The Bank has two Global Public Private Partnerships for youth employment. Until December 2011, the Social Development Network had a Global Public Private Partnership for Youth Investment. The Human Development Network manages the Global Partnership for Youth Employment. In 2001, the World Bank, together with the United Nations, the International Labor Organization, and other development partners,[2] launched the Youth Employment Network (YEN). The YEN is mainly a platform for data collection and information sharing that provides technical advice to find new solutions to the youth employment challenge. Whether these Partnerships and YEN had an impact on labor markets for youth has not been assessed.

In 2008, the Adolescent Girls Initiative (AGI) was created to promote the transition of adolescent girls from school to productive wage, or self-employment. It currently operates in nine participating countries. AGI offers training sessions in basic numeracy and literacy skills, technical skills,[3] life skills, and business skills. The number of beneficiaries per country ranges from approximately 900 in Jordan to 3,500 women in Nepal. Implementation started in 2010 in selected countries, and impact evaluations are ongoing. Appendixes C and D provide more detailed information on the Bank's support to priority country needs. Appendix E describes the IFC portfolio in detail.

## Notes

1.  The impact evaluation was not finalized because the Kenya project did not perform as well as expected.

2.  The Danish-Led Africa Commission, the International Olympic Committee, Jacobs Foundation, Swedish International Development Agency (SIDA), the World Bank Development Grant Facility, United Nations Industrial Development Organization (UNIDO), BASF-The Chemicals Company, and BMZ- German Federal Ministry for Economic Cooperation and Development.

3.  The type of skills is targeted to sectors with high demand. For example, the program in Liberia includes skills development on hospitality, house painting, professional driving, office/computer skills, and security guard services. In Rwanda, the technical training is in areas such as horticulture, agro-processing, tourism, arts and crafts, technical servicing, and solar technology, information and communications technology, and secretarial services.

## References

Betcherman, Gordon, Martin Godfrey, Susana Puerto, Friederike Rother, and Antoneta Stavreska. 2007. "A Review of Interventions to Support Young Workers: Findings of the Youth Employment Inventory." SP Discussion Paper No. 0715. Washington, DC: World Bank.

Holzmann, Robert. 2007. MILES: Identifying Binding Constraints to Job Creation and Productivity Growth. An Introduction. Washington, DC: World Bank.

Independent Evaluation Group. 2012. "World Bank and IFC Support for Youth Employment Programs." Background Paper. Country Case Study: Ghana. Forthcoming.

International Finance Corporation (IFC). IFC Education Investment Strategy. 2012.

———. 2006. "PEP- MENA Annual Report." http://ifcnet.ifc.org/intranet/changemo .nsf/AttachmentsByTitle/OneIFCWeek_VirualFail_IFCDevelopmentImpactSource Study/$FILE/IFC+source+study+fact+sheet.pdf

World Bank. 2012. Building Resilience and Opportunity. The World Bank's Social Protection and Labor Strategy 2012–2022. Executive Summary. Draft for SPL Board/HD Council. February 3, 2012.

———. 2010. Learning for All: Investing in People's Knowledge and Skills to Promote Development: World Bank Education Strategy 2020. Education Strategy. Human Development Network, Education. Washington, DC.

———. 2009a. "The Dominican Republic: Country Partnership Strategy for the Dominican Republic for the Period FY10–13." Report No. 49620-DO, Washington, D.C.: World Bank.

———. 2009b. "Morocco: Country Partnership Strategy for the Kingdom of Morocco for the Period FY10–13." Report No. 50316-MA. Washington, D.C.: World Bank.

———. 2009c. "Nigeria: Country Partnership Strategy for the Federal Republic of Nigeria for the Period FY2010–13." Report No. 46816-NG. Washington, D.C.: World Bank.

———. 2009d. "Tunisia: Country Partnership Strategy for the Republic of Tunisia for the Period FY10–13." Report No. 50223-TUN. Washington, D.C.: World Bank.

———. 2008. "Turkey: Country Partnership Strategy for the Republic of Turkey for the Period FY2008–11." Report No. 42026-TR. Washington, D.C.: World Bank.

———. 2007. *World Development Report 2007: Development and the next generation.* Washington, DC.

———. 2006. "Création d'emplois pour la Réduction de la Pauvreté au Burkina Faso." Employment Program Review. Washington, DC.

# Chapter 4

What is the Evidence on the
Effectiveness of Bank and IFC Support
to Youth Employment?

This chapter presents findings from the IEG systematic review of impact evaluations and from World Bank Group projects. Evidence is presented by single interventions. This follows the interventions listed in table 4.1, which were introduced in chapter 2.

Evidence on the results from the Bank and IFC project portfolio on youth employment has been difficult to obtain, mainly because the data are lacking or because almost two-thirds of the selected projects are ongoing. More detailed information is in appendix F. Appendix D, table D.12 provides an overview of the type of interventions supported by Bank projects in the different regions.

| Table 4.1 | Youth Employment Intervention Categories | |
|---|---|---|
| Demand-side: Fostering job creation/work opportunities (I) | Smoothing school-to-work transition and job mobility (L) | Supply-side: Fostering skill development and labor market relevance of skills (E) |
| • Improving the business and investment climate<br>• Regulations to encourage the hiring of young people<br>• Fostering self-employment and entrepreneurship<br>• Training in entrepreneurship or business management<br>• Support to start businesses and farms<br>• Providing wage subsidies<br>• Direct job creation (public works programs) | • Counseling, job search skills, information on vacancies, placement<br>• Improving information on the labor market<br>• Program for overseas employment of young people | • Improving the quality of formal technical and vocational education and training (TVET)<br>• Expanding/improving work-based learning in vocational and apprenticeship schemes<br>• Certification of skills<br>• Remedial education/second chance/non-formal technical and vocational training programs<br>• Providing information on training<br>• Training subsidies and vouchers<br>• Support for transportation and change of residence |

*Source:* IEG.

## Fostering Job Creation and Work Opportunities (I)

Firms' demand for youth and self-employment is unevenly covered in the Bank's analytical reports, which focus more on the skills gap constraint for employers. The Bank's Investment Climate Assessment reports examine whether entrepreneurs see the lack of skills as a constraint to investment. They identify the sectors that are likely to grow, the kinds of skills needed, and whether young employees are learning these skills (for example, in Mongolia). Where there is little prospect for increasing formal sector jobs as, for example, in sub-Saharan Africa, some Bank reports argue for more focus on raising the productivity and incomes of youth working in the informal sector or in agriculture.

Improving the business and investment climate has been linked to investment and employment growth (Bruhn 2008), but the impact on youth employment is unknown. Four Bank operations supported trade reforms in youth-intensive industries. However, the effect on employment and earnings is unknown. In Liberia, Mali, and Sierra Leone, the Bank facilitated the export of fish and local artisanal products. Reforms in export competitiveness in Turkey contributed to a one percentage point increase in private spending on research and development. In Armenia, an enterprise incubator helped 18 local information technology companies attract foreign investors, resulting in a 15 percent annual increase in graduates employed in information technology. In Bhutan, which has the highest youth-to-adult unemployment ratio (8.7) in the world, the Bank helped shortening the administrative time to recruit foreign workers, thereby increasing the labor supply. The substitution effect on Bhutanese youth is unknown.

Data on job creation for most IFC investment climate advisory projects have not been tracked. IFC-supported investment climate reforms in four African countries (Burkina Faso, Liberia, Rwanda, and Sierra Leone) created roughly 60,000 jobs for all age groups through newly established businesses across different sectors. However, no information is available on the distributional aspects.

Regulations to encourage hiring of youth allow greater flexibility and reduce segmentation in middle-income countries, but the impact on youth employment is not clear. Labor market regulations mainly protect formal sector "insider" workers, and can make it more difficult for youth to enter the market. For example, in Latin America, the unemployment effect of stricter regulations is almost two times larger for youth than for adult workers (Heckman and others 2000). Based on data from 17 OECD countries, Neumark and Wascher (2004) found that the negative employment effect of minimum wages on youth can be reduced by a youth sub-minimum wage. Higher youth minimum wages in Portugal led to a flatter wage profile over time as firms would compensate a higher initial wage with a slower wage progression (Cardoso 2009). The Bank did not collect any information on the youth employment effect from Bank-supported regulatory reforms in Eastern Europe and Central Asia.

IFC supports the Better Work program, which improves compliance with labor standards and overall competitiveness in global supply chains in Cambodia, Haiti, Indonesia, Jordan, and Vietnam. The program does not have a youth focus, but data in Haiti, Indonesia, and Jordan indicate that the main beneficiaries are women (70–90 percent) and youth 15–30 years of age (60 percent).

The Bank's analytical work proposes easing regulations for hiring youth, but does not provide guidance for implementation. Several Bank reports (such as the Ghana and Serbia labor market reports) analyze labor market regulations, hiring and firing procedures, and minimum wages in relation to their impact on youth informality. Reports conclude and recommend easing the negative impact of public employment on youth, preventing discrimination of labor market regulations and taxes against youth, and improving school-to-work transition through career counseling, internships, and job search assistance. None of the analytical work discusses how alternative regulations should be formulated or what their fiscal impact would be.

Entrepreneurship training has demonstrated small effects for some groups and limited effects on business performance. An impact evaluation of Mexico's Probecat program (Delajara and others 2006) found no self-employment effect. Rather, on-the-job training for unemployed youth in larger firms increased their employment and income. Bank support to business training for young ex-combatants in Côte d'Ivoire and Sierra Leone does not identify employment effects. However, in Eritrea, 85 percent of participating ex-combatants were economically active after training.

The Bank supported entrepreneurship training in Colombia, Tunisia, and Uganda. In Colombia and Uganda, start-up capital and entrepreneurship training facilitate access to training and employment in rural areas. In Northern Uganda (appendix F, box F.2), the Youth Opportunity Program provides unconditional cash grants to underemployed youth groups to pay for about 10 weeks of full-time vocational training, tools, and business start-up costs. Almost 80 percent of the treatment group enrolled in vocational training (mainly tailoring and carpentry) compared to 17 percent in the control group, who did not receive the cash grant. The employment and earning effect was strong for the treatment group (1,300 youth). About two-thirds found skilled work compared to one-third of the control group. The treatment group reported a 45 percent increase in net earnings compared to their status before enrolling in the program; however, women saw no earning impact, probably because tailoring pays less well than carpentry (Blattman and others 2011). In Colombia, the Bank supported the Young Rural Entrepreneurs training programs, which increased participants' employment rate by about 14 percentage points compared to the control group (Castañeda and others 2010).

In Tunisia, the effect of the entrepreneurship training program for University students is negligible and the cost unknown. An impact evaluation found that training offered to about 800 university students in Tunisia led to a 3 percentage point increase in their probability of becoming self-employed (about 24 additional self-employed) from a low baseline of 4 percent. The result was stronger for men than for women. The training affected neither the probability of students finding a job nor their earnings (Premand and others 2012). The analysis lacks information on cost, cost-effectiveness, and distributional effects.

Only a few IFC projects sought to provide opportunities to young entrepreneurs, mostly through the Grassroots Business Initiative, and more recently through the Business Edge program in Yemen, and the e4e Initiative for Arab Youth in the Middle East and North Africa region. The 10 IFC advisory projects sought to provide opportunities to youth by supporting capacity-building grants or through loan guarantees and technical assistance to financial institutions and business development service providers. Most of these projects were provided under the Grassroots Business Initiative, which has been spun-off.[1] There are other channels through which IFC creates employment opportunities, directly or indirectly, such as through investment climate reforms, and access to finance and infrastructure. IFC's linkage and supply chain programs account for its most comprehensive effort to create jobs, develop SMEs, and support entrepreneurship through packages of interventions including training, finance, and supplier development.

It is too early to draw conclusions about the effectiveness of IFC's e4e Initiative for Arab Youth program, as implementation has only recently begun. Although the rest of the projects have not explicitly targeted youth as part of their objectives, it is likely that the jobs created would benefit youth. For instance, an IFC agribusiness investment-advisory project with a tea plant in India created 3,000 jobs for youth, which represented 10 percent of the total workforce at the plant.

Temporary wage subsidies paid to employers to hire youth can have a short-term positive employment impact in countries with a formal sector—mainly if the work provides youth with higher-level skills. However, low uptake among employers is a challenge. Kluve (2006), in a review of European countries, found private sector incentive schemes to have a 30 to 50 percentage-point higher employment effect than skills-training programs offered under active labor market programs. In contrast, under the Swedish Youth Practice Program, subsidized youth were less likely to find employment compared to youth who received job search assistance, which was explained by insufficient planning and follow-up and low-quality work without building any higher-level skills (Larsson 2003). The U.K. New Deal includes a wage subsidies program that positively affects youth employment, but it suffered from low uptake among employers (Van Reenen 2003).

South Africa is considering a youth wage subsidy, which is planned to be a voucher that can be cashed by the hiring employer. The introduction is blocked by the South African labor unions.[2] The Bank supported wage subsidies in

Argentina, Bulgaria, Colombia, and Turkey; however, the youth impact is unknown. In Colombia, the subsidy program benefited more than 100,000 workers, but the program was stopped due to low uptake among employers.

Subsidized internships for tertiary students mainly cater to the upper income groups and result in being regressive. The governments of Rwanda and Tunisia are subsidizing internships in the public and private sector for university graduates (IEG 2012a; IEG 2012b; IEG 2012c; IEG 2012d). Findings from Tunisia suggest very low placement rates at below 15 percent in disadvantaged regions compared to the OECD benchmark placement rate of 80 percent for on-the-job training programs (World Bank 2011).

Public works programs provide short-term employment. These programs have been recommended by the Bank in rural areas. In Europe, the employment effect of public works programs, which form part of ALMPs, is negative for youth and scores below other interventions, including wage subsidies and skills training programs (Kluve 2010). Van Reenen (2003) finds a positive employment effect of the public works "environmental task force," which is part of the U.K. New Deal program. The Bank supported public works programs for all age groups in Argentina, Bulgaria, Colombia, El Salvador, Kenya, and Turkey. Impact evaluations in Argentina and Colombia only report short-term positive income effects related to the income transfer received, but no information on post-program employment. Various Bank reports recommend self-targeted, low-wage public works programs in rural areas instead of the high-cost and poorly targeted active labor market programs.

The coverage of Active Labor Market Programs is generally thorough and systematic in the Bank's analytical program. Much of the analytic work reviewed (appendix B) added value through the systematic treatment of ALMPs. Some reports describe and analyze the range of programs that are available. In the Kosovo report, for example, a large number of donors have each been supporting different ALMPs. The report analyzes each of these programs, describing how they operate and reporting data on cost per beneficiary and employment impact. The Ghana study provides a separate paper evaluating the National Youth Employment Program and deals with cost-effectiveness issues.

Few Bank reports focus explicitly on rural youth and on youth employment opportunities in the agriculture and agribusiness sectors although the majority of low-income youth live in rural areas. In the Africa region, analytic work tends to focus on formal employment in the urban areas, where political interest and the data can be found. Few reports examine youth employment in rural low-income areas. In Africa, it is most likely that youth will continue to be absorbed in agriculture, non-farm work, or self-employment. Too little is known about what this implies. The Bank could consider studies on the work and earnings situation of youth in agriculture and off-farm activities, and examine rural growth policy and investment to inform future lending for youth employment programs.

## Smoothing School-to-Work Transition and Job Mobility (L)

Although little is known from Bank support, evidence from the OECD and middle-income countries suggests adding school-to-work interventions to skills building increases the employment effect of skills building in a positive growth context. In the U.K. New Deal program, for example, unemployed youth enter a four-month "gateway" with a personal advisor who assists in the job search. The gateway significantly raised transition to employment. If still unemployed after the gateway period, youth either have to enroll in second-chance education or in subsidized job placement (van Reenen 2003; Blundell and others 2004).

The U.S. Center for Employment Training (CET) keeps youth in training for employment-relevant skills until they find a position. They are assisted in the process by a counselor (Miller and others 2003). The U.S. Job Corps is a multi-intervention program for disadvantaged youth with vocationally focused training and job placement assistance in a residential setting. Participation increases educational attainment, reduces criminal activity, and increases earnings. However, the job placement service was weak and strengthening it could enhance program results (Schochet and others 2008; Lee 2009). A positive growth environment supported the success of these programs.

Although 70 percent of Bank projects support "improving information on the labor market," little is known about how accessible and helpful job information is to job seekers, particularly in low-income areas with few formal sector jobs. Only in the case of Turkey did the analytic work examine this topic in depth. Even so, it is an area often supported by Bank lending (figure 2.2). The analysis of Bank reports identifies extensive coverage of the education system, whereas the school-to-work transition represents a gap in the analytical framework of youth employment.

Job search assistance, better information, and on-the-job training helped reintegrate ex-soldiers in the former Yugoslavia. In Bosnia and Herzegovina from 1996–1999, the Bank supported the re-integration of 300,000 ex-combatants into the workforce, among them 50,000 youth. The program included a municipal-level labor market information system with job vacancies and job seeker registration, education and retraining services with counseling, and a job-finding service. An impact evaluation found youth had the smallest program impacts, though still significant, with an increase in 28 percentage points in employment and a 42 DM (Deutsch Mark) increase in monthly income (Benus and others 2001).

Without tracer surveys, little is known about the employment and earnings effects of job search assistance. The Bank supported job search assistance in 40 percent of 90 projects, including in Armenia, Bulgaria, El Salvador, Maldives, and Turkey. However, only a few projects report information on job placement rates. In Honduras, the employment service reports a 33 percent placement rate for youth. In Tunisia, the employment service facilitated 69 foreign work contracts to France where 24 percent of youth are unemployed. During a job fair in Serbia, about 12 percent of participants found a job. In Indonesia, private sector providers in the Life Skills Education for Employment and Entrepreneurship program train, certify, and match unemployed youth with domestic and overseas jobs. IFC's Business Edge program for unemployed youth in Yemen provides training and job placement services and reports a placement rate of 45 percent. Most of these job search interventions reach a small number of youth, and they are only helpful in positive job growth environments.

## Fostering Skill Development and Labor Market Relevance of Skills (E)

The World Bank Group supports three main types of technical skills building in all regions (see appendix F, table F.2):[3]

- Formal technical education and vocational education training at the junior, secondary, or tertiary education level (comparable to TVET in OECD countries)—for example, the Technical Education III project in India (IEG 2011b).

- Short-term skills training targeted to unemployed youth, comparable to the SENA (Servicio Nacional De Aprendizaje) Colombia program (Medina and Núñez 2001).

- Remedial skills training targeted to disadvantaged youth comparable to the U.S. Job Corps and the Jovenes en Accion programs in Latin America.

### FORMAL TECHNICAL EDUCATION AND VOCATIONAL TRAINING

Evidence suggests TVET is more effective if provided comprehensively. The OECD (2010) defines a comprehensive approach to TVET as:

- Workplace training (because it provides learning opportunities for technical and soft skills and facilitates recruitment);

- Professional career guidance;

- Effective training of TVET teachers who should work part-time to sustain their industrial know-how;

- Incentives to employers to offer workplace learning; and

- Standardized assessments for TVET qualifications.

In some countries, high private returns to TVET education are observed, but information on costs is needed to draw policy conclusions. A study on the private returns to investment in education from 16 countries in East Asia and Latin America suggests that TVET seems to serve students better in entering wage employment compared with general secondary education (Patrinos and others 2006). Private returns do not take into account the often substantial public costs associated with TVET and related fiscal implications (Mingat and others 2010). Most Bank analytic work reviewed finds low returns to primary education in the countries studied, and hardly any difference between no education and primary education for employment or lifetime earnings. Returns increase with secondary education. However, Bank work does not examine the costs and cost-effectiveness of formal TVET.

The few tracer studies find positive employment and earning effects of TVET reforms supported by the Bank and IFC. The Bank supported TVET reforms through private sector involvement in management and governance boards in several countries, including India, Ghana, and Zambia. The five TVET projects that tracked employment outcomes all demonstrated improvement; however, the causal chain is difficult to establish without trend and comparison group data. The IEG project performance evaluation in India found an increase in employment rates for polytechnic graduates from 37 to 70 percent over six years (IEG 2011b). In Mauritania, the employment rate for TVET graduates increased from 60 to 80 percent. IFC support to TVET in Latin America increased student enrollment and the student earnings potential (appendix F, box F.5). IFC has reached 1.5 million students through its education investments. However, with a few exceptions, the ultimate impacts of these IFC projects on jobs and wages are not yet known (see appendix E). Bank reports recommend that governments routinely undertake tracer studies to judge the effectiveness of policies and allocate funding.

Workplace training responds to employer needs and increases the effectiveness of formal TVET. The Honduras training program EPEM (Entrenamiento para el Empleo) (not supported by the Bank), provides workplace training for unemployed youth that is designed and delivered by employers. An impact evaluation found that participation in EPEM increased post-training wages, the probability of employment, and the likelihood of a formal sector job with social security and benefits (Rozada 2011). In many low-income areas, the small formal sector limits the number of work-based learning opportunities.

Skills certification of TVET programs needs to be credible to have a signaling effect for employers, but they can suffer from manipulation. Bank-supported TVET programs emphasize accreditation. However, the potential for manipulation in the accreditation process can devalue its legitimacy as an instrument for accountability. The IEG review of Bank analytical reports found that recommendations in those products focused on the governance of TVET to enhance quality of training, though often in countries with weak governance systems. In India, Crisil India, a Standard and Poor's company with an established reputation for providing unbiased credit ratings of companies, has recently started rating Master in Business Administration (MBA) institutes to ensure that these institutes meet the needs of the market (IEG 2011b). IFC has not worked on skills certification systems.

Unrestricted vouchers in Kenya are increasing TVET training uptake in the private sector where dropout rates are lower. Kenya's Technical and Vocational Voucher Program supported by the Bank (Hicks and others 2011) randomly awarded vouchers to about 1,000 out-of-school youth for technical and vocational training. Among voucher winners, a random half were awarded a voucher that could only be used in public vocational institutions, whereas the voucher for the other half could be used in both private and public schools. The unrestricted group had a significantly higher training uptake of 79 percent compared to 69 percent in the public institution-only group. Students in private sector training reported lower dropout rates. Females have higher returns to training than males do, but males report higher returns for self-employment. The evaluation for labor market outcomes is ongoing and results are expected by September 2012.[4]

Information about returns to training affects choices by young women, and labor outcomes. In Kenya, girls received information on the relative returns to vocational training on female- and male-dominated trades. The informed girls were five percentage points more likely to enroll in male-dominated courses (Hjort and others 2010). Peru's ProJoven program provides skills training and internships. It encouraged equal participation between men and women in its training courses—especially for traditionally male-dominated occupations. Eighteen months later, girls reported a 15 percent increase in employment and 93 percent higher earnings (Ñopo and others 2007).

### SHORT-TERM SKILLS BUILDING PROGRAMS

Short-term skills building programs are more effective when three features are present (Fares and Puerto 2009; Betcherman and others 2007), but few Bank projects contain all of them. They include: (i) private sector involvement in training; (ii) classroom instruction combined with employer attachment (internship, apprenticeship); and (iii) training combined with other services, such as job counseling. Almost 40 percent of Bank-supported skills-building projects provide work-based training, but only 17 percent of projects use a comprehensive approach with the private sector participating in education, counseling, and work-based training (appendix F, table F.3). However, the private sector is still small in many low-income countries.

The few studies of the employment effects of Bank-supported short-term skills building for unemployed youth suggest questionable results. In Turkey, 12,453 unemployed youth received skills training supported by the Bank. The dropout rate was 12 percent and the placement rate 43 percent in 2006. However, no medium-term information is available on employment. The remaining one-third of the project portfolio with short-term skills building did not track employment data. Many skills-building programs support the transport and residential expenses of trainees, which is helpful for youth from lower-income groups. However, no information is collected on the distributional impact of skills building.

Three Bank impact evaluations suggest short-term skills building has had limited effects in Latin America (appendix F, table F.4). The Chile Califica evaluation found no employment impact and only positive monthly wage impacts for participants older than 40 years of age (Santiago Consultores 2009). The Juventud y Empleo program in the Dominican Republic features several weeks of basic skills training by a private provider followed by a two-month internship with fully subsidized wage and limited follow-up with counseling and technical assistance. Nearly all interns were let go after the internship. The program had no effect on participants' employment, but a modest impact on earnings (Card and others 2011). The IDB-supported Colombia Jovenes en Accion program reached 80,000 participants over four years with classroom training by a private provider and on-the-job training in a registered company. The main impact is a shift from informal to formal employment, but there was no overall employment effect. Job quality improved through an increase in formal sector employment by 6.8 percentage points and in earnings by 19.6 percent. Effects were stronger for women than for men (Attanasio and others 2011).

Women are often benefiting more than men are from non-formal, short-term skills training. Latin America has several short-term training programs that are part of ALMPs. These courses provide basic job readiness skills for unemployed and disadvantaged youth. For example, the Mexican Probecat offers short-term, on-the-job training complemented by internships in the private sector (Delajara and others 2006). El Salvador and Honduras have introduced such programs as well. These short-term training programs generally report higher employment rates for women, better earnings, and shorter cost-recovery times.

There has been a lack of attention in collecting labor market outcome and cost-effectiveness data in skills development projects (see appendix F for more details), which was similarly noted in other recent IEG evaluations (IEG 2010; IEG 2011c).

## The Bank's Impact Evaluations on Youth Employment

The Bank's impact evaluations examine short-term effects, find limited positive results, and often fail to address issues important for policymaking. All seven impact evaluations examine short-term effects. Two of them (Uganda and Kenya) currently collect follow-up data collection. Early findings on what works are inconclusive. In sum:

- Short-term training with internships seems to work in Colombia, but not in the Dominican Republic.

- Entrepreneurship training for university graduates in Tunisia has a negligible self-employment effect and no employment and earning effect;

- Entrepreneurship training appears promising in rural areas in Uganda and Colombia.

- Men report better labor market outcomes for self-employment than women, who do better in skills training.

- Comparing the interventions analyzed by these evaluations with the most frequent interventions in Bank projects (figure 2.2) suggests that impact evaluations are not focusing on the "high-frequency or high-cost" interventions supported by Bank projects, which questions their strategic relevance.

Cost and cost-effectiveness analysis of youth employment interventions are not calculated in Bank operations. IEG's analysis of 39 impact evaluations of youth employment programs found that 20 percent include cost-benefit analysis. None of the 90 Bank projects in the portfolio reports cost and cost-benefit analysis of interventions. Since evaluating the social returns to investment in alternative youth employment programs is critical for both policy makers and international organizations aiming to facilitate employment for young people, future studies should adopt a more substantive focus on this aspect, thereby enabling a comprehensive analysis on the program effectiveness based on the costs and benefits. Given the high cost of impact evaluations, they should be applied selectively to scalable interventions.

The link between the ongoing impact evaluation program and the need for information for future lending is not clear. The Social Protection Network, with the support of the Spanish Impact Evaluation Fund, is conducting additional impact evaluations including on the India Employment Guarantee Program (no information on youth), the Malawi Apprenticeship Program, the Turkey TVET program (only baseline available), and the South Africa Wage Subsidy program. However, this evaluation has not been implemented as the subsidy is blocked by the labor unions. It is not always clear how the selection of these interventions for impact evaluations is related to the sector strategies and future lending.

## Notes

1. In 2008, the GBI department was transformed into an independent organization called the Grassroots Business Fund.

2. Democratic Alliance: South Africa: COSATU's opposition to youth wage subsidy is hurting the poor. 13 March 2012. http://allafrica.com/stories/201203131263.html

3. The World Bank Group supports the entire education sector including higher education facilities, for example in Vietnam, to bringing advanced technologies to developing regions. The recent IEG Education Portfolio Review (2011) examines the effectiveness of this support.

4. The Technical and Vocational Vouchers Program was launched in late 2008. The majority of voucher winners were still in school until December 2011 when the evaluations were done.

## References

Attanasio, Orazio, Adriana Kugler, and Costas Meghir. 2011. "Subsidizing Vocational Training for Disadvantaged Youth in Colombia: Evidence from a Randomized Trial." *American Economic Journal: Applied Economics* 3(3): 188–220.

Benus, Jacob, James Rude and Satyendra Patrabansh. 2001. "Impact of the Emergency Demobilization and Reintegration Project in Bosnia and Herzegovina." Department of Labor Bureau of International Affairs. Development Impact Evaluation (DIME).

Betcherman, Gordon, Martin Godfrey, Susana Puerto, Friederike Rother, and Antoneta Stavreska. 2007. "A Review of Interventions to Support Young Workers: Findings of the Youth Employment Inventory." SP Discussion Paper No. 0715. Washington, DC: World Bank.

Blattman, Christopher, Nathan Fiala, and Sebastian Martinez. 2011. "Can Employment Programs Reduce Poverty and Social Instability Experimental Evidence from a Ugandan Aid Program." World Bank Policy Research Working Paper series.

Blundell, Richard, Monica Costa Dias, Costas Meghir, and John Van Reenen. 2004. "Evaluating the Employment Impact of a Mandatory Job Search Assistance Program." *Journal of the European Economic Association* 2(4): 569–606.

Bruhn, Miriam. 2008. "License to Sell: The Effect of Business Registration Reform on Entrepreneurial Activity in Mexico." Policy Research Working Paper 4538. World Bank, Washington, DC.

Card, David, Pablo Ibarrarán, Ferdinando Regalia, David Rosas, and Yuri Soares. 2011. "The Labor Market Impacts of Youth Training in the Dominican Republic." *Journal of Labor Economics* 29(2): 267–300.

Cardoso, Ana Rute. (2009). "Long-Term Impact of Youth Minimum Wages: Evidence from Two Decades of Individual Longitudinal Data." IZA Discussion Paper No. 4236.

Castañeda, Carlos, José González, and Norberto Rojas. 2010. "Evaluación de Impacto del Programa Jóvenes Rurales Emprendedores del SENA." Fedesarrollo Working Paper No. 53 de 2012–2, Bogotá, Colombia.

Delajara, Marcelo, Samuel Freije, and Isidro Soloaga. 2006. "An Evaluation of Training for the Unemployed in Mexico." Working Paper: OVE/WP-09/06. Inter-American Development Bank, Office of Evaluation and Oversight.

Fares, Jean, and Susana Puerto. 2009. "Towards Comprehensive Training." Social Protection Discussion Papers 52188. World Bank.

Heckman, James and Carmen Pagés-Serra. (2000). "The Cost of Job Security Regulation: Evidence from Latin American Labor Markets." *Economia* 1(1) 109-144.

Hicks, Joan Hamory, Michael Kremer, Isaac Mbiti, and Edward Miguel. 2011. "Vocational Education Voucher Delivery and Labor Market Returns: A Randomized Evaluation among Kenyan Youth, Report for Spanish Impact Evaluation Fund (SIEF) Phase II." Policy Note Human Development Network. World Bank.

Hjort, Jonas, Michael Kremer, Isaac Mbiti, and Edward Miguel. 2010. "Vocational Education Vouchers and Labor Market Returns: A Randomized Evaluation among Kenyan Youth." Harvard University and Southern Methodist University, Berkeley, CA.

Independent Evaluation Group (IEG). 2012a. "Project Performance Assessment Report on Colombia Higher Education Improving Access Project (HEIAP) and Chile Lifelong Learning and Training Project (LLTP) and Chile Science for the Knowledge Economy Project (SKEP)." Report No. 68251. Washington, DC: World Bank.

———. 2012b. "World Bank and IFC Support for Youth Employment Programs." Background Paper. Country Case Study: Ghana. Forthcoming.

———. 2012c. "World Bank and IFC Support for Youth Employment Programs." Background Paper. Country Case Study: Rwanda. Forthcoming.

———. 2012d. "World Bank and IFC Support for Youth Employment Programs." Background Paper. Country Case Study: South Africa. Forthcoming.

———. 2011a. "Project Performance Assessment Report on Higher Education Enhancement Project (HEEP) in Egypt, Higher Education Learning and Innovation Project (HELIP) in Yemen, and Higher Education Project in the Hashemite Kingdom of Jordan." Report No. 62651. Washington, DC: World Bank.

———. 2011b. "Project Performance Assessment Report on India's Third Technician Education Project (TTEP) and Technical/Engineering Education Quality Improvement Project I (TEQIP I)." Report No. 66056. Washington, DC: World Bank.

———. 2011c. "World Bank Support to Education since 2001: A Portfolio Note." Washington, DC: World Bank.

———. 2010. "Gender and Development." An Evaluation of World Bank Support, 2002–2008. The Washington DC: World Bank.

International Finance Corporation. 2011. "Education for Employment (e4e): Realizing Arab Youth Potential—Executive Summary." www.e4earabyouth.com

Kluve, Jochen. 2010. "The effectiveness of European active labor market programs." *Labour Economics* 17: 904–918.

———. 2006. "The Effectiveness of European Active Labor Market Policy." Discussion Paper No. 2018. Institute for the Study of Labor.

Larsson, Laura. 2003. "Evaluation of Swedish Youth Labor Market Programs." *The Journal of Human Resources* 38(4): 891–927.

Lee, David S. 2009. "Training, Wages, and Sample Selection: Estimating Sharp Bounds on Treatment Effects." *Review of Economic Studies* 76(3): 1071–1102.

Medina, Carlos, and Jairo Núñez. 2001. "The Impact of Public and Private Job Training in Colombia." Inter-American Bank, Research Network Paper.

Miller, Cynthia, Johannes M. Bos, Kristin E. Porter, Fannie M. Tseng, Fred C. Doolittle, Deana N. Tanguay, and Mary P. Vencill. 2003. "Working with Disadvantaged Youth Thirty-Month Findings from the Evaluation of the Center for Employment Training Replication Sites." Manpower Demonstration Research Corporation Working Paper.

Mingat, A., B. Ledoux, R. Rakotomalala. 2010. "Developing Post-Primary Education in Sub-Saharan Africa: Assessing the Financial Sustainability of Alternative Pathways." Africa Human Development Series. Washington, DC: World Bank.

Neumark, David and William Wascher. (2004). "Minimum Wages, Labor Market Institutions, and Youth Employment: A Cross-National Analysis." *Industrial and Labor Relations Review* 57( 2): 223–248.

Ñopo, Hugo, Miguel Robles, and Jaime Saavedra. 2007. "Occupational Training to Reduce Gender Segregation: The Impacts of ProJoven." *Economia* XXI (62): 33–54.

Organisation for Economic Co-operation and Development (OECD). 2010. Education at a Glance 2010. OECD Indicators.

Patrinos, Harry Anthony, Cris Ridao-Cano, and Chris Sakellariou. 2006. "Estimating the Returns to Education: Accounting for Heterogeneity in Ability." Unpublished report.

Premand Patrick, Stefanie Brodmann, Rita Almeida, Rebekka Grun, and Mahdi Barouni. 2012. "Entrepreneurship training and self-employment among university graduates: Evidence from a randomized trial in Tunisia." World Bank Impact Evaluation Report. Washington, DC: World Bank.

Rozada, Martin-Gonzalez. 2011. "Evaluación de impacto del programa EPEM y Análisis Costo-Beneficio." Draft paper. Inter-American Development Bank.

Santiago Consultores 2009. Evaluación en Profundidad Programa ChileCalifica. Santiago. Chile. www.sca.cl

Schochet, Peter, John Burghardt, Steven Glazerman. 2000. "National Job Corps Study: The Short-Term Impacts of Job Corps on Participants' Employment and Related Outcomes. Final Report." Princeton: Mathematica Policy Research.

Van Reenen, John. 2003. "Active Labour Market Policies and the British New Deal for the Young Unemployed in Context." NBER Working Paper Series. Working Paper 9576.

World Bank. 2011. Governance and Opportunity Development Policy Loan. Program Document. May 26.

# Chapter 5
Recommendations

This evaluation examines youth employment issues in the World Bank and IFC's lending and investment support and analytical work program. Over the fiscal years 2001–2011, the World Bank loaned $2.85 billion to youth employment programs in 57 countries, and provided an active analytical and advisory program.

The evaluation recognizes that the priority condition for expanding employment, including youth employment, is through sound macroeconomic management, effective public institutions, and good governance. But these are not enough to address the situation of youth. As youth are worse off than adults in the labor, credit, and asset markets, specific interventions for youth are needed. Accordingly, the evaluation focuses on the investment climate, labor market, and education in examining the support for and results of youth employment programs.

The evaluation shows that evidence is scant on what works in Bank and IFC projects and programs, and that better diagnostics are needed to inform policy. Hence, there is a critical need to strengthen evidence-based feedback loops to the strategic planning process in Bank lending and IFC investment. Sound analysis and identifying key aspects of country context are particularly important for countries with relatively weak institutional capacity and macroeconomic management. For example, in much of sub-Saharan Africa, robust analytic work should underpin youth employment interventions because of the greater institutional risks they face.

The evaluation finds that a comprehensive approach to youth employment is more effective than isolated interventions, and a positive growth environment helps ensure their success (box 3.1). Factors contributing to better labor market outcomes for youth include participation of the private sector in skills building, monitoring and follow up of individual program participants, and a combination of complementary interventions, such as training with job search and placement assistance. Programs that combine smoothing the transition from school to work with work-based skills development appear to be most effective for youth employment and earnings. However, its applicability to developing countries with a large informal sector and rural areas is limited. In low or no growth environments in which there are no jobs, wage subsidies, skills training, and job search will matter very little to getting a job. In rural low-income areas, where most youth are active in agriculture and non-farm employment or self-employment in the informal sector, stimulating the market for the growth of farms, non-farm household enterprises, and rural agribusinesses is essential. The Bank and IFC could support the expansion of rural and urban jobs in these sectors.

Youth employment projects could benefit more from multisectoral thinking and coordination. This might include, for example, cross-sector collaboration in project support to youth in small-scale agriculture, vocational schooling, access to credit and land markets, as well as support between farm and non-farm self-employment and employment and earnings, and between rural employment and skills requirements.

Two main recommendations are offered to guide the Bank Group's future work on youth employment in countries where youth employment is a concern to the government and/or the World Bank/IFC.

## IEG Findings, Conclusions, and Recommendations

| IEG Findings and Conclusions | IEG Recommendations |
|---|---|
| **The paucity of data limits the ability to assess the impact of Bank Group support to youth employment.**<br>• Although most Bank projects support information on the labor market, little is known about how data is being used. Few projects or analytic products include tracer studies to track the subsequent employment history of youth.<br>• IFC does not disaggregate employment data by age groups, and the majority of Bank projects with youth employment interventions provide no information on youth as a beneficiary group. If reported, outcome indicators are generally not disaggregated by age.<br>• Diagnostic work on youth employment is insufficient. It does not identify how the recommended interventions should be formulated or discuss related cost and fiscal impacts.<br>• Few Bank and IFC operations do identify whether youth employment interventions reached low-income youth or women. Only one (Uganda) impact evaluation conducted quantile analysis. | **Apply an evidence-based approach to youth employment programs.**<br>• Improve knowledge about youth employment by supporting government collection of labor market outcome data for youth in relevant surveys.<br>• Monitor the employment situation by age groups by providing statistics for inclusion in country strategies and Country Economic Memorandums.<br>• Ensure that World Bank and IFC youth employment interventions are informed by relevant analytical work or due diligence on their strategic relevance that also addresses likely costs of possible interventions.<br>• Monitor or evaluate age-specific employment and earning outcomes in Bank operations, IFC investments, and Bank analytic and advisory activities and IFC Advisory Services designed to address youth employment issues. This would include measures on gender and socioeconomic groups. |
| **Most country strategies do not identify youth employment as a strategic issue. A combination of complementary interventions works best, and implementation benefits from multisector teams.**<br>• A comprehensive approach is missing in the Bank's youth employment projects. Most projects include isolated interventions. Collaboration across sector teams is limited.<br>• Subgroups of youth are always worse off. These include the low-income youth in rural areas without the necessary skills and connections to find work, or access credit and land. | **At the country level, take a strategic approach to youth employment by addressing the issue comprehensively, working across teams.**<br>• Help countries address youth employment issues comprehensively, from the demand and supply side. This requires greater cross-sectoral collaboration within the World Bank Group and with other donors as appropriate.<br>• Help countries design interventions targeted to low-income youth. Examples for the private sector could include closing the gap between skills demanded by the private sector and those acquired through the educational system. |

# Appendix A

Conceptual Foundation of the
Evaluation Framework

This appendix presents the factors that determine youth employment outcomes, which contributed to the framework used in the evaluation. Youth employment outcomes are determined by many factors and some of them may not be specifically categorized as youth-focused. Thus, the MILES framework, shown in figure 2.1 of the main text, helps provide the context for this evaluation.

## The Determinants of Youth Employment Outcomes

The youth employment situation in different countries is determined by demand and supply factors, as well as by labor markets. The relative importance of these factors, and how they play out in a dynamic growth context, will vary across countries and regions. It is important for governments to know and understand these factors when they design youth employment programs tailored to the youth groups most affected. Governments can then better incorporate in the design specific interventions to address the underlying causes of youth employment problems.

### LABOR DEMAND SIDE: ECONOMIC GROWTH AND NET JOB CREATION BY FIRMS

The aggregate demand is a main determinant of youth employment and depends on a favorable investment climate. The strength of the economy and its capacity to increase labor demand, and create work opportunities has an impact on youth employment. During the recent global economic crisis, the demand for labor collapsed because product demand fell due to credit rationing, falling consumer confidence, and delayed monetary interactions (Bell and Blanchflower 2010). A business environment favorable to investment and job creation in youth-intensive sectors is thus vital in absorbing young labor market entrants.

Structural changes in the economy affect the skills needed in the labor market. The impact of growth on youth employment is affected by the openness of the economy and technological change. Industrial changes and the resulting changing structure of labor demand (for example, for more-skilled or less-skilled workers) also affect young people's labor market prospects. Depending on the availability of skills, the demand for youth labor may be skill-biased in a changing economy, and unskilled youth are most at risk, benefiting less in business upswings, and suffering more in downswings.[1]

Sustained growth and skills investment are important in developing a formal sector and creating work opportunities for youth. The type of work opportunities—whether they provide regular wages and stable employment or low and uncertain income—will largely depend on the stage of a given country's economic development. In developing countries, a large fraction of the labor market is informal and a large proportion of the labor force has low levels of education. Thus, many youth enter the labor market informally and change jobs frequently. Even among those countries experiencing rapid growth, such as India,[2] casual jobs with low pay and self-employment are the most common type of employment. In many low-income countries, growth has not been accompanied by a sufficient increase in formal employment, especially for the millions of youth who enter the labor force. It is only after a long period of sustained growth and human capital investment that countries can expect to see a formal sector gradually develop and an increasing number of stable and better-paid jobs created.

Youth employment is skill-biased in a growing and open economy. The extent to which the economy is open to international trade and sensitive to technology affects youth. Industries with more rapidly growing productivity demand more educated workers, and tend to substitute physical and human capital for less-skilled labor (World Bank 2007). As younger cohorts are more educated than older cohorts, the demand for young educated workers increases relative to the demand for less-educated workers.

Young people do not have the experience employers are looking for and face more difficulties obtaining a job that would give them the experience. Among the reasons for higher youth to adult unemployment rates are employers' preference for experienced workers, "last-in-first-out policies" and, in some countries, young people waiting for public sector jobs, as for example in Sri Lanka (box A.1) and the Middle East and North Africa.

Access to credit and infrastructure are major constraints for young firms. In low-income and rural areas, investors rarely have access to credit, telecommunications (enterprises using the Internet grow significantly faster), export markets, and essential business services such as International

---

| Box A.1 | Educated and Unemployed Youth Waiting for Government Jobs in Sri Lanka |

The unemployment rate in Sri Lanka for educated youth is twice the national average unemployment rate.[a] In the past, high youth unemployment has led to serious social unrest among young people and university students. To relieve political pressure, the government has employed graduates in the public sector, which has created an overstaffed civil service system.

Private sector employers report that students leave secondary school and university without the English and computer technology skills needed in a globalized economy. In addition, social skills such as teamwork, diligence, and discipline are sought after by private sector employers, but not emphasized by secondary and tertiary education. Although there are vacancies in the private sector, university graduates favor government employment because of more favorable terms and lower intensity of work. Thus, university graduates queue and wait for these jobs to open. In 2006, the new government followed through on its campaign promise to provide public sector jobs to unemployed university graduates.

*Source:* IEG 2012b.

a. In 2009, the unemployment rate for young adults (25-29 years) was 11.6 percent and 17.6 percent for those youth with A-Level or higher.

Organization for Standardization (ISO) management certification and formal training programs with Internet use. These factors are especially important for young firms and small and medium enterprises (SMEs) (Dutz and others 2011). Youth who cannot find work in rural areas tend to migrate (box A.2).

## LABOR SUPPLY SIDE: EDUCATION AND SKILLS

Employers identify the lack of skilled labor as a major constraint to doing business. Country program analysis indicates that workers without a completed primary education do not qualify for most wage jobs in medium and large enterprises. Many workers lack *cognitive skills* regardless of their level of educational attainment. The lack of *catalytic skills* is particularly harmful for the development of the service sector—where communication and other social abilities are important. School dropouts are not trained in financial literacy, including spending and saving, and they lack information on the variables that affect business development.

The level of education and skills can have a positive impact on youth employment. Rising levels of education of youth cohorts can respond to the demand for more educated workers in growing economies (as human capital complements physical capital). Education is also closely tied to upward mobility in income and occupation, increasing the probability that workers can move out of agriculture, casual, and low-wage jobs into better-paid jobs and more stable employment. Thus, productivity can be augmented through education and training. In addition, education may permit a better job match as educated youth tend to be more efficient in acquiring and processing job search information. Firms also tend to engage in greater hiring efforts for higher-wage, skilled jobs (the cost of keeping unfilled vacancies is higher).

| Box A.2 | Rural Investment and Employment Opportunities Affect Youth Migration |
|---|---|

Rural areas generally offer fewer employment opportunities, causing young people to either migrate to urban areas or work locally in lower-income agriculture and informal sector jobs. If jobs were available in rural areas, young people might remain in place, as suggested by Facebook users who responded to an IEG poll. Urban areas in Africa have been very slow to create jobs to accommodate the increasing numbers of young male migrants. As a result, migrants are more likely to be unemployed and out of the labor force than their non-migrant counterparts (World Bank 2008–09).

**Would you stay in rural areas if there were jobs for youth?**

No (n = 39), 22%

Yes (n = 140), 78%

*Sources:* IEG; Facebook Users, 2012. See appendix G.

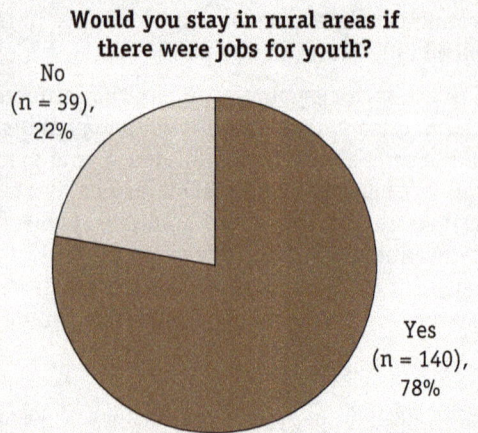

Finally, during business downswings, greater firm attachment and a higher level of skills reduce the probability of being laid off.

Education is less beneficial to employment if there is an oversupply and low-quality training. Depending on the context, education brings several benefits: a lower probability of unemployment, lower job turnover, higher wages, and greater upward mobility in income and occupation. However, these benefits may be reduced (or not arise) when the supply of skills outpaces the demand or when the education and training system fails to produce the skills required by the labor market (such as a low quality of education and obsolete skills). Furthermore, the efficiency of the job search process can be reduced when diplomas and certificates are no longer reliable indicators of qualifications and skills.

The mismatch between the skill composition of the labor force and the needs of a changing labor market affect employment. One could expect that wage premiums for different education and training levels would adjust to changes in demand, creating incentives or disincentives to acquire the corresponding skills. The severity and duration of unemployment will then depend on the capacity of response in the education and training sector to build the relevant skills for a fast-changing labor market. However, wage premiums are not the only market signal. Other factors such as a heightened prestige for a specific profession play a role in the education and career decisions of young people, which may lead to a mismatch with the needs of the labor market.

### Labor Supply Side: Size and Composition of Youth Cohorts

The extent to which demographic factors affect youth employment depends on country context, including the magnitude of the demographic change, the capacity of the economy to create jobs (box A.3), the flexibility of the labor market, and the pay determination process. In the countries of the Middle East and North Africa, in a context of lower growth rates in the 1980s and 1990s, the demographic expansion led to both higher unemployment rates and lower returns to investment in education. In South Asia, demographic factors have not affected employment as large cohorts of new entrants have been absorbed by a dynamic labor market able to create some 800,000 new jobs a month for a decade (Nayar and others 2012). In the United States, which is characterized by a flexible wage determination process, the primary impact of large cohorts of new entrants in the 1970s has been to depress youth wages relative to adult wages, rather than to affect employment rates (Freeman and Wise 1982).

Youth cohorts—as well as the whole labor force—are heterogeneous with regard to gender, social class, and other cultural and personal characteristics. To the extent that specific youth groups have different behavioral patterns or that employers value differently their characteristics, their employment opportunities will differ. Possible youth employment solutions have to account for these heterogeneities.

Rwanda reported a high population growth rate of 2.6 percent and high fertility rates of 6.1 children per woman in 2005, which decreased to 4.6 in 2010 (DHS 2010). About 64 percent of the population is below the age of 25, pointing to a high dependency ratio. High fertility rates and dependency ratios limit savings, and increase the demographic burden for households.

Rwanda has a dividend opportunity if the young find work with higher earnings. Economic growth averaged around 6 percent in the past decade, but the formal private sector is still small. The government has to promote investment policies to create jobs for the growing youth cohort. Since most of these children are from poor families, inclusive growth is needed to help them find jobs with higher earnings.

Only about 10 percent of the labor force has a post-primary education and the critical workforce skills, though this is expected to increase to 20 percent by 2020. High population growth puts fiscal pressure on the government to increase investments in primary and secondary education, and affects the composition of public spending.

Rwanda and other low-income countries can reap the demographic dividend if fertility rates fall and the children of today work in productive jobs with higher earnings, and generate savings.

*Sources:* IEG 2012a; National Institute of Statistics, Rwanda 2012.

## LABOR MARKET INSTITUTIONS

Labor market information can decrease job search costs, shorten unemployment spells, and reduce job turnover. Imperfect information increases the time and resources for employees to find a job and for firms to find appropriate workers. Mechanisms that facilitate access to information about job opportunities (such as job search assistance) can reduce the length of the search period, and facilitate both labor market entrance and mobility between jobs. Similarly, mechanisms that can help employers "detect" the skills of potential employees, can reduce hiring costs and increase the speed at which vacancies are filled as well as ensure the probability of a good match. Therefore, information and lower costs of job search and hiring can promote youth employment both through shorter unemployment spells and less job turnover.

Labor market regulations are usually found to inhibit labor market flexibility by reducing the ability of firms to hire and fire workers. Although regulations aim at protecting workers by reducing economic uncertainty and enhancing job and income security, they can also adversely affect workers by reducing their ability to find a new job. Stable employment relationships can be an asset to a firm as they are preconditions for trust, loyalty to the firm, and cooperation. For the worker, they reduce the probability of being laid off. However, while protecting workers with jobs, the adverse impact is likely to be greater for younger than for more experienced workers.[3]

Flexibility in work contracts (fixed-term and temporary contracts) and low severance payments in case of dismissal may affect youth employment.

Contract flexibility and low firing costs allow employers to check whether the skills of a young worker are a good match for the job and whether the increase in the firm's economic activity is sustainable. Less rigid labor market regulations allow employers to respond to short-term increases in the demand for products without having to suffer high costs of dismissal. Similarly, part-time contracts can attract particular types of workers, such as young women with children.

Pay may affect employment. Whether wage-setting mechanisms are centralized or coordinated through collective bargaining, whether a minimum wage is imposed or not, and at what level, will matter. A minimum wage (depending on its level relative to average pay) can negatively affect young workers more than older workers if young workers' marginal productivity is below the wage level. A youth sub-minimum wage may lead employers to substitute lower-salaried youth for low-skilled adult employees (Neumark and Wascher 2004). In the United Kingdom, no significant impact was found from the influx of less-skilled workers from European Union accession countries on the employment of the least-skilled youth; however, it did have a slightly negative impact on wages (Nickell and Saleheen 2008).

In sum, the three main determinants that affect the demand for youth employment are economic growth, structural changes, and employer preferences. On the supply side, the main determinants are the level of education and the relevance of skills, the size of the youth cohort, and individual attributes. In addition, institutional factors in the labor and credit market matter— including information, regulations, wage levels, and credit costs.

As these factors are influenced by overall development efforts, including macroeconomic support to countries and World Bank Group support to the public and private sectors, a full picture of the Bank Group's effects on youth employment outcomes presents a considerable challenge. It would only be possible to do so if the impact of each of these interventions on youth employment could be identified. Unfortunately, they cannot. Thus, the evaluation needs a framework to identify what can be evaluated in the broader context. The following section presents the framework, categorizes youth employment problems based on the determinants, and proposes strategic directions and interventions to address the issue.

## Government Policies to Address Youth Employment

Governments use three main strategic directions—investment climate policies, labor market reforms, and education reforms—to tackle youth employment depending on the country context. Table A.1 categorizes youth employment problems and related determinants, taking into account the issues youth face when entering the labor market. It suggests the main strategic directions to address these issues. In all five contexts, policies to improve the business environment, increase trade, and foster

| Table A.1 | Types of Youth Employment Problems, Determinants, and Main Strategic Directions | |
|---|---|---|
| Nature of problem | Related determinants | Main strategic directions |
| Youth unemployment high (or rising) for all groups of young workers | • Lack of growth and net job creation<br>• Business recession<br>• Large cohorts of new entrants not absorbed by job supply<br>• Restrictive labor legislation | • Policies improving investment climate and business environment (political stability, security, tax, infrastructure, openness to trade)<br>• Labor market reforms providing more flexibility (contracting, pay) |
| High youth unemployment, mostly for less educated | • Skill-biased growth (demand for unskilled workers increasing less than for skilled workers)<br>• Downturn of business cycle | • Growth and investment policies<br>• Education and training policies to increase human capital of youth<br>• Flexible labor market with wage premiums for higher levels of skills |
| High youth unemployment concentrated in subgroups of youth population (minorities, poor) | • Demand for workers (usually with low education levels) increasing little with growth, and disproportionately affected during recessions<br>• Discrimination | • Policies improving investment climate and fostering growth<br>• Targeted education and training programs to raise human capital and employability<br>• Antidiscrimination policies |
| High youth unemployment for highly-educated young workers | • Lack of (or slow) growth and insufficient job creation<br>• Segmented labor market with different work conditions and pay across sectors<br>• Inefficient education and training sector (inadequate skills) | • Policies to improve investment climate, business environment, and promote growth<br>• Labor market policies to increase flexibility and reduce segmentation<br>• Quality and relevance of education and training programs, information about labor market opportunities |
| Large number of casual, low-productivity, low-paid jobs held by youth | • Stage of economic development with a large informal sector<br>• Low level of education of youth cohorts<br>• Phenomenon accentuated in case of segmentation of labor market and restrictive labor legislation in the formal sector | • Policies fostering job creation to induce gradual transformation of the economy (move from casual to more formal jobs)<br>• Education and training policies and programs to raise the human capital level of youth cohorts<br>• Labor market reforms to allow greater flexibility and reduce segmentation. |

*Source:* Riboud 2012.

entrepreneurship and growth are crucial to increasing net job creation and labor demand. In some contexts, they may need to be accompanied by education policies and labor market reforms.

## YOUTH EMPLOYMENT INTERVENTIONS

This evaluation has categorized interventions into three areas: investment climate, labor market, and education (see table 4.1 in the main text).

## INVESTMENT CLIMATE: "FOSTERING JOB CREATION AND WORK OPPORTUNITIES"

Investment climate interventions include measures to increase labor demand for youth, provide new self-employment opportunities, or reduce labor market rigidities. The goal is to improve the business environment, open the economy to trade, foster investment and growth, and create jobs with increased earning power. Without net job creation, all other interventions can only have a limited impact. Interventions to foster entrepreneurship help young entrepreneurs who lack finance and experience to start new businesses. Such interventions can also support small enterprises through appropriate training. Reforms to reduce labor market rigidities have been advocated and implemented in less-developed countries where regulations discourage hiring and firing, and encourage noncompliance with labor legislation and the expansion of the informal sector.

Incentives to firms to hire youth and public works programs are temporary employment measures. Wage subsidies and a sub-minimum wage for youth aimed at encouraging employers to hire young workers are more common in OECD and middle-income countries with large formal sectors. Direct job creation and public works programs that provide work and income for a finite period seek to provide an immediate relief to the most disadvantaged as part of an active labor market policy.

### LABOR MARKET: "SMOOTHING THE SCHOOL-TO-WORK TRANSITION AND JOB MOBILITY"

School-to-work transition interventions aim to shorten the job search period. Labor market interventions include: improvements to information about the labor market and reduction of the costs of job search for both workers and employers; helping youth to overcome obstacles to job taking; and removing discriminatory barriers to employment. Their objective is to reduce the period of search and the duration of unemployment spells, thereby facilitating a better match. Where large youth cohorts exceed the capacity of the labor market to absorb them, some governments (for instance, the Philippines and some countries in the Middle East and North Africa) have put in place programs to help young workers with finding overseas employment.

### EDUCATION: "FOSTERING SKILL DEVELOPMENT AND LABOR MARKET RELEVANCE OF SKILLS"

The objective of education interventions, which governments rely heavily on, is to ensure that there is a skills-needs match between potential youth employees and their employers. Interventions include wide-ranging reforms in the education and training systems to improve the quality and relevance of skills acquired, as well as governance reforms, with increased participation of the private sector in decisions on curricula and occupational standards, as well as more competition between public and private providers. Some countries have opted for vocational training with a mix of classroom and work-based learning, including the use of apprenticeship systems.

Training programs are frequently designed to address the specific needs of a particular population group (for example, long-term unemployed youth with a low level of general education or migrants). Remedial programs and short-term training programs are introduced to help them re-engage into the world of work. Training and subsidies often accompany these programs to encourage participation.

# Notes

1. This phenomenon could be less important if skills are defined as comprising both education and work experience. Youth's lack of experience could then outweigh the benefits of their increased education. This hypothesis called "the double-skill bias" has hardly been submitted to empirical verification (See Ryan 2001).

2. Where still about 90 percent of the labor force works in the informal sector.

3. Although measuring and isolating the effects of employment protection legislation is difficult, a number of studies find employment lower when the employment protection legislation is strict. There is also evidence of changes in the dynamics of unemployment with lower inflows and outflows, and longer duration of unemployment spells (Bentolila and Bertola 1990; Nickell and Layard (1998), changes in the composition of unemployment with youth most adversely affected (Scarpetta 1996; Heckman and Pagés-Serra 2000). The OECD study (1999) suggests that employment protection legislation protects the jobs of prime-age men at the cost of reducing employment for youth.

# References

Bell, David, and David Blanchflower. 2010. Youth Unemployment: "Déjà vu?" IZA DP No. 4705. Forschungsinstitut zur Zukunft der Arbeit: Bonn, Germany.

Dutz, Mark, Ioannis Kessides, Stephen O'Connell and Robert Willig. 2011. "Competition and Innovation-Driven Inclusive Growth." World Bank Policy Research Working Paper 5852.

Freeman, Richard, and David Wise. 1982. "The Youth Labor Market Problem: Its Nature, Causes, and Consequences." National Bureau of Economic Research (NBER). http://www.nber.org/chapters/c7869.pdf

Heckman, Jame J. and Carmen Pages-Serra. 2000. "The Cost of Job Security Regulation: Evidence from Latin American Labor Markets." *Economica* 1(1):109-144.

Independent Evaluation Group. 2012a. "World Bank and IFC Support for Youth Employment Programs." Background Paper. Country Case Study: Rwanda. Forthcoming.

———. 2012b. "Project Performance Assessment Report, Sri Lanka Education." Forthcoming.

Nayar, Reema, Pablo Gottret, Pradeep Mitra, Gordon Betcherman, Yue Man Lee, Indhira Santos, Mahesh Dahal, and Maheshwor Shrestha. 2012. "More and Better Jobs in South Asia." South Asia Development Matters. Washington, DC: World Bank.

Neumark, David and William Wascher. (2004). "Minimum Wages, Labor MarketInstitutions, and Youth Employment: A Cross-National Analysis." *Industrial and Labor Relations Review* 57( 2): 223–248.

Nickell, Stephen, and Jumana Saleheen. 2008. "The Impact of Immigration on Occupational Wages: Evidence from Britain." Working Paper No. 08–6. Federal Reserve Bank of Boston.

Riboud, Michelle. 2012. "A taxonomy of youth employment interventions. Background paper prepared for the IEG youth employment evaluation." Unpublished report.

World Bank. 2008–09. "ADI Africa Development Indicators 2008/09. Youth and Employment in Africa: The Potential, the Problem, the Promise." Washington, DC: World Bank.

———. 2007. *World Development Report 2007: Development and the next generation.* Washington, DC.

# Appendix B

Evaluation Data Sources and Methods

This appendix describes the sources of data and the methodology used in the evaluation.

## Data Sources and Limitations

The evaluation focuses on fiscal years (FY) 2001 to 2011. It covers the youth employment-relevant portfolio of closed and ongoing operations approved since FY01, relevant economic and sector work (ESW), and the World Bank and IFC's engagement in the youth employment dialogue at the country level. Much of the World Bank Group's work on youth employment is of recent nature, thus the evaluation has a strong formative and prospective focus. Evidence from a variety sources has been collected:

- A **literature review** of evaluations of job creation, including youth, and projects that have involved the private sector.

- A **portfolio review of IFC's projects** with explicit objectives of job creation or skills upgrading, and IFC investments in education. A review of relevant IFC project self- and independent assessments, including Project Completion Reports (PCRs), Extended Project Supervision Reports (XPSRs), and the Development Outcome Tracking System (DOTS).

- A **portfolio review of 90 Bank loans** (investment and policy-based) directly supporting youth employment programs.

- A **review of 21 Economic and Sector Work (ESW) reports** with an analytical focus on youth employment.

- **Eighteen purposefully selected country case studies**, five of which were field studies, and 13 in-depth desk studies. Case studies involved extensive document review and interviews with World Bank Group staff, management, other donors, and clients.

- A **systematic review of 38 impact evaluations** of youth employment programs. This review examines evidence on what works in which context, and under what circumstances.

- **Project Performance Assessment Reports (PPARs)** on post-primary education in Chile, Colombia, Egypt, India, Jordan, Sri Lanka, Yemen, and Zambia.

- An **electronic survey of Bank task team leaders** of youth employment operations and ESW products included in this evaluation to better understand Bank and country support to promote youth employment.

- **Semi-structured key informant interviews** with a randomly selected small group of Bank directors and chief economists. The objective was to identify common issues and concerns for the evaluation. The field-based country case studies and PPARs provided opportunities to interview key stakeholders among government and private sector representatives and donors.

## Identification and Analysis of the World Bank Lending Portfolio

**Identification.** All IBRD and IDA projects are coded by the originating unit using a standard set of codes for sectors and themes. Project coding is verified during the project approval process by the Bank teams. To identify the youth employment portfolio, IEG searched all active and closed investment and policy operations approved between FY01–FY11 containing the sector or theme codes listed in table B.1. That search identified 1,585 operations with the relevant codes.

The search software "Atlas TI" was then used to review the objectives, components, and research frameworks of the 1,585 projects to select those projects directly supporting youth employment. Projects were retained for further review if their development objectives or components contained any of the following search terms: vocational training, skills building, skills development, school-to-work transition, active labor market policies, labor market policies, wage subsidies, employment service, job search assistance, public works, youth employment, youth unemployment, self-employment, entrepreneurs, micro-enterprise development, investment climate, firms, or job creation. This review produced a list of 140 projects for additional detailed document review, distributed as shown in table B.2.

| Table B.1 | Sector and Theme Codes Used to Identify Youth Employment Projects | | | | |
|---|---|---|---|---|---|
| Sector | Education | Social protection and risk management | Agriculture and rural development (n=767) | Social development, gender, and inclusion(n= 418) | Innovation, technology, and entrepreneurship practice |
| Sector Code | Vocational training (n=89) | | | | |
| Theme code | | Improving labor markets (n=149) | Rural markets | Participation and civic engagement | Micro, small and medium enterprise support (n=162) |
| | | | Rural non-farm income generation | Conflict prevention and post conflict reconstruction | |
| | | | Rural policies and institutions | Gender | |
| | | | Rural services and infrastructure | Indigenous peoples | |
| | | | Other rural development | Social analysis and monitoring | |
| | | | | Other social development | |

*Source:* World Bank data.

| Table B.2 | Distribution of Projects Selected for Review at Each of Three Stages | | | | | |
|---|---|---|---|---|---|---|
| Number of Operations | TVET | ILM | ARD | SD | SMEs | Total |
| Projects reviewed from Business Warehouse | 89 | 149 | 767 | 418 | 162 | 1,585 |
| Operations identified for detailed document review | 59 | 51 | 11 | 4 | 15 | 140 |
| Operations included in portfolio review | 37 | 30 | 11 | 4 | 8 | 90 |

*Source:* World Bank data.
*Note:* ARD= Agriculture and rural development; ILM= Improving labor markets; SD= Social development, gender, and inclusion; SME= small and medium enterprise; TVET= technical and vocational education training.

For the final detailed review, IEG examined the Project Appraisal Document (PAD), last Implementation Status Report (ISR) of active projects, and the Implementation Completion and Results Report (ICR) of closed operations. Projects were selected for the portfolio review if they included the terms "employment" and/or "youth" either in the project objective or in any component, youth as a target group, or an indicator in the results framework on youth employment or earnings. Ninety operations were selected for the portfolio review (see table B.3).

**Excluded Projects.** Some youth projects may not have been included in the portfolio review for this evaluation because they did not have the relevant sector and theme codes (table B.1), or did not mention the relevant terms related to youth employment in the objective, components, target groups or indicators. Many World Bank and IFC operations have an indirect effect on youth employment (for example, infrastructure and labor market operations). These operations were not included in the Bank portfolio review, as their effect on youth employment cannot be disentangled from their overall effect on the working population.

**Coding Objectives.** The stated objectives in the PAD for the 90 portfolio projects were coded using the following five categories:

- **Supply of skills**—Projects aimed at: (i) improving the relevance of skills and learning outcomes for the labor market, or the functional application of literacy skills and response to employer needs for skilled graduates, and improvement in their satisfaction; (ii) developing or strengthening different aspects (quality, sustainability, efficiency, access) of vocational education training.

- **Individual attributes**—Projects targeted to individual attributes that affect employment outcomes, such as youth, and disadvantaged or vulnerable groups (such as the disabled, females, or the poor).

- **Making the labor market work better**—Projects aimed at: (i) improving the employability and employment opportunities, or increasing the productivity of employment; (ii) information and transparency; building institutional capacity, labor market strategies, policies and laws; and improving fiscal sustainability or management; and (iii) employment services, job search assistance, or employment programs.

- **Firms and entrepreneurs**—Projects with objectives to support :(i) entrepreneurs, start-ups, and self-employment; enterprises and small and medium businesses; and (ii) the investment climate including access to credit and other resources, contributing to growth and competitiveness.

- **Efficiency**—Internal and external efficiency of skills building, labor market programs, or service provision by the government.

**Coding Interventions.** IEG reviewed the project documents for the 90 projects to determine the planned activities it would support, its intended beneficiaries, and expected outcomes. The activities were categorized using the MILES framework and were coded into one of the following three intervention categories:

**Fostering skill development and labor market relevance of skills (E):** (i) improving quality in formal secondary and post-secondary vocational or technical education; (ii) expanding/improving work-based learning in post-secondary or secondary vocational education and training and apprenticeship systems, including the private sector; (iii) recognition and certification of skills (including improving education signaling, establishing school-employer networks); (iv) remedial/second chance/non-formal technical and vocational and non-technical programs (including literacy programs and language programs for migrants and minorities); (v) providing information on training opportunities for youth; (vi) training subsidies and vouchers (including credit for access to training); and (vii) support for transportation and residential movement.

**Fostering job creation and work opportunities (I):** (i) improving the investment/business climate, including sector policies with high job-growth potential and access to credit; (ii) enacting regulations to provide incentives to firms to hire young people (including changes in rules for dismissal and wage setting to reduce layoff costs, introducing flexible contracting rules); (iii) fostering entrepreneurship through training in entrepreneurial or business management skills or support for start-up businesses, including access to credit; (iv) supporting wage subsidies (including social security payments waivers); and (v) creating public works programs and direct job creation which are part of Active Labor Market Programs (ALMP).

**Smoothing the transition from school to work and facilitating job mobility (L):** (i) counseling, job search skills, matching, placement and outreach programs (including by public or private employment agencies, or career counseling in schools, information about job opportunities); (ii) building administrative capacity in monitoring and evaluation and labor market information; and (iii) supporting programs for overseas employment of young people.

**Evaluation Approach.** The small number of closed Bank projects reviewed by IEG does not allow for an objective-based portfolio analysis. Only 36 of the 90 projects reviewed are closed. IEG has prepared an Implementation Completion and Results Report review for 29 of the closed projects, of which 17 have skills building or youth employment in their project objectives. Thus, a full assessment of outcomes against intended objectives using data from ICR reviews is impossible, as operations are still ongoing and are not expected to have achieved their results yet. The evaluation therefore uses a formative and prospective approach.

| Table B.3 | | List of Projects in Portfolio Review, by Fiscal Year (FY) of Bank Approval | | |
|---|---|---|---|---|
| Approval FY | Project ID | Project name | Country | Youth employment |
| 2001 | P005750 | Agricultural Support Services | Tunisia | Target |
| 2001 | P050474 | Education Reform | Russian Federation | Skill development |
| 2001 | P050658 | Technical Education III | India | Project Development Objective and target |
| 2001 | P057167 | Technical and Vocational Education and Training Sector Investment and Maintenance Loan | Zambia | Target |
| 2001 | P065593 | Education Action Project | West Bank and Gaza | Target |
| 2001 | P065372 | Social Action Fund Specific Investment Loan | Tanzania | Target |
| 2002 | P044852 | Enterprise Incubator Leaning and Innovation Loan | Armenia | Skill development |
| 2002 | P068271 | Lifelong Learning and Training | Chile | Skill development |
| 2002 | P071308 | Education Sector Development Adaptable Program Loan | Mauritania | Skill development |
| 2002 | P073604 | Emergency Demobilization and Reintegration Economic Recovery Loan | Eritrea | Target |
| 2002 | P074006 | Emergency Infrastructure Rehabilitation and Living Conditions | Congo, Republic of | Target |
| 2002 | P074408 | Social Risk Mitigation Project | Turkey | Target |
| 2003 | P067575 | Private Sector Adjustment Loan 2 | Romania | Beneficiary |
| 2003 | P069374 | Employment Promotion Learning and Innovation Loan | Serbia | Target |
| 2003 | P072317 | Northwest Mountainous and Forest Areas Development | Tunisia | Target |

| Table B.3 | | List of Projects in Portfolio Review, by Fiscal Year (FY) of Bank Approval (cont.) | | |
|---|---|---|---|---|
| Approval FY | Project ID | Project name | Country | Youth employment |
| 2003 | P079335 | National Social Action | Sierra Leone | Target |
| 2004 | P049702 | Skills Development | Egypt | Skill development |
| 2004 | P075387 | E-Learning Support Adaptable Program Loan | Russian Federation | Target |
| 2004 | P081269 | Education Sector Development Project II Adaptable Program Loan | Lesotho | Target |
| 2004 | P087620 | Social Protection Administration | Armenia | Target |
| 2005 | P066149 | Secondary Education | Turkey | Target |
| 2005 | P074065 | Poverty Reduction Support Credit 1 Development Policy Loan | Senegal | Target |
| 2005 | P078523 | Integrated Human Development | Maldives | Skill development |
| 2005 | P080935 | Growth Support | Mali | Target |
| 2005 | P081482 | Community-Based Rural Development | Ghana | Skill development |
| 2005 | P082865 | Labor and Social Development Reform II | Colombia | Target |
| 2005 | P084317 | Basic Education Support | Congo, Republic of | Target |
| 2005 | P088857 | Technical Assistance Loan to support the 2nd Programmatic Structural Adjustment Loan | Colombia | Skill development |
| 2006 | P079275 | Capacity Building for Agriculture Services | Ethiopia | Target |
| 2006 | P082242 | Nutrition and Social Protection | Honduras | Project Development Objective and target |
| 2006 | P085009 | Private Sector/Micro, Small, and Medium Enterprise Competitiveness | Tanzania | Target |
| 2006 | P087347 | Technical and Vocational Education and Training | Mozambique | Target |
| 2006 | P096605 | Youth Development Project | Dominican Republic | Project Development Objective and target |
| 2006 | P098956 | Post Primary Education Specific Investment Loan | Burkina Faso | Target |
| 2007 | P073458 | Private Sector Development | Bhutan | Skill development |
| 2007 | P074132 | Science and Technical Education in Post-Basic Education | Nigeria | Target |
| 2007 | P087479 | Education Sector Support Project | Kenya | Target |
| 2007 | P086308 | Second Vocational Training Project | Yemen | Target |
| 2007 | P086875 | Education and Training Development Policy Loan | Namibia | Target |
| 2007 | P092999 | Bor Region Development Project | Serbia | Target |
| 2007 | P094097 | Labor and Social Development III | Colombia | Target |

(*Continues on the following page.*)

| Table B.3 | | List of Projects in Portfolio Review, by Fiscal Year (FY) of Bank Approval (cont.) | | |
|---|---|---|---|---|
| Approval FY | Project ID | Project name | Country | Youth employment |
| 2007 | P095514 | Lifelong Learning Project | Argentina | Project Development Objective and target |
| 2007 | P095873 | Education Sector Support | Timor-Leste | Target |
| 2007 | P097141 | Organization of Eastern Caribbean States Skills for Inclusive Growth | St. Lucia | Project Development Objective and target |
| 2007 | P099047 | Vocational Training | India | Target |
| 2007 | P104931 | Second Development Policy Grant | Bhutan | Beneficiary |
| 2008 | P052608 | Antioquia Secondary Education Project | Colombia | Project Development Objective and target |
| 2008 | P082817 | Post-Conflict Assistance | Côte d'Ivoire | Target |
| 2008 | P085376 | Migrant Skills Development and Employment | China | Skill development |
| 2008 | P085539 | City-Port Integrated Infrastructure | Costa Rica | Target |
| 2008 | P100534 | Employer Driven Skills Development | Jordan | Skill development |
| 2008 | P101084 | Investing in Children and Youth | Bolivia | Project Development Objective and target |
| 2008 | P102573 | Skills Development Project | Afghanistan | Target |
| 2008 | P105116 | Social Protection Development | Azerbaijan | Target |
| 2008 | P108791 | Regional Training Center International Institute for Water and Environmental Engineering Specific Investment Loan | Burkina Faso | Target |
| 2009 | P095681 | Organization of Eastern Caribbean States Skills for Inclusive Growth | Grenada | Project Development Objective and target |
| 2009 | P096707 | Technical and Vocational Education and Training | China | Target |
| 2009 | P096840 | Competitiveness and Employment Development 2 | Turkey | Target |
| 2009 | P102331 | Madhya Pradesh District Poverty Initiatives II | India | Target |
| 2009 | P105036 | Education Reform for the Knowledge Economy II | Jordan | Target |
| 2009 | P105075 | Pakistan Poverty Alleviation Fund III | Pakistan | Project Development Objective |
| 2009 | P109333 | Support of Education and Training Skills and Innovation Policy 1 Development Policy Loan 2 | Namibia | Target |
| 2009 | P111222 | Development Policy Grant /Credit | Bhutan | Target |
| 2009 | P111633 | Second Northern Uganda Social Action Fund | Uganda | Skill development |
| 2009 | P115183 | Basic Protection Project | Argentina | Beneficiary |
| 2009 | P115400 | Social Sectors Institutional Reform Development Policy Loan 3 | Bulgaria | Target |

| Table B.3 | | List of Projects in Portfolio Review, by Fiscal Year (FY) of Bank Approval (cont.) | | | |
|---|---|---|---|---|---|
| Approval FY | Project ID | Project name | Country | | Youth employment |
| 2010 | P086446 | Chongqing Urban-Rural Integration Program | China | | Skill development |
| 2010 | P087145 | Second Community Development and Livelihood Improvement | Sri Lanka | | Target |
| 2010 | P090807 | Skills and Training Enhancement Project | Bangladesh | | Skill development |
| 2010 | P106063 | West Africa Fisheries - Phase 1 | Africa | | Target |
| 2010 | P106708 | Social Development Policy Loan | Colombia | | Target |
| 2010 | P111546 | Youth Empowerment Project | Kenya | | Project Development Objective and target |
| 2010 | P112495 | Restoring Equitable Growth and Employment Development Policy Loan | Turkey | | Target |
| 2010 | P114987 | Rapid Employment Project | Solomon Islands | | Target |
| 2010 | P115247 | Social Opportunities Project | Ghana | | Beneficiary |
| 2010 | P117107 | Technical and Vocational Education | China | | Target |
| 2010 | P117440 | Income Support and Employability | El Salvador | | Target |
| 2010 | P121052 | Youth Employment Support | Sierra Leone | | Project Development Objective and target |
| 2010 | P121686 | Youth, Employment, Skills Project | Liberia | | Project Development Objective and target |
| 2011 | P102177 | Technical and Vocational Education Modernization | Kazakhstan | | Target |
| 2011 | P104015 | Enhanced Vocational Education and Training | Nepal | | Target |
| 2011 | P114042 | Urban Youth Employment Project | Papua New Guinea | | Project Development Objective and target |
| 2011 | P117161 | Employment Development Policy Loan | Tunisia | | Target |
| 2011 | P118101 | Skills Development Project | Rwanda | | Target |
| 2011 | P118112 | Skills and Technology Development | Ghana | | Target |
| 2011 | P118177 | Skills Development Project | Pakistan | | Project Development Objective and target |
| 2011 | P118974 | Skills Development Support Project | Mauritania | | Target |
| 2011 | P120005 | Gas and Oil Capacity Building | Ghana | | Target |
| 2011 | P122326 | Private Sector Development Support | Togo | | Target |
| 2011 | P126094 | Governance and Opportunity Development Policy Loan | Tunisia | | Target |

*Source:* World Bank.

A limitation of the review is that IFC has not identified youth as a priority, and available data have not been categorized by age. Therefore, the review is not restricted to those projects with demonstrated "youth employment" results. In addition, IFC's investment operations and advisory services implicitly have the objective of job creation based on the premise that investments result in private sector development, higher growth, and greater employment opportunities, which may have created opportunities for youth directly or indirectly. Therefore, the evaluation reviews and assesses IFC private sector projects with components focused on job creation and skills development. The portfolio review used the evaluation's MILES-based conceptual framework as follows:

**Investment Climate:** The review included investment and advisory services projects that either had job creation as an objective or tracked job creation as an indicator. The review also looked at the type of investment done in countries with high youth unemployment and at the number of jobs created in sectors and industries (agriculture, information technologies, tourism, and textiles) with the highest proportion of youth employment (sectors as identified by the Organization for Economic Cooperation and Development). Although this did not yield a complete picture of IFC's contribution to youth employment, it identified the investments that may result in youth employment. The review also included investment climate and access to finance projects regardless of their job and youth focus, since evidence indicates that these sectors lead to employment creation that may also benefit youth.

**Labor:** IFC's involvement with labor market policies is limited, but the review looked for any relevant project.

**Education and skills:** IFC's education sector and advisory services provide skills training or assistance to entrepreneurs and institutions that, in turn, deliver skills training and education programs for youth. IFC's education portfolio was included since most of the universities that IFC has invested in offer courses to current workers to upgrade skills, and/or offer TVET courses.

Given the limitations noted above, the portfolio review was done in two steps. As shown in table B.4, the first-level analysis identified 1,148 investment and 159 advisory services operations with job/employment creation objectives, and 50 investment and 18 advisory services operations in education and skills development. Additional analyses were conducted at this level to gain insight into whether youth benefitted from any of the interventions designed to improve skills and employment. The second-level analysis specifically focused on operations that targeted youth as a beneficiary or tracked youth in its results indicators. This analysis identified 10 projects.

IDENTIFICATION AND ANALYSIS OF WORLD BANK ECONOMIC AND SECTOR WORK

**Identification.** Published studies undertaken by the Bank between 2005 and 2011 on topics of youth employment, job skills, or labor markets were

| Table B.4 | IFC Portfolio Review | | | | |
|---|---|---|---|---|---|
| | | Portfolio reviewed | Level 1 focus | Level 2 focus |
| (I)nvestment Climate | All investment operations | Projects with employment data (company level) approved between FY01–FY11 | Employment/ job N= 853 clients (corresponding to 1148 investment operations); N= 159 advisory services projects | YOUTH N=10 |
| | All advisory services | Projects with: (i) job creation objective and/or; (ii) job relevant indicator, and approved between FY06–FY11* | | |
| (L)abor market | Investment climate advisory services | Investment climate advisory services portfolio approved between FY06–FY11* | Labor market N=0 | |
| (E)ducation and skills | Education sector advisory services | Access to finance, public-private partnerships, investment climate, and sustainable business advisory services projects listed under education | N=50 investment operations, 18 advisory services | |
| | Education investment operations | Entire portfolio approved between FY01–FY11 | | |

*Source:* IEG.

\* IFC's advisory services review covers FY06–11, as the corporate data system for advisory services was established in only in FY06.

identified. This yielded 34 studies from all six Bank regions. Most studies were produced by the Africa, Europe and Central Asia, and East Asia regions, so these regions accounted for a majority of the sample. The 21 studies in the sample were selected to include the topics most relevant to youth employment.[1] Table B.5 shows the number of studies from each region in the sample.

The 21 reports related to one of five categories (table B.6 lists the reports) include:

- **General Labor Market Assessments** provide some specific coverage of youth issues including employability of young labor market entrants; labor market institutions affecting youth (such as sub-minimum wages and hiring and firing rules); reviews of TVET and apprenticeship sys-

| Table B.5 | Distribution of Sample by Region | | | | | | |
|---|---|---|---|---|---|---|---|
| Region | | AFR | LAC | MENA | ECA | EAP | SAR |
| Number of Economic and Sector Work (ESW) products reviewed | | 8 | 2 | 2 | 3 | 4 | 2 |

*Source:* World Bank data.
*Note:* AFR=Africa; EAP= East Asia and Pacific; ECA= Europe and Central Asia; LAC= Latin America and Caribbean; MENA= Middle East and North Africa; SAR= South Asia Region.

tems; ALMPs; and informal sector employment. However, they do not cover school-to-work transitions, and cover only to a limited extent unemployed out-of-school youth (Ghana, Jordan, Nigeria, Serbia, and Tunisia).

- **General Youth Assessments** relate to the broader topic of youth empowerment, of which employment is a central feature. There is limited coverage of labor market policies and regulations, skill building relevant to labor markets, and links between employment and growth (Argentina, Timor-Leste, and Zambia).

- **Youth Employment Assessments** conducted in countries where youth employment is a pillar in a country program or poverty reduction strategy program. The focus is on skills building, school-to-work transitions, labor market regulations, and demand for youth by firms. These assessments also examine sectoral growth patterns, unemployment, and financing of youth employment programs (Burkina Faso, The Gambia, Kosovo, Sierra Leone, Sri Lanka, and Tanzania).

- **Skills Development Assessments** identify the demand for skills and education and TVET systems. Studies develop strategies to ensure relevant skills for rapidly growing economies (Bangladesh, Cambodia, Indonesia, and Mongolia).

- **Special Studies** focusing on a particular aspect of youth employment, such as school-to-work transition, the nexus between child labor and youth employment, and the relationship between economic growth, the business cycle and youth employment (Brazil, Ethiopia, and Turkey).

**Analysis.** Each report was reviewed with respect to four dimensions: (i) strategic relevance, consisting of timeliness, government ownership, and strategic coherence; (ii) quality of contextual and diagnostic analysis including coverage of relevant factors such as data, hypotheses testing, and clarity of presentation; (iii) quality of conclusions and recommendations for youth employment with regard to macroeconomic conditions, the investment climate, labor market institutions, education, and social protection; and (iv) dialogue and dissemination, including consultation with stakeholders, public availability of the report and national awareness, and the degree of follow-up in implementing recommendations.

### IDENTIFICATION AND ANALYSIS OF COUNTRY CASE STUDY PROGRAMS

Countries face different youth employment issues and challenges. The evaluation takes these differences into account with 18 country case studies to understand the nature of the World Bank Group's work on youth employment in client countries from 2001 to 2011, as well as the relevance of the youth employment program given the countries' needs. The case studies use the MILES framework to provide information on the types and causes of youth unemployment, the strategies used by countries with and without World Bank and IFC support to promote youth employment through

| Table B.6 | List of Economic Sector Work Analyzed | | |
|---|---|---|---|
| Country | Fiscal year | Abbreviated title | Category |
| Argentina | 2009 | Argentine Youth: An Untapped Potential | GYA |
| Bangladesh | 2008 | Learning for Job Opportunities | SDA |
| Brazil | 2008 | Is the Window of Opportunity Closing for Youth | SSY |
| Burkina Faso | 2007 | Creating Better Jobs for Poverty Reduction | YEA |
| Cambodia | 2011 | Providing Skills for Equity and Growth | SDA |
| Ethiopia | 2007 | The Twin Challenges of Child Labor and Youth Employment | SSY |
| The Gambia | 2011 | Youth Employment and Skills Development | YEA |
| Ghana | 2009 | Job Creation and Skills Development | GLMA |
| Indonesia | 2011 | Education, Training and Labor Market Outcomes | SDA |
| Jordan | 2009 | Resolving Jordan's Labor Market Paradox | GLMA |
| Kosovo | 2009 | Youth in Jeopardy | YEA |
| Mongolia | 2007 | Building the Skills for the New Economy | SDA |
| Nigeria | 2010 | Putting Nigeria to Work | GLMA |
| Serbia | 2007 | Labor Market Assessment | GLMA |
| Sierra Leone | 2009 | Youth Employment in Sierra Leone | YEA |
| Sri Lanka | 2010 | The Challenge of Youth Employment in Sri Lanka | YEA |
| Tanzania | 2007 | Youth in the Labor Market | YEA |
| Timor-Leste | 2008 | Youth in Crisis | GYA |
| Tunisia | 2004 | Employment Strategy | GLMA |
| Turkey | 2008 | Investing in Turkey's Next Generation | SSY |
| Zambia | 2008 | The Economic Empowerment of Young People | GYA |

Source: IEG 2012.
Note: GLMA=General Labor Market Assessment (GLMA); GYA= General Youth Assessment ; SDA=Skills Development Assessment; ; SSY= Special Studies on Youth Employment ; YEA=Youth Employment Assessment.

firms, self-employment, and effective skills building systems to enhance employability in higher quality jobs and entrepreneurship.

**Identification.** The 119 countries with populations greater than 1 million that were also eligible borrowers between 2001 to 2011were categorized based on high, low, or no engagement with the Bank on youth employment issues. Countries were grouped into one of the Bank's regions, resulting in 12 strata. Countries were classified as having high youth employment engagement if they had at least two lending operations with youth employment programs. They were classified as having low youth employment engagement if they had one lending operation or AAA on youth employment.

A sample of 18 countries was selected from the 119 countries from among both high and low engagement countries in each World Bank region (table B.7). The following criteria were used for the selection process:

| Table B.7 | | List of Countries for Country Case Studies and Project Performance Assessment Reports, by Region and Level of World Bank Group Engagement on Youth Employment | |
|---|---|---|---|
| | World Bank engagement level | Purposefully selected countries | Total case studies |
| AFR | High | Burkina Faso, Ghana, Rwanda | 6 |
| | Low | Liberia, Nigeria, South Africa | |
| EAP | High | China | 2 |
| | Low | Indonesia | |
| ECA | High | Turkey, Armenia | 4 |
| | Low | FYR Macedonia, Romania | |
| LAC | High | Colombia | 3 |
| | Low | Dominican Republic, Brazil | |
| MENA | High | Tunisia | 2 |
| | Low | Morocco | |
| SAR | High | | 1 |
| | Low | Bangladesh | |

*Source:* World Bank data.
*Note:* AFR= Africa; EAP= East Asia and Pacific; ECA= Europe and Central Asia; LAC= Latin America and the Caribbean; MENA= Middle East and North Africa; SAR= South Asia Region.

- High official youth unemployment rates as reported by the International Labor Organization and World Development Indicators statistics (the former Yugoslav Republic of Macedonia, Armenia, South Africa, Dominican Republic);

- Large youth cohorts and high youth inactivity rates (Nigeria, Morocco, Bangladesh);

- Introduction of reforms and programs related to youth employment (Ghana, Liberia, Indonesia, Turkey, Romania, Rwanda);

- High Bank involvement in youth employment (Colombia, China, Tunisia, Burkina Faso).

More countries in Sub-Saharan Africa (6 countries) were selected to reflect the large World Bank Group involvement and high youth population. Field visits were undertaken to the Dominican Republic, Ghana, Liberia, Rwanda, and Tunisia. Comprehensive desk reviews were conducted for the remaining 13 countries. Each desk-based case study took approximately 10 days to complete, while field-based case studies took 15–17 days for both desk and field work. The data sources consulted for the case studies included:

- Substantial in-depth reviews of World Bank Group project and program documents of operations managed by sectors such as Human Development, Private Sector Development, and Agriculture that became effective since 2001 (including PADs, concept notes, program documents, ICRs, ICR reviews, implementation status reports, PPARs, and country strategies).

- Reviews of project documents and studies of projects and programs undertaken by other institutions, such as bilateral donor agencies, development banks, the ILO, and so on.

- Reviews of research documents, AAA documents, evaluations, reports published in the peer-reviewed literature by the World Bank Group and other institutions. The analytical material consulted included, among others: youth employment reviews, poverty assessments, country education sector reviews, country labor market reviews, public expenditure reviews, country economic memoranda, beneficiary assessments, impact evaluations, and country social protection strategies.

- Interviews with key World Bank Group staff involved in youth employment support to the countries (3–5 interviews per country). The countries that involved field missions also included extensive interviews with clients, key stakeholders, and development partners.

**Analysis.** The case studies used a 17-page structured questionnaire based on the MILES framework. The survey covered: (i) issues in youth employment; (ii) government and private sector interventions to promote youth employment; (iii) support by the World Bank Group and other development partners to promote youth employment and; (iv) evaluation of World Bank Group support to youth employment. Some questions were factual while others required an evaluative judgment based on data and evidence to support the assessment.

Seven IEG staff and consultants undertook the 18 case studies. At the start of the work, IEG organized a one-day workshop for the team to review the case study questionnaire, data sources, and methodology, and reach a common understanding of required information and the basis for assessment. One panel reviewer vetted all 18 draft case studies to ensure consistency and evidence base.

At the end of the process, detailed information was compiled about youth employment issues and interventions in the 18 countries. Issue notes were prepared related to the main evaluation questions. Analytical evidence from the case studies was triangulated with evidence from other evaluation inputs and incorporated into the final report.

SYSTEMATIC-REVIEW OF IMPACT EVALUATIONS

**Identification of Impact Evaluations.** The English language evaluation literature written since 2000 was reviewed for inclusion in this systematic review. The literature was identified with an online search using EconLit, Google Scholar, Journal Storage (JSTOR), Development Impact Evaluation (DIME), ILO, the Institute for the Study of Labor (IZA), the Abdul Latif Jameel

Poverty Action Lab (J-PAL), the National Bureau of Economic Research (NBER), the International Initiative for Impact Evaluation (3iE), Innovations for Poverty Action, and the Youth Employment Inventory.

The key words used to identify relevant articles were "labor markets," "ALMP," "youth employment," "job search assistance for youth/young," "self-employment/entrepreneurship," "vocational training," "apprenticeship," "school-to-work transition," "wage," and "market earning" with the cross-cutting terms "impact evaluation" or "evaluation."

An initial list of 59 evaluations was identified for further review. Both their abstracts and summaries were reviewed to discern whether the evaluation was specifically related to youth employment. Each study was reviewed to identify whether youth were explicitly targeted and, if not, whether youth were identified in the analysis as beneficiaries of the intervention. Studies were excluded if they did not explicitly measure outcomes for youth or if they did not disentangle youth employment interventions from other labor market interventions.

Evaluations that did not provide sound information on intervention objectives, design, and target criteria were excluded, as were studies that did not report employment or earning outcomes for beneficiary groups. Thirty-eight evaluations were retained for the systematic review, among them 16 articles from peer-reviewed journals (42 percent), 5 World Bank working papers and reports (13 percent), and 17 working papers and reports from other institutions (45 percent).

**Categorizing Studies by Methodology.** The methodology of each study was analyzed. The 38 studies were reviewed and categorized as one of three types based on the methodology used:

- Impact evaluations with experimental or quasi-experimental design using individual micro-data with no cost-benefit analysis (22 studies);
- Impact evaluations with cost-benefit analysis (10 studies); and
- Other evaluations with outcomes measures (6 studies)

Studies were classified as impact evaluations if they constructed a counterfactual to program participation using experimental or quasi-experimental methods, such as randomization, propensity score matching, difference-in-difference, instrumental variables, or regression discontinuity. Impact evaluations identify a comparison group of non-beneficiaries that resembles the without-program scenario for beneficiaries. Further, to be categorized as an impact evaluation, the regression must use micro-data and include robustness tests. Results should be robust on a variety of factors, including changes in econometric methods and specification, endogeneity issues, context, and implementation aspects. The impact evaluation category was further broken down into evaluations that included a cost-benefit analysis and those that did not.

Other evaluations with outcome measures used surveys or national or regional time series data to report the outcomes of an intervention. Impact evaluations without micro-data or a robustness test were included in this category. The outcome evaluation may also include a cost-benefit analysis.

**Categorizing Studies by Intervention Evaluated.** Each of the 38 studies was reviewed to identify the youth employment interventions evaluated (see table 4.1). The interventions were categorized into three groups, following the MILES framework (box 2.1):

- Fostering job creation/work opportunities (I)
- Smoothing the transition from school to work and facilitating job mobility (L)
- Fostering skill development and labor market relevance of skills (E).

The 38 studies were reviewed to code the interventions, methodology, time period, target groups, and employment and earning outcomes. The results were then entered in a spreadsheet. Coding was based on information taken directly from the text of the evaluation report. Target groups of the interventions described in the 38 studies included the poor, females, specific age groups, youth (both highly educated and those with little education), certain ethnic or racial groups, and specific geographic areas. Table B.8 is an overview of the 38 studies by country retained for the systematic review. For some youth employment programs, several studies have been conducted, with some analyzing different interventions in the same program.

| Table B.8 | Youth Employment Impact Evaluations | | | | | | |
|---|---|---|---|---|---|---|---|
| Country | Evaluation study | Interventions | Target group | Observation period | Evaluation method | Employment effect | Earnings effect |
| Argentina | Aedo and Núñez (2004) | Skills development Remedial TVET, training subsidies, and vouchers | Youth | 1996–1997 | Matching estimators | Positive (for adult females only) | Positive (for young males and adult females) |
| | Alzua and Brassiolo (2006) | Skills development Remedial TVET, training subsidies, and vouchers | Youth | 1990s | Propensity score matching | Insignificant | Insignificant |
| | Elías and others (2004) | Skills development Remedial TVET, training subsidies, and vouchers | Youth | 1997 | Propensity score matching Difference in difference | NA | Positive |

*(Continues on the following page.)*

| Table B.8 | | Youth Employment Impact Evaluations (cont.) | | | | | |
|---|---|---|---|---|---|---|---|
| Country | Evaluation study | Interventions | Target group | Observation period | Evaluation method | Employment effect | Earnings effect |
| | Jalan and Ravallion (2003) | Fostering job creation/work opportunities Direct job creation | Self-selected unemployed workers from poor families | 1997 | Propensity score matching | NA | Positive |
| Bosnia and Herzegovina | Benus and others (2001) | Smoothing transition from school to work and facilitating job mobility Counseling Skills development Remedial TVET | Demobilized soldiers and displaced workers | 1996–1999 | Mean differences | Positive | Positive |
| China | Bidani and others (2009) | Skills development Remedial TVET | Youth | 1994–1996 | Propensity score matching Ordinary least square | Positive (in Wuhan) | Positive (in Shenyang) |
| Colombia | Attanasio and others (2011) | Skills development Remedial TVET | Youth | 2004–2006 | Experiment | Positive (for women) | Positive (for women) |
| | Kugler (2005) | Fostering job creation/work opportunities Regulations to provide incentives to firms to hire young people (job security regulations, severance payments) | All workers hired after 1990 and covered by the legislation (formal-sector workers) | 1988–1996 | Difference in difference | Varies (depending on gender, age, education level, industry, and firm size) | NA |
| | Medina and Núñez (2001) | Skills development Remedial TVET | Youth | 1997 | Propensity score matching | NA | Insignificant |
| Dominican Republic | Card and others (2011) | Smoothing transition from school to work and facilitating job mobility Counseling Skills development Remedial TVET, training subsidies, and vouchers | Youth | 2004–2005 | Experiment | Insignificant | Positive |
| | Tesliuc (2011) | Skills development Remedial TVET, training subsidies, and vouchers | Youth | 2008–2011 | Experiment | Insignificant | Positive |

| Country | Evaluation study | Interventions | Target group | Observation period | Evaluation method | Employment effect | Earnings effect |
|---|---|---|---|---|---|---|---|
| France | Brodaty and others (2001) | Fostering job creation/work opportunities Wage subsidies Skills development Remedial TVET | Youth | 1986–1988 | Matching estimators | Varies | NA |
| Kenya | Hicks and others (2011) | Skills development Training subsidies and vouchers | Youth | 2008–2010 | Ordinary least square Random/fixed effect | Negative (short-run) | NA |
| Mexico | Delajara and others (2006) | Fostering job creation/work opportunities Training in entrepreneurship Skills development Remedial TVET | Youth | 1999–2004 | Propensity score matching Selection correction | Positive | Positive |
| Panama | Ibarraran and Rosas (2007) | Skills development Work-based TVET Remedial TVET | Youth | 2004–2005 | Mean differences Dynamic random coefficient logit model | Insignificant Positive for females | Insignificant Positive for females |
| Peru | Chong and Galdo (2006) | Skills development Work-based TVET Remedial TVET | Youth | 1996–2004 | Propensity score matching Difference in difference | NA | Positive |
| | Díaz and Jaramillo (2006) | Skills development Work-based TVET Remedial TVET | Youth | 1999–2004 | Propensity score matching Difference in difference | Positive | Positive |
| Portugal | Cardoso (2009) | Fostering job creation/work opportunities Regulations to incentivize firms to hire young people (minimum wage) | Youth | 1987–2005 | Ordinary least square | NA | An overall wage premium and a flatter tenure-earnings profile (long-run) |
| Romania | Malamud and Pop-Eleches (2010) | Skills development Improving the quality of formal TVET | Youth | 1992–2002 | Regression discontinuity | Insignificant | Insignificant |
| Sri Lanka | de Mel and others (2010) | Fostering job creation/work opportunities Wage subsidies | Youth | 2008–2010 | Description | Positive | NA |

*(Continues on the following page.)*

| Country | Evaluation study | Interventions | Target group | Observation period | Evaluation method | Employment effect | Earnings effect |
|---|---|---|---|---|---|---|---|
| | World Bank South Asia Region (2011f) | Skills development Improving the quality of formal TVET Remedial TVET | All labor market participants (youth and prime-aged adults) | 1992–2004 | Propensity score matching Parametric survival models | Positive (formal training on full-time salaried employment for all working age population) Insignificant (time to find a first job for youth) | Positive (formal training for all working age population) |
| Sweden | Larsson (2003) | Fostering job creation/work opportunities Wage subsidies Skills development Remedial TVET | Youth | First half of the 1990s | Propensity score matching | Negative (short-run) Insignificant (medium-run) | Negative (short-run) Insignificant (medium-run) |
| Tunisia | Premand and others (2012) | Fostering job creation/work opportunities Training in entrepreneurship Support to start up businesses | Youth | 2009–2011 | Ordinary least square | Insignificant Positive in self-employment | Positive in private sector reservation wage of participants |
| United Kingdom | Blundell and others (2004) | Fostering job creation/work opportunities Wage subsidies Direct job creation Smoothing transition from school to work and facilitating job mobility Counseling Skills development Remedial TVET | Youth | 1997–1998 | Difference in difference combined with various methods | Positive | NA |
| | Van Reenen (2003) | Fostering job creation/work opportunities Wage subsidies Direct job creation Smoothing transition from school to work and facilitating job mobility Counseling Skills development Remedial TVET | Youth | 1998–2002 | Difference in difference | Positive | NA |

| | Table B.8 | Youth Employment Impact Evaluations (cont.) | | | | | | |
|---|---|---|---|---|---|---|---|---|
| Country | Evaluation study | Interventions | Target group | Observation period | Evaluation method | Employment effect | Earnings effect |
| United States | Burghardt and Schochet (2001) | Smoothing transition from school to work and facilitating job mobility Counseling Skills development Remedial TVET Support to transportation and changes of residence | Youth | 1994–1998 | Mean differences | NA | Positive |
| | Gritz and Johnson (2001) | Smoothing transition from school to work and facilitating job mobility Counseling Skills development Remedial TVET Support to transportation and changes of residence | Youth | 1994–1998 | Propensity score matching | NA | Positive |
| | Lee (2009) | Smoothing transition from school to work and facilitating job mobility Counseling Skills development Remedial TVET Support to transportation and changes of residence | Youth | 1994–1998 | Trimming estimator | NA | Positive |
| | Miller and others (2003) | Smoothing transition from school to work and facilitating job mobility Counseling Skills development Remedial TVET | Youth | 1990s | Mean differences | Positive (female) Negative (male and low-educated) | Positive (female) Negative (male and low-educated) |
| | Rodriguez-Planas (2010) | Skills development Remedial TVET, training subsidies, and vouchers | Youth | 1995–2005 | Mean differences | Positive (female) Negative (male) | NA |

*(Continues on the following page.)*

| Country | Evaluation study | Interventions | Target group | Observation period | Evaluation method | Employment effect | Earnings effect |
|---|---|---|---|---|---|---|---|
| | Schochet and others (2000) | Smoothing transition from school to work and facilitating job mobility Counseling Skills development Remedial TVET Support to transportation and changes of residence | Youth | 1994–1998 | Ordinary least square | Positive | Positive |
| | Schochet and others (2008) | Smoothing transition from school to work and facilitating job mobility Counseling Skills development Remedial TVET Support to transportation and changes of residence | Youth | 1993–2003 | Mean differences | Positive | Positive |
| | Department of Labor US (2005) | Skills development Remedial TVET | Youth | 2004–2005 | Description | Positive | NA |
| Uganda | Blattman and others (2011) | Fostering job creation/work opportunities Training in entrepreneurship Support to start up businesses Skills development Training subsidies and vouchers | Youth | 2008–2010 | Mean differences | Positive | Positive |
| 16 East Asian and Latin American countries | Patrinos and others (2006) | Skills development Improving the quality of formal TVET | Youth | Varies (1998–2005) | Ordinary least square | NA | NA |
| 17 OECD countries | Neumark and Wascher (2004) | Fostering job creation/work opportunities Regulations to provide incentives to firms to hire young people (minimum wage) | All labor market participants (youth and prime-aged adults) | 1975–2000 | Ordinary least square Fixed effect Generalized Method of Moments | Negative | NA |

| Country | Evaluation study | Interventions | Target group | Observation period | Evaluation method | Employment effect | Earnings effect |
|---|---|---|---|---|---|---|---|
| **Table B.8** | | Youth Employment Impact Evaluations (cont.) | | | | | |
| European countries | Kluve (2010) | Fostering job creation/work opportunities Wage subsidies Direct job creation Smoothing transition from school to work and facilitating job mobility Counseling Skills development Remedial TVET | Youth | Varies (1984–2004) | Ordered probit models | Varies depending on program type | NA |
| Latin American and the Caribbean countries | Heckman and Pagés-Serra (2000) | Fostering job creation/work opportunities Regulations to provide incentives to firms to hire young people (job security regulations) | All labor market participants (youth and prime-aged adults) | 1980s and 1990s | Ordinary least square Random/fixed effect | Negative | NA |

*Source:* World Bank data.
*Note:* NA = not the focus of the evaluation; TVET= technical and vocational education training.

## KEY INFORMANT INTERVIEWS AND SURVEYS

Interviews with senior Bank managers and a survey of operational staff (Task Team Leaders) were conducted to understand World Bank corporate thinking on youth employment, issues related to collaboration across sectors, and implementation successes and challenges. The findings from the survey and interviews were analyzed and triangulated with other sources of data before incorporation in the report.

**Interviews with Bank Management.** Regions and networks were selected for interviews if they had a youth employment operation in the past 10 years. In December 2011, IEG sent a total of 59 interview invitations to each regional chief economist and network director and to a random selection of regional sector directors and managers and country directors. Questions were shared with interviewees in advance. Two IEG representatives (one interviewer and one note taker) conducted the face-to-face interviews in January and February 2012. Each interview took 40–60 minutes. Twelve interviews were held.

**Task Team Leader Survey.** Seventy-nine Task Team Leaders (TTLs) of youth employment lending operations or ESW were sent an email in January 2012 requesting that they complete an online survey to provide their views and implementation experiences. A reminder email was sent prior to closing the survey on February 24, 2012. Twenty-six TTLs participated in the survey, a 33 percent response rate. Table B.10 shows the number of survey respondents by region and sector board.

| Table B.9 | Number of Survey Respondents by Primary Sector Board and Region | | | | | | | | |
|---|---|---|---|---|---|---|---|---|---|
| Sector Board | AFR | EAP | ECA | HDN | LAC | MENA | PREM | SAR | Total |
| Social Protection | 4 | 1 | 1 | 2 | 2 | 2 | | 1 | 13 |
| Education | 3 | 1 | 1 | | 2 | | | 1 | 8 |
| Social Development | 2 | | | | | | | | 2 |
| Economic Policy | | | 1 | | | | 1 | | 2 |
| Agriculture and Rural Development | | | | | | | | 1 | 1 |
| Total | 9 | 2 | 3 | 2 | 4 | 2 | 1 | 3 | 26 |

Source: IEG.
Note: AFR= Africa; EAP= East Asia and Pacific; ECA= Europe and Central Asia; HDN= Human Development Network; LAC= Latin America and the Caribbean; MENA= Middle East and North Africa; PREM= Poverty Reduction and Economic Management; SAR= South Asia Region.

## Note

1. This approach left the Middle East and North Africa region with only one study (Jordan) included in the sample. It was decided to look at earlier years for additional studies. On this basis, a 2004 study on the Tunisian Labor Market was included in the sample.

## References

Aedo, Cristian, and Sergio Núñez. 2004. "The impact of training policies in Latin America and the Caribbean: the Case of Programa Joven." Research Network Working Paper R-483. Inter-American Development Bank.

Alzua, Maria Laura, and Pablo Brassiolo. 2006. "The Impact of Training Policies in Argentina: An Evaluation of Proyecto Joven." IADB Office of Evaluation and Oversight Working Paper OVE/WP-15/06, Argentina.

Attanasio, Orazio, Adriana Kugler, and Costas Meghir. 2011. "Subsidizing Vocational Training for Disadvantaged Youth in Colombia: Evidence from a Randomized Trial." *American Economic Journal: Applied Economics* 3(3): 188–220.

Benus, Jacob, James Rude and Satyendra Patrabansh. 2001. "Impact of the Emergency Demobilization and Reintegration Project in Bosnia and Herzegovina." Department of Labor Bureau of International Affairs. Development Impact Evaluation (DIME).

Bidani, Benu, Niels-Hugo Blunch, Chor-ching Goh and Christopher J. O'Leary. 2009. "Evaluating Job Training in Two Chinese Cities." *Journal of Chinese Economic and Business Studies* 7 (1): 77–94.

Blattman, Christopher, Nathan Fiala, and Sebastian Martinez. 2011. "Can Employment Programs Reduce Poverty and Social Instability Experimental Evidence from a Ugandan Aid Program." World Bank Policy Research Working Paper series.

Blundell, Richard, Monica Costa Dias, Costas Meghir, and John Van Reenen. 2004. "Evaluating the Employment Impact of a Mandatory Job Search Assistance Program." *Journal of the European Economic Association* 2(4): 569–606.

Brodaty, Thomas, Bruno Crépon, and Denis Fougère. 2001. "Using Matching Estimators to Evaluate Alternative Youth Employment Programs: Evidence from France, 1986–1988." In *Econometric Evaluation of Labour Market Policies,* eds. M. Lechner and F. Pfeiffer. Heidelberg and New York: Physica-Verlag and Centre for European Economic Research.

Burghardt, John, and Peter Z. Schochet. 2001. "National Job Corps Study: Impact by Center Characteristics." US Department of Labor, Employment, and Training Administration. Washington, DC.

Card, David, Pablo Ibarrarán, Ferdinando Regalia, David Rosas, and Yuri Soares. 2011. "The Labor Market Impacts of Youth Training in the Dominican Republic." *Journal of Labor Economics* 29(2): 267–300.

Cardoso, Ana Rute. (2009). "Long-Term Impact of Youth Minimum Wages: Evidence from Two Decades of Individual Longitudinal Data." IZA Discussion Paper No. 4236.

Chong, Alberto and Jose Galdo. 2006. "Does the Quality of Training Programs Matter? Evidence from Bidding Processes Data." IZA Discussion Papers 2202. Institute for the Study of Labor (IZA), Latin America.

de Mel, Suresh, David McKenzie, and Christopher Woodruff. (2010). "Wage Subsidies for Microenterprises." *American Economic Review: Papers & Proce*edings 100 (2): 614-18.

Delajara, Marcelo, Samuel Freije, and Isidro Soloaga. 2006. "An Evaluation of Training for the Unemployed in Mexico." Working Paper: OVE/WP-09/06. Inter-American Development Bank, Office of Evaluation and Oversight.

Díaz, Juan José, and Miguel Jaramillo. 2006. "Evaluation of the Peruvian Youth Labor Training Program – ProJoven." Working Paper #1006. Inter-American Development Bank, Office of Evaluation and Oversight.

Elías, Víctor, Fernanda Ruiz Núñez, Ricardo Cossa, and David Bravo. 2004. "An Econometric Cost- Benefit Analysis of Argentina's Youth Training Program." Working Paper #R-482. Inter-American Development Bank.

Gritz, Mark, and Terry Johnson. 2001. "National Job Corps Study Assessing Program Effects on Earnings for Students Achieving Key Program Milestones." Impact evaluation submitted to U.S. Department of Labor. Battelle Memorial Institute, Seattle, Washington.

Heckman, James and Carmen Pagés-Serra. (2000). "The Cost of Job Security Regulation: Evidence from Latin American Labor Markets." *Economia* 1(1) 109-144.

Hicks, Joan Hamory, Michael Kremer, Isaac Mbiti, and Edward Miguel. 2011. "Vocational Education Voucher Delivery and Labor Market Returns: A Randomized Evaluation among Kenyan Youth, Report for Spanish Impact Evaluation Fund (SIEF) Phase II." Policy Note Human Development Network. World Bank.

Ibarraran, Pablo, and David Rosas. 2007. "Impact Evaluation of a Labor Training Program in Panama." OVE Inter-American Development Bank, Washington DC.

Independent Evaluation Group. 2012. "World Bank and IFC Support for Youth Employment Programs." Background Paper. Country Case Study: Ghana. Forthcoming.

Jalan, Jyotsna and Martin Ravallion. 2003. Estimating the Benefit Incidence of an Antipoverty Program by Propensity-Score Matching. *Journal of Business and Economic Statistics, American Statistical Association* 21(1) 19–30.

Kluve, Jochen. 2010. "The effectiveness of European active labor market programs." *Labour Economics* 17: 904–918.

Kugler, Adriana D. 2005. "The Effect of Job Security Regulations on Labor Market Flexibility. Evidence from Colombia Labor Market Reform." In *Law and Employment: Lessons from Latin American and the Caribbean*, eds. James J. Heckman and Carmen Pagés. Chicago: University of Chicago Press.

Larsson, Laura. 2003. "Evaluation of Swedish Youth Labor Market Programs." *The Journal of Human Resources* 38(4): 891–927.

Lee, David S. 2009. "Training, Wages, and Sample Selection: Estimating Sharp Bounds on Treatment Effects." *Review of Economic Studies* 76(3): 1071–1102.

Malamud, Ofer, and Cristian Pop-Eleches. 2010. "General Education versus Vocational Training: Evidence from an Economy in Transition." *Review of Economics and Statistics* 92(1): 43–60.

Medina, Carlos, and Jairo Núñez. 2001. "The Impact of Public and Private Job Training in Colombia." Inter-American Bank, Research Network Paper.

Miller, Cynthia, Johannes M. Bos, Kristin E. Porter, Fannie M. Tseng, Fred C. Doolittle, Deana N. Tanguay, and Mary P. Vencill. 2003. "Working with Disadvantaged Youth Thirty-Month Findings from the Evaluation of the Center for Employment

Training Replication Sites." Manpower Demonstration Research Corporation Working Paper.

Neumark, David and William Wascher. (2004). "Minimum Wages, Labor Market Institutions, and Youth Employment: A Cross-National Analysis." *Industrial and Labor Relations Review* 57( 2): 223–248.

Patrinos, Harry Anthony, Cris Ridao-Cano, and Chris Sakellariou. 2006. "Estimating the Returns to Education: Accounting for Heterogeneity in Ability." Unpublished report.

Premand Patrick, Stefanie Brodmann, Rita Almeida, Rebekka Grun, and Mahdi Barouni. 2012. "Entrepreneurship training and self-employment among university graduates: Evidence from a randomized trial in Tunisia." World Bank Impact Evaluation Report. Washington, DC: World Bank.

Rodriguez-Planas, Nuria. 2010. "Longer-Term Impacts of Mentoring, Educational Services, and Incentives to Learn: Evidence from a Randomized Trial." IZA Discussion Paper No. 4754, United States.

Schochet, Peter, John Burghardt, Steven Glazerman. 2000. "National Job Corps Study: The Short-Term Impacts of Job Corps on Participants' Employment and Related Outcomes. Final Report." Princeton: Mathematica Policy Research.

Schochet, Peter, John Burghardt, and Sheena McConnell. 2008. "Does Job Corps Work? Impact Findings from the National Job Corps Study." *American Economic Review* 98(5): 1864–1886.

Tesliuc, Cornelia. 2011. "Impact Evaluation Report on Dominican Republic Programa Juventud y Empleo (PJE)." Summary Note Human Development Network. World Bank.

United States Department of Labor. 2005. "Performance and Accountability Report." Department of Labor Annual Report. Fiscal Year 2005.

Van Reenen, John. 2003. "Active Labour Market Policies and the British New Deal for the Young Unemployed in Context." NBER Working Paper Series. Working Paper 9576.

World Bank. 2011. "Sri Lanka: Education, Training and Labor Market Outcomes." World Bank South Asia Region.

# Appendix C
Strategies and Collaboration

Appendix C provides additional information on strategic thinking and collaboration in youth employment.

## Strategic Thinking on Youth Employment

The *World Development Report 2007: Development and the Next Generation* (World Bank 2007) emphasized the urgency of investing in youth. The report highlighted the fact that young people make up nearly half of the unemployed worldwide, and that decisions about continuing to learn and starting to work have the biggest long-term impact on how human capital is developed and deployed. To support youth, the report presents three strategic policies to enhance investment. These include expanding opportunities, improving capabilities, and offering second chances for young people who have fallen behind due to difficult circumstances or poor choices. During the past decade, other World Development Reports also raised the issue (box C.1).

The Bank's Human Development Network has produced several regional reports about skills development. *Putting Higher Education to Work: Skills and Research for Growth in East Asia* (World Bank 2012) identifies the functional skills needed for employability and discusses how higher education systems can produce these skills. It also addresses research to promote growth. *More and Better Jobs in South Asia* (Nayer and others 2012) examines what needs to be done to meet the region's employment challenge of large demographic pressures. Reforms that cut across sectors are needed; some include improving early child nutrition and improving the quality of education to equip workers with relevant skills. *Skills Not Just Diplomas: Managing Education for Results in Eastern Europe and Central Asia* (Sondergaard and Murthi 2012) argues for

---

**Box C.1**　　Other World Development Reports

The *World Development Report 2004: Making Service Work for Poor People* indicated that many governments are falling short in ensuring basic education services, especially for poor people. One of the key messages of the *World Development Report 2005: A Better Investment Climate for Everyone* was that a top priority for governments is to improve the opportunities and incentives for companies to invest productively, create jobs, including for young people. The *World Development Report 2006: Equity and Development* emphasized that excessively stringent forms of employment protection legislation can make it costly to hire unskilled, young, and female workers—exactly those groups the laws seek to protect.

The *2008 World Development Report: Agriculture for Development* argued that agriculture has features that make it a unique instrument for development. It is a source of livelihoods for an estimated 86 percent of rural people and provides jobs for 1.3 billion. The 2013 *World Development Report* on jobs sets out to explore the notion of the quality of jobs and the connection between jobs and economic and social development.

*Sources:* World Bank 2013; World Bank 2008; World Bank 2006; World Bank 2005; World Bank 2004; World Bank 2000-2001.

*Note:* WDR= World Development Report.

reform of the Eastern Europe and Central Asia education and training systems to support the competitiveness of their economic systems.

*Skills for the 21st Century in Latin America and the Caribbean Region* (Aedo and Walker 2012) highlights the large achievement gap between the Latin America and Caribbean region and advanced economies and East Asia, which keeps the former region from developing cutting-edge industries. The report recommends the need to address problems of quality and relevance in secondary and tertiary education. These recent Bank reports contribute to the discussion about what is needed on a regional level to improve youth employment.

## Collaboration in Youth Employment

The full extent of cross-sector collaboration in youth employment operations is not known. Most operations are multisectoral and support some interventions in skills building, school-to-work transition, and investment climate reforms. When Bank teams prepare and implement these operations, they generally include Bank staff, consultants, and government counterparts, who can have different sector expertise. IEG reviewed the Implementation Completion Reports of 36 closed projects to identify the number of staff from different sectors working on a project team. The data in these reports do not identify how long staff from other sectors spent on a team, the sector specialty of consultants, or the contribution of government counterparts. Thus, the full extent of cross-sector collaboration in youth employment projects is unknown.

Institutional structures and lack of incentives to work across sectors can be addressed. Youth employment issues can benefit from cross-sectoral collaboration. Discussions with key informants and the results of the survey of task team leaders suggest that the Bank's sector organization is perceived to constrain cross-sector collaboration in multisectoral projects. Credit for an operation goes to the units that officially manage the tasks. Indeed, few connections are built across sectors to address youth employment. Cross-sector collaboration and coordination in both the Bank and the client country are useful in addressing youth employment in a comprehensive way. In Brazil, for example, matching the Bank team with the client "teams" (representatives from different ministries) helped support cross-sector projects and enhanced coordination within both the Bank and the government.

The Bank is participating in international initiatives relevant for youth employment (boxes C.2 and C.3).

In 2008, the Adolescent Girls Initiative (AGI) was created as part of the World Bank Group's Gender Action Plan, "Gender Equality as Smart Economics." It is cofinanced by the NIKE Foundation and the governments of Australia, Denmark, Norway, Sweden, and the United Kingdom. AGI aims to promote the transition of adolescent girls from school to productive employment in wage-

## Box C.2 — Global Partnership for Youth Employment (GPYE)

The partnership was established in 2008 as an alliance between the International Youth Foundation, the YEN, the Arab Urban Development Institute, and the Understanding Children's Work (UCW) Project. It is funded by the World Bank's Development Grant Facility with $8 million over five years. GPYE aims to build and disseminate evidence on youth employment outcomes and effective programs. Focus countries are in the Middle East and North Africa region and Sub-Saharan Africa. The GPYE works in three key areas:

- **Applied research and learning:** Generates knowledge on the constraints youth are facing in their transition to work, and on "what works" to increase their employability. Several studies have been produced (for example, Senegal, Sudan, Rwanda, and Lebanon).

- **Policy dialogue:** Promotes effective policy dialogue among stakeholders to raise awareness and share knowledge about youth employment issues and policies. Several conferences were organized to promote evidence-based policy dialogue.

- **Local engagement:** Support technical assistance for local governments, innovative pilot projects, and capacity building for stakeholders from the public sector and civil society.

Technical assistance is provided to local governments in the Middle East (for example, in Tripoli, Aleppo, and Cairo).

*Source:* http://www.gpye.org/.

or self-employment in participating countries, including Afghanistan, Jordan, Lao PDR, Liberia, Nepal, Rwanda, South Sudan, Haiti, and Papua New Guinea. The number of beneficiaries per country ranges from approximately 900 in Jordan to 3,500 women in Nepal. AGI includes a skills development component focused on developing basic numeracy and literacy skills, technical skills,[1] life skills, and business skills during training sessions lasting up to one year. Implementation started in 2010 in selected countries, and impact evaluations are ongoing.

Box C.3     The Youth Employment Network

The Youth Employment Network (YEN) emphasizes four global priorities—employability, entrepreneurship, employment creation, and equal opportunities.

It is comprised of the following four areas:

The **Lead Country Network** includes countries[a] that have committed to prioritize youth employment. Network countries share learning and experiences on youth employment through the benchmarking exercise, focusing on collecting: (i) eight youth labor market indicators;[b] and (ii) narrative information on youth employment interventions. Countries have to commit to the preparation and implementation of a National Action Plan (NAP) on youth employment with a coherent set of policies that are integrated in national development policies and budgets. A review of 41 such plans finds that most address education, vocational training, work experience, career guidance, job counseling, and the school-to-work transition. Many countries also have initiatives to address equal opportunities and encourage entrepreneurship (United Nations 2007).

The **Evaluation Clinics** provide technical and financial support to policymakers to help countries design and implement impact evaluations.

The **Youth to Youth Fund** provides grants to fund small-scale youth entrepreneurship projects in East and West Africa. The funds are allocated based on competition among a pool of applicants. About 70 percent of the proposals are from rural areas.

The **YEN Marketplace** is an online space for the global youth employment community to exchange or offer innovative ideas, best practice, expertise, and advice, as well as collaboration and partnership.

Since the inception of the YEN, the ILO has hosted the YEN Secretariat. Although YEN has had some success in resource mobilization, the funding issue remains a major obstacle to the sustainability of YEN and its Secretariat.

*Source:* ILO Youth Employment Network, http://www.ilo.org/public/english/employment/yen/.

a. Bangladesh, Democratic Republic of Congo, Ecuador, Egypt, Ghana, Indonesia, Jamaica, Kiribati, Liberia, Mali, Nigeria, Rwanda, Senegal, Sri Lanka, Syria, Togo, Tanzania, Turkey, Vanuatu, and Zambia.

b. Indicators include the distribution of youth by primary activity, youth unemployment rate, relaxed youth unemployment rate (the number of unemployed youth plus the number of discouraged youth divided by the youth labor force), youth employment-to-population ratio, status of young workers in employment, youth employment by sector, mean earnings for wage and salaried workers, and educational attainment of the youth labor force.

## Note

1. The type of skills is targeted to sectors with high demand. For example, the program in Liberia includes skills development on hospitality, house painting, professional driving, office/computer skills, and security guard services. In Rwanda, the technical training is in areas such as horticulture, agro-processing, tourism, arts and crafts, technical servicing, and solar technology, information and communications technology, and secretarial services.

# References

Aedo, Cristian, and Ian Walker. 2012. "Skills for the 21st Century in Latin America and the Caribbean." Directions in Development Human Development Network. Washington, DC: World Bank.

Nayar, Reema, Pablo Gottret, Pradeep Mitra, Gordon Betcherman, Yue Man Lee, Indhira Santos, Mahesh Dahal, and Maheshwor Shrestha. 2012. "More and Better Jobs in South Asia." South Asia Development Matters. Washington, DC: World Bank.

Sondergaard, Lars, and Mamta Murthi. 2012. "Skills, Not Just Diplomas Managing Education for Results in Eastern Europe and Central Asia." Directions in Development Human Development Network: World Bank.

United Nations. 2007. Review of National Action Plans on Youth Employment. Putting Commitments into Action. Department of Economic and Social Affairs, New York.

World Bank. 2013. *World Development Report on Jobs*. Washington, D.C.: World Bank. Forthcoming Autumn 2012.

World Bank. 2012. "Putting Higher Education to Work: Skills and Research for Growth in East Asia" World Bank East Asia and Pacific Regional Report. Washington, DC.

World Bank. 2008. *World Development Report: Agriculture for Development*. Washington, D.C.: World Bank

World Bank. 2006. *World Development Report: Equity and Development*. Washington, D.C.: World Bank.

World Bank. 2005. *World Development Report: A Better Investment Climate for Everyone*. Washington, DC.

World Bank. 2004. *Making Services Work for Poor People*. Washington, D.C.: World Bank. World Bank. 2000–2001. *World Development Report: Attacking Poverty*. Washington, D.C.: World Bank.

# Appendix D
The World Bank Portfolio for
Youth Employment

This appendix provides additional information on the scope and trends in World Bank support to youth employment programs.

## World Bank Group Support to Youth Employment in Client Countries

Table D.1 lists the number of youth employment projects by country. IEG calculated total financial commitment to youth employment based on actual costs for activities focused solely on youth employment. This amount includes disbursed and committed amounts for youth employment activities as reported in PADs, ICRs for closed projects, and the Bank's operation portal for ongoing projects.

| Table D.1 | Youth Employment Operations and Spending, IBRD and IDA, in US$ millions | | |
|---|---|---|---|
| Country | Number of projects | Total actual spending for youth employment | Average actual spending for youth employment |
| **IBRD** | **34** | **1,731.7** | **50.9** |
| Argentina | 2 | 169.0 | 84.5 |
| Bangladesh | 1 | 70.9 | 70.9 |
| Bulgaria | 1 | 100.0 | 100.0 |
| Chile | 1 | 41.7 | 41.7 |
| China | 4 | 151.9 | 38.0 |
| Colombia | 5 | 181.0 | 36.2 |
| Costa Rica | 1 | 2.0 | 2.0 |
| Dominican Republic | 1 | 25.0 | 25.0 |
| Egypt, Arab Republic of | 1 | 5.5 | 5.5 |
| El Salvador | 1 | 37.0 | 37.0 |
| Jordan | 2 | 67.5 | 33.8 |
| Kazakhstan | 1 | 29.3 | 29.3 |
| Namibia | 2 | 3.0 | 1.5 |
| Romania | 1 | 60.0 | 60.0 |
| Russian Federation | 2 | 80.5 | 40.2 |
| Tunisia | 4 | 104.8 | 26.2 |
| Turkey | 4 | 602.7 | 150.7 |
| **IDA** | **53** | **1,107.9** | **20.9** |
| Afghanistan | 1 | 20.0 | 20.0 |
| Africa | 1 | 3.0 | 3.0 |
| Armenia | 2 | 2.7 | 1.3 |
| Azerbaijan | 1 | 17.0 | 17.0 |
| Bhutan | 3 | 6.0 | 2.0 |
| Bolivia | 1 | 4.1 | 4.1 |
| Burkina Faso | 2 | 7.0 | 3.5 |
| Congo, Republic of | 2 | 19.8 | 9.9 |

| Table D.1 | Youth Employment Operations and Spending, IBRD and IDA, in US$ millions  (cont.) | | |
|---|---|---|---|
| Country | Number of projects | Total actual spending for youth employment | Average actual spending for youth employment |
| Côte d'Ivoire | 1 | 40.0 | 40.0 |
| Eritrea | 1 | 12.0 | 12.0 |
| Ethiopia | 1 | 4.3 | 4.3 |
| Ghana | 4 | 123.6 | 30.9 |
| Grenada | 1 | 3.0 | 3.0 |
| Honduras | 1 | 7.0 | 7.0 |
| India | 3 | 334.3 | 111.4 |
| Kenya | 2 | 111.0 | 55.5 |
| Lesotho | 1 | 0.8 | 0.8 |
| Liberia | 1 | 6.0 | 6.0 |
| Maldives | 1 | 5.8 | 5.8 |
| Mali | 1 | 3.5 | 3.5 |
| Mauritania | 2 | 27.7 | 13.9 |
| Mozambique | 1 | 20.3 | 20.3 |
| Nepal | 1 | 1.0 | 1.0 |
| Nigeria | 1 | 120.0 | 120.0 |
| Pakistan | 2 | 31.0 | 15.5 |
| Papua New Guinea | 1 | 1.0 | 1.0 |
| Rwanda | 1 | 30.0 | 30.0 |
| Senegal | 1 | 4.0 | 4.0 |
| Sierra Leone | 2 | 51.5 | 25.8 |
| Solomon Islands | 1 | 6.0 | 6.0 |
| Sri Lanka | 1 | 4.4 | 4.4 |
| St. Lucia | 1 | 5.0 | 5.0 |
| Tanzania | 2 | 14.1 | 7.1 |
| Timor-Leste | 1 | 2.2 | 2.2 |
| Togo | 1 | 4.0 | 4.0 |
| Uganda | 1 | 20.0 | 20 |
| Yemen, Republic of | 1 | 15.0 | 15.0 |
| Zambia | 1 | 19.8 | 19.8 |
| Blend | 3 | 9.8 | 3.3 |
| Serbia | 2 | 7.0 | 3.5 |
| West Bank and Gaza | 1 | 2.8 | 2.8 |

*Source:* IEG portfolio review based on World Bank data.
*Note:* IBRD= International Bank for Reconstruction and Development; IDA= International Development Association. Total actual spending = Project amount allocated (disbursed and planned) to youth employment activity as identified in PAD or ICR; Average actual spending = Total actual spending divided by the number of projects.

The number of projects and total lending for youth employment increased over time (figure D.1).

Most lending is managed by the Human Development Network (HDN), 73 percent), which implements 63 operations (70 percent). The Sustainable Development Network (SDN) follows with 14 operations (3 percent of total lending), and Finance and Private Sector Development (FPD) with 8 operations accounting for 13 percent of total lending. More recently, 5 PREM operations also started to incorporate youth employment, reflecting 11 percent of total youth employment lending (figure D.1 and table D.2).

Most youth employment projects are in Africa, and most lending went to Europe and Central Asia (ECA). Africa had more than one-third of the projects. The ECA Region leads slightly with 31 percent of lending, followed by Africa with 23 percent of total lending (figure D.3). The average youth employment loan commitment ranges from $20 million in Africa to $64 million in ECA (table D.3 and figure D. 3).

## Who is Borrowing for Youth Employment Programs?

IDA countries are more likely to borrow for youth employment. Although IBRD countries received 61 percent of total youth employment lending, IDA countries are more likely to receive Bank support to promote youth employment. More than half of IDA countries (59 percent) report at least one

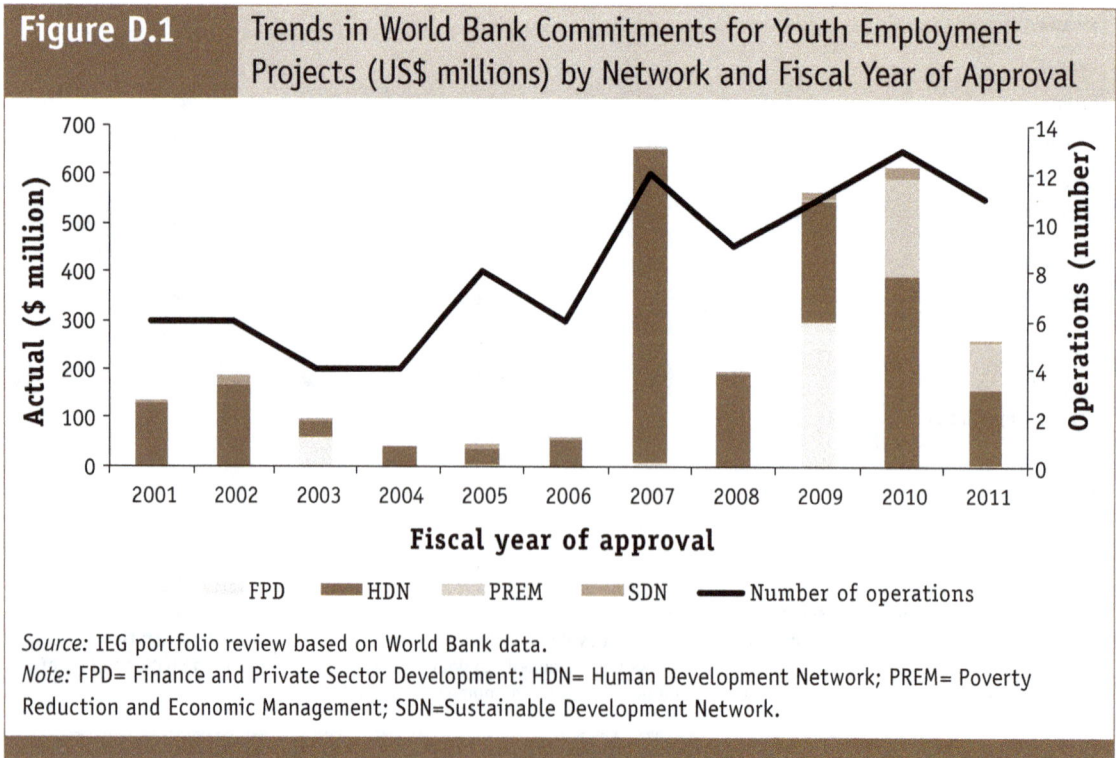

**Figure D.1** Trends in World Bank Commitments for Youth Employment Projects (US$ millions) by Network and Fiscal Year of Approval

FPD ▮ HDN ▒ PREM ▒ SDN ━ Number of operations

*Source:* IEG portfolio review based on World Bank data.
*Note:* FPD= Finance and Private Sector Development: HDN= Human Development Network; PREM= Poverty Reduction and Economic Management; SDN=Sustainable Development Network.

| Sector Board | ED | SP | FPD | PREM | SDN | Total |
|---|---|---|---|---|---|---|
| **Distribution of operations** | | | | | | |
| Number of operations | 37 | 26 | 8 | 5 | 14 | 90 |
| Distribution (percent) | 41 | 29 | 9 | 6 | 16 | 100 |
| FY01–05 (percent; total operations = 28) | 39 | 32 | 11 | 4 | 14 | 100 |
| FY06–11 (percent; total operations = 62) | 42 | 27 | 8 | 7 | 16 | 100 |
| Percent Development Policy Operations | 13 | 40 | 13 | 33 | 0 | 100 |
| **Distribution of actual support** | | | | | | |
| Average support per operation ($ millions) | 34 | 32 | 47 | 62 | 6 | 32 |
| FY01–05 (percent; total actual support = $ 502 million) | 43 | 37 | 13 | 1 | 6 | 100 |
| FY06–11 (percent; total actual support = $ 2.35 billion) | 44 | 28 | 13 | 13 | 2 | 100 |

**Table D.2 Distribution of Youth Employment Operations and Actual Support by Sector Board, FY01–11 Approvals**

*Source:* IEG portfolio review based on World Bank data.
*Note:* ED= Education; FPD= Finance and Private Sector Development; PREM= Poverty Reduction and Economic Management; SDN= Sustainable Development Network; SP= Social Protection.

youth employment operation in the past decade, compared to 29 percent of IBRD countries, and 1 blend economy that has both IBRD and IDA projects (West Bank and Gaza).[1] See table D.4.

Many middle-income countries, especially those in Latin America, already have youth employment programs in place, and their effectiveness has been

**Table D.3 Distribution of Youth Employment Operations and Actual Support by Region FY01–11 Approvals**

| | AFR | EAP | ECA | LAC | MENA | SAR | Total |
|---|---|---|---|---|---|---|---|
| **Distribution of operations** | | | | | | | |
| Number of operations | 32 | 7 | 14 | 15 | 9 | 13 | 90 |
| Distribution (percent) | 36 | 8 | 16 | 17 | 10 | 14 | 100 |
| FY01–05 (percent; total operations = 28) | 39 | 0 | 29 | 11 | 14 | 7 | 100 |
| FY06–11 (percent; total operations = 62) | 34 | 11 | 10 | 19 | 8 | 18 | 100 |
| Percent DPOs | 20 | 0 | 33 | 20 | 13 | 13 | 100 |
| **Distribution of actual support** | | | | | | | |
| Average actual support per operation ($ millions) | 20 | 23 | 64 | 32 | 22 | 36 | 32 |
| FY01–05 (percent; total actual support = $ 502 million) | 25 | 0 | 49 | 12 | 3 | 11 | 100 |
| FY06–11 (percent; total actual support = $ 2.35 billion) | 22 | 7 | 28 | 18 | 8 | 18 | 100 |

*Source:* IEG portfolio review based on World Bank data.
*Note:* AFR= Africa; DPO= Development Policy Operation; EAP= East Asia and Pacific; ECA= Europe and Central Asia; LAC= Latin America and the Caribbean; MENA= Middle East and North Africa; SAR= South Asia Region.

## Figure D.2 — World Bank Youth Employment Distribution by Region

**A. Operations**

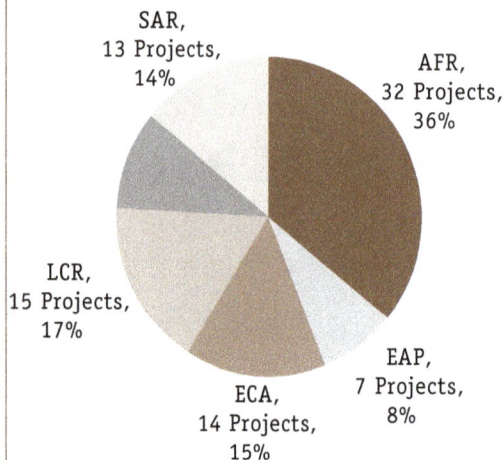

- SAR, 13 Projects, 14%
- AFR, 32 Projects, 36%
- EAP, 7 Projects, 8%
- ECA, 14 Projects, 15%
- LCR, 15 Projects, 17%

**B. Commitments**

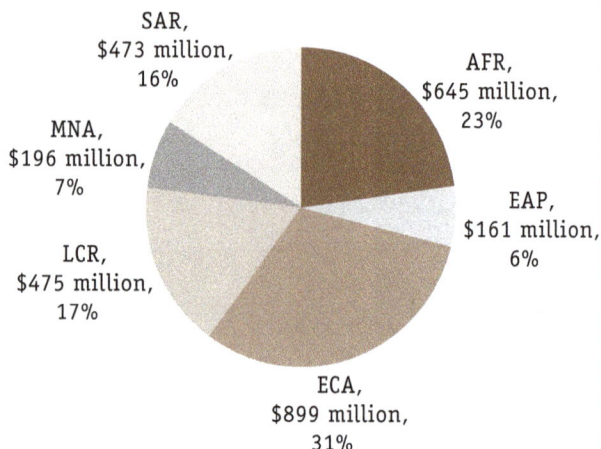

- SAR, $473 million, 16%
- AFR, $645 million, 23%
- EAP, $161 million, 6%
- ECA, $899 million, 31%
- LCR, $475 million, 17%
- MNA, $196 million, 7%

*Source:* IEG portfolio review based on World Bank data.

*Note:* AFR= Africa; EAP= East Asia and Pacific; ECA= Europe and Central Asia; LAC= Latin America and the Caribbean; MNA= Middle East and North Africa; SAR= South Asia Region.

## Table D.4 — Scale of World Bank Engagement in Youth Employment, FY01–11 Approvals

|  | IDA | IBRD | Total |
|---|---|---|---|
| Countries with youth employment operations | 38.5 | 18.5 | 57 |
| Youth employment lending (in US$ millions) | $1,112.53 | $1,736.87 | $2,849.39 |
| Youth employment lending as a percentage of total Bank lending | 0.95% | 0.86% | 0.90% |
| Youth employment operations, number | 53.5 | 36.5 | 90 |
| Youth employment operations as a percentage of total Bank operations | 2.85% | 2.97% | 2.90% |
| Top 10 borrowers, number | 4 | 6 | 10 |
| Most used interventions | Information on labor market | Improve quality of formal TVET | Information on labor market |
| Economic sector work (youth employment activities) | 14 | 7 | 21 |

*Source:* IEG.

*Note:* West Bank and Gaza was 50/50 blend and is allocated accordingly between IDA and IBRD. Serbia had one IDA operation and one 25/75 IDA/IBRD blend. The loan amount is allocated based on the percentage, and Serbia is counted under IBRD based on its current status. IDA includes one operation in the Africa region.

IBRD= International Bank for Reconstruction and Development; IDA= International Development Association; TVET= technical and vocational education training.

evaluated. Also, in middle-income countries, unemployed youth are more visible to policy makers through labor force survey results, and by the large number of youth in coffee shops.

The Bank supports youth employment programs in many fragile and post-conflict settings. Youth employment support went to 10 of the 35 settings considered fragile by the Bank's definition.[2] Most of these countries are IDA-eligible and are located in Sub-Saharan Africa (box D.1). Fragile states implemented 12 of the 90 youth employment operations and about 6 percent of total youth employment lending (table D.5).

## What Objectives Do Youth Employment Operations Aim to Achieve?

Most projects aim to build relevant skills for the labor market and generate employment opportunities and economic integration for youth. In line with the MILES framework, the objectives of the 90 operations in the identified portfolio were grouped into three categories. Most operations had an objective related to "school–to-work transition" (82 percent) and a majority had a "skills development" objective (59 percent). Within these categories, objectives to build the relevant skills, find employment, and encourage economic integration were most frequent. Objectives related to "fostering job creation/work opportunities" (17 percent) were less often mentioned. Also prominent were objectives to improve vocational education and to enhance institutional capacity, including labor market policies and laws.

All regions have a strong focus on school-to-work transitions and many attend to skills development. Analyzing the objectives by region shows that skills development objectives are most prevalent in the East Asia and

---

**Box D.1**    Youth Employment in Fragile States

Youth in fragile settings face different obstacles in the labor market. The risk of resurgent violence is a common concern among policy makers in these countries, which makes job creation an urgent priority to promote social and political stability.

Donors have supported short-term, labor-intensive public works programs that can provide a "quick win." In Sierra Leone, the National Social Action Project has created temporary employment for over 12,000 individuals, and the Youth Employment Support project is expected to provide employment to about 30,000–35,000 youth over the period 2010–13. However, given the need to structure long-term solutions to job creation, these short-term programs should be the initial step toward a longer-term employment generation strategy that includes the promotion of a positive investment climate to encourage private investment.

Addressing youth employment in fragile states requires a holistic approach to economic recovery and employment generation. Improved governance and institutions matter.

*Source:* World Bank 2011.

| | Table D.5 | Youth Employment Interventions Supported by Projects Conducted in Fragile States (n=20) | |
|---|---|---|---|

| Intervention category | Number of projects |
|---|---|
| **1. Fostering job creation/work opportunities** | **8** |
| i. Improving the business environment and investment climate | 1 |
| ii. Regulations to provide incentives to firms to hire young people | 0 |
| iii. Fostering entrepreneurship | |
|     Training in entrepreneurship/business management skills | 2 |
|     Support to start up businesses | 2 |
| iv. Wage subsidies | 0 |
| v. Direct job creation | 7 |
| **2. Smoothing the transition from school-to-work and facilitating job mobility** | **10** |
| i. Counseling, job search skills, matching, placement | 3 |
| ii. Program for overseas employment of young people | 0 |
| iii. Improving information on the labor market | 10 |
| **3. Fostering skill development and labor market relevance of skills** | **10** |
| i. Improving the quality of formal secondary and post-secondary vocational education and training including through the private sector | 6 |
| ii. Expanding/improving work-based learning in post-secondary and secondary vocational training and apprenticeship | 4 |
| iii. Recognition and certification of skills | 2 |
| iv. Remedial education/second chance/non-formal technical and vocational training | 5 |
| v. Providing information on training opportunities | 5 |
| vi. Training subsidies and vouchers | 2 |
| vii. Support to transportation and changes of residence | 1 |

*Source:* IEG portfolio review based on World Bank data.

Pacific region (86 percent), followed by Latin America and the Caribbean (73 percent). However, "school–to–work transition" is the top objective in both regions. "Fostering job creation and employment opportunities" was most prominent in Europe and Central Asian countries, followed by the Middle East and North Africa. Projects in Africa show lower frequencies because projects have more single objectives than those in other regions where multiple sub-objectives are more common (tables D.7 and D.8).

Objectives reflect the priority of the managing Sector Board. All projects managed by the Education Sector Board support relevant skills building for the labor market, and those managed by Social Protection support improved school–to–work transition and job mobility. However, these Human Development-led operations include very few job creation or work opportunity objectives, which are more prominent in FPD and PREM-led operations. To some extent, this reflects the sector expertise in the teams.

## Table D.6 — Prevalence of Project Objectives (percent)

| Percent of operations with objective | 2001–2011 (n=90) |
|---|---|
| **Fostering job creation/work opportunities (I)** | **17** |
| Entrepreneurs start up firms, self employment | 2 |
| Enterprises; small-medium enterprises | 7 |
| Investment climate, access to credit | 10 |
| Growth and competitiveness | 8 |
| **School-to-work transition/job mobility (L)** | **82** |
| Employment/economic integration | 50 |
| Individual earnings | 20 |
| Information, transparency | 8 |
| Institutional capacity/labor market policy/laws | 29 |
| Fiscal management, financial sustainability | 1 |
| Employment service/job search | 3 |
| Employment programs | 9 |
| Productivity | 6 |
| Efficiency | 13 |
| **Skill development (E)** | **59** |
| Relevant skill building | 51 |
| Improve technical and vocational education | 29 |

*Source:* IEG portfolio review based on World Bank data.

## Table D.7 — Prevalence of Project Objectives, by Sector Board (percent)

| Percent of projects with objective | Education (n=37) | Social Protection (n=26) | Finance and Private Sector Development (n=8) | Economic Policy (n=5) | Social Development (n=14) |
|---|---|---|---|---|---|
| **Fostering job creation/work opportunities (I)** | **3** | **8** | **88** | **60** | **14** |
| Entrepreneurs start up firms, self employment | 0 | 0 | 13 | 0 | 7 |
| Enterprises; small and medium enterprises | 0 | 0 | 50 | 20 | 7 |
| Investment climate, credit access | 0 | 0 | 75 | 60 | 0 |
| Growth/competitiveness | 3 | 8 | 38 | 20 | 0 |
| **School-to-work transition/job mobility (L)** | **70** | **100** | **75** | **80** | **86** |
| Employment/economic integration | 35 | 73 | 50 | 60 | 43 |
| Earnings, wealth | 3 | 27 | 13 | 40 | 50 |
| Information, transparency | 3 | 15 | 0 | 20 | 7 |
| Institutional capacity/Labor policy/laws | 27 | 38 | 38 | 40 | 7 |
| Fiscal management, financial sustainability | 0 | 0 | 13 | 0 | 0 |
| Employment service/job search | 0 | 12 | 0 | 0 | 0 |

*(Continues on the following page.)*

| Percent of projects with objective | Education (n=37) | Social Protection (n=26) | Finance and Private Sector Development (n=8) | Economic Policy (n=5) | Social Development (n=14) |
|---|---|---|---|---|---|
| Employment programs | 0 | 23 | 13 | 0 | 7 |
| Productivity | 3 | 4 | 25 | 0 | 7 |
| Efficiency | 19 | 15 | 13 | 0 | 0 |
| **Supply of skills (E)** | **97** | **35** | **25** | **20** | **36** |
| Relevant skills building | 81 | 35 | 25 | 20 | 29 |
| Improve technical and vocational education training | 62 | 4 | 0 | 0 | 14 |
| **Objective targeted to individual attributes** | **35** | **50** | **0** | **20** | **43** |
| Youth | 16 | 23 | 0 | 0 | 14 |
| Disadvantaged, vulnerable or disabled | 11 | 19 | 0 | 20 | 14 |
| Gender | 5 | 0 | 0 | 0 | 7 |
| Poor | 5 | 23 | 0 | 20 | 29 |
| Equity | 16 | 8 | 0 | 0 | 0 |

*Source:* IEG portfolio review based on World Bank data.
*Note:* n=the number of projects.

## Youth as a Target Group in Project Objectives and Interventions

Youth are often not mentioned as a target group in project objectives. About one-third of the reviewed operations mentioned a target group in their objective, and only 16 percent explicitly targeted youth in their objectives. Even fewer (3 percent) targeted young women. Young people were more frequently targeted over time (table D.9). Social Protection-led operations more often cite youth as a target group than other operations, whereas none of the FPD-led operations had objectives targeting a specific group. Youth are most often targeted in Latin America and the Caribbean (47 percent), but they were not targeted in any of the operations in MENA and ECA. However, if not targeted in the objective, project documents still describe the target groups for their components; here youth are targeted.

Few projects collect indicators to assess the effect on target groups. Of the three projects with a gender emphasis in their objectives, only the Technical Education III Project in India (P050658) has followed through and targeted interventions to young women and collected relevant indicators.

| Table D.8 | Prevalence of Project Objectives, by Region (percent) | | | | | |
|---|---|---|---|---|---|---|
| Percent of projects with objective | AFR (n=32) | EAP (n=7) | ECA (n=14) | LAC (n=15) | MENA (n=9) | SAR (n=13) |
| **Fostering job creation/work opportunities (I)** | 9 | 0 | 36 | 13 | 33 | 15 |
| Entrepreneurs start up firms, self employment | 0 | 0 | 7 | 0 | 11 | 0 |
| Enterprises; small and medium enterprises | 6 | 0 | 14 | 7 | 0 | 8 |
| Investment climate, credit access | 6 | 0 | 29 | 0 | 11 | 15 |
| Growth/competitiveness | 6 | 0 | 14 | 7 | 22 | 0 |
| **School to work transition/job mobility (L)** | 66 | 100 | 79 | 100 | 89 | 92 |
| Employment/economic integration | 28 | 57 | 50 | 87 | 44 | 62 |
| Earnings, wealth | 19 | 43 | 14 | 13 | 11 | 31 |
| Information, transparency | 0 | 0 | 7 | 27 | 22 | 0 |
| Institutional capacity/Labor mobility policy/laws | 22 | 57 | 36 | 40 | 22 | 15 |
| Fiscal management, financial sustainability | 0 | 0 | 7 | 0 | 0 | 0 |
| Employment service/job search | 0 | 14 | 0 | 13 | 0 | 0 |
| Employment programs | 13 | 0 | 21 | 7 | 0 | 0 |
| Productivity | 3 | 0 | 14 | 7 | 0 | 8 |
| Efficiency | 13 | 0 | 21 | 13 | 11 | 15 |
| **Supply of skills (E)** | 50 | 86 | 43 | 73 | 56 | 69 |
| Relevant skills building | 38 | 86 | 43 | 73 | 33 | 62 |
| Improve technical and vocational education training | 31 | 29 | 29 | 13 | 33 | 38 |
| **Objective targeted to individual attributes** | 34 | 29 | 7 | 73 | 11 | 54 |
| Youth | 9 | 14 | 0 | 47 | 0 | 23 |
| Disadvantaged, vulnerable or disabled | 6 | 14 | 0 | 40 | 11 | 15 |
| Gender | 3 | 0 | 0 | 0 | 0 | 15 |
| Poor | 9 | 0 | 7 | 27 | 11 | 31 |
| Equity | 13 | 0 | 0 | 20 | 0 | 8 |

*Source:* IEG portfolio review based on World Bank data.
*Note:* AFR= Africa; EAP= East Asia and Pacific; ECA=Europe and Central Asia; LAC= Latin America and Caribbean; MENA= Middle East and North Africa; SAR= South Asia Region.

More than half of the projects (60 percent) mentioned young women as a target group in their interventions, but only six collected outcome indicators to assess the extent to which young women have benefited from interventions [the Competitiveness and Employment Sector Development Policy Loan (CEDPL2) in Turkey (P096840); the Social Risk Mitigation Project (SRMP) in Turkey (P074408); the Technical Education III Project in India (P050658), the Post-Basic Education Project in Nigeria (P074132); the Income Support and Employability Project in El Salvador (P117440), and the Skills Development Project in Pakistan (P118177)].

| Table D.9 | Target Groups of Project Objectives over Time (percent) | | |
|---|---|---|---|
| | 2001–05 (n=28) | 2006–11 (n=62) | 2001–11 (n=90) |
| Percent of operations with individual attributes in project objective | 32 | 39 | 37 |
| Youth | 4 | 21 | 16 |
| Disadvantaged, vulnerable or disabled | 14 | 13 | 13 |
| Gender | 4 | 3 | 3 |
| Poor | 18 | 13 | 14 |
| Equity | 7 | 10 | 9 |

*Source:* IEG portfolio review based on World Bank data.

## What Types of Youth Employment Interventions Are Bank Projects Supporting?

In line with objectives, interventions mainly focus on skill development and school-to-work transition. Bank projects include several components with activities to support youth employment interventions in countries. Projects generally include several interventions. Using the MILES framework, the portfolio review found that most Bank projects include interventions in skills development (82 percent), and school–to-work transition (79 percent). About half of the projects include interventions to foster job creation and work opportunities for youth (table D.10). It is likely that this share is lower because youth are beneficiaries of other Bank support, which does not explicitly target youth, or identify youth as a beneficiary.

Interventions reflect the priority of the managing sector. Education-managed operations mostly include interventions in skill development and school-to-work transition, but relatively few interventions that seek to create jobs. Operations managed by Social Protection, FPD, PREM, and SDN are more balanced across all three intervention categories and have a stronger focus on job creation. All five regions emphasize skill development and school–to-work transition, whereas job creation is most prominent in ECA (tables D.11 and D.12).

Formal vocational training reform is most often supported in DPOs. The 15 DPOs supported 115 prior actions, of which 30 (26 percent), mostly in Africa, emphasized the need to "improve the quality of formal secondary and post-secondary vocational education and training." Other relevant prior actions were mentioned considerably less often, among them, the need to "improve information on the labor market" (five times) and support for "counseling, job search skills, matching and placement" (four times). Prior actions to support job creation and the investment climate were only mentioned four times (table D.13).

Projects equally target their interventions to young women and men, but little is known about whether women have benefited. Youth employment

| Table D.10 | Type of Intervention Supported by Youth Employment Projects (percent of projects) | |
|---|---|---|
| Intervention type | 2001–2011 (n=90) |
| **Fostering Job Creation/Work Opportunities (I)** | 54 |
| Business environment and investment climate | 7 |
| Regulations to provide incentives to firms to hire young people | 18 |
| Training in entrepreneurship or business management | 21 |
| Support business start up and access to credit | 18 |
| Wage subsidies and minimum wages | 6 |
| Direct job creation and public works programs | 23 |
| **School to Work Transition and Job Mobility (L)** | 79 |
| Counseling, job search skills, matching, placement | 38 |
| Improving information on labor market | 76 |
| Overseas employment programs | 1 |
| **Skill Development and Labor Market Relevance of Skills (E)** | 82 |
| Improving quality formal vocational education | 73 |
| Expanding work-based vocational education | 34 |
| Skills recognition and certification | 41 |
| Remedial/second chance/non-formal technical and vocational education training programs | 33 |
| Providing information on training and outreach | 50 |
| Training subsidies and vouchers | 28 |
| Support transportation and residential changes | 7 |

*Source:* IEG portfolio review based on World Bank data.
*Note:* n=the number of projects.

interventions were fairly equally targeted to young women. The four most frequently mentioned interventions for women are all in the skills development category, including "providing information on training opportunities," "recognition and certification of skills," "training subsidies and vouchers," and "expanding work-based learning." However, the results framework in projects is weak in identifying gender-specific project benefits. Nonetheless, the systematic review of impact evaluations shows that skills training programs generally have stronger employment effects for women.

## What Types of Skills Are Being Trained?

Technical skills training is most commonly provided in Bank projects. According to project documents and Implementation Completion Reports, technical skills training is the most common type provided, followed by

| Table D.11 | Type of Interventions Supported by Youth Employment Projects by Sector Board (percent) | | | | |
|---|---|---|---|---|---|
| Percent of projects with interventions | Education (n=37) | SP (n=26) | FPD (n=8) | PREM (n=5) | SD (n=14) |
| **Type of Interventions Supported by Youth Employment Projects by Sector Board (percent)** | **3** | **92** | **100** | **100** | **79** |
| Business environment/investment climate | 0 | 0 | 38 | 20 | 14 |
| Regulations to provide incentives to firms to hire young people | 0 | 35 | 25 | 80 | 7 |
| Training in entrepreneurship or business management skills | 3 | 23 | 63 | 40 | 36 |
| Support business start up and access to credit | 0 | 15 | 38 | 40 | 50 |
| Wage subsidies and minimum wages | 0 | 15 | 0 | 20 | 0 |
| Direct job creation and public works programs | 0 | 50 | 25 | 40 | 29 |
| **School to work transition and job mobility (L)** | **76** | **96** | **63** | **80** | **64** |
| Counseling, job search skills, matching | 27 | 62 | 13 | 60 | 29 |
| Improving information on labor market | 70 | 96 | 50 | 80 | 64 |
| Overseas employment programs | 0 | 4 | 0 | 0 | 0 |
| **Skill development and labor market relevance of skills (E)** | **100** | **73** | **63** | **80** | **64** |
| Improving quality formal vocational education | 92 | 65 | 63 | 80 | 43 |
| Expanding work-based vocational education | 32 | 42 | 25 | 80 | 14 |
| Skills recognition and certification | 49 | 46 | 25 | 80 | 7 |
| Remedial/second chance/non-formal technical and vocational training programs | 22 | 50 | 0 | 60 | 43 |
| Providing Information on training | 49 | 58 | 50 | 80 | 29 |
| Training subsidies and vouchers | 32 | 31 | 13 | 40 | 14 |
| Support transportation and residential changes | 11 | 8 | 0 | 0 | 0 |

*Source:* IEG portfolio review based on World Bank data.
*Note:* n=the number of projects. FPD= Finance and Private Sector Development; PREM= Poverty Reduction and Economic Management; SDN= Sustainable Development Network; SP= Social Protection.

entrepreneurial, basic, and information technology skills. Eighty percent of the operations with skills development interventions focused on technical skills building. About half of the projects with interventions to foster job creation mention offering entrepreneurial skills (figure D.7).

| Table D.12 | Type of Interventions Supported by Youth Employment Projects by Region (percent) | | | | | |
|---|---|---|---|---|---|---|
| Percent of projects with interventions | AFR (n=32) | EAP (n=7) | ECA (n=14) | LAC (n=15) | MENA (n=9) | SAR (n=13) |
| **Fostering job creation/work opportunities (I)** | 53 | 43 | 71 | 53 | 44 | 54 |
| Business environment and investment climate | 9 | 0 | 7 | 0 | 11 | 8 |
| Regulations to provide incentives to firms to hire young people | 6 | 14 | 43 | 27 | 11 | 15 |
| Training in entrepreneurship or business management skills | 19 | 0 | 29 | 20 | 33 | 23 |
| Support business start up and access to credit | 16 | 0 | 21 | 7 | 33 | 31 |
| Wage subsidies and minimum wages | 0 | 0 | 14 | 20 | 0 | 0 |
| Direct job creation and public works programs | 28 | 29 | 36 | 13 | 22 | 8 |
| **School to work transition and job mobility (L)** | 72 | 71 | 71 | 87 | 100 | 85 |
| Counseling, job search skills, matching, placement | 13 | 43 | 57 | 67 | 33 | 46 |
| Improving information on labor market | 69 | 71 | 64 | 87 | 100 | 77 |
| Overseas employment programs | 0 | 0 | 0 | 0 | 11 | 0 |
| **Skill development/labor market relevance of skills (E)** | 84 | 100 | 71 | 87 | 67 | 85 |
| Improving quality formal vocational education | 69 | 71 | 71 | 80 | 67 | 85 |
| Expanding work-based vocational education | 38 | 57 | 21 | 27 | 33 | 38 |
| Skills recognition and certification | 31 | 57 | 36 | 67 | 11 | 54 |
| Remedial/second chance/non-formal technical and vocational training programs | 25 | 57 | 21 | 67 | 11 | 31 |
| Providing Information on training and outreach | 44 | 86 | 43 | 60 | 22 | 62 |
| Training subsidies and vouchers | 13 | 71 | 29 | 40 | 11 | 38 |
| Support transportation and residential changes | 6 | 0 | 0 | 20 | 0 | 8 |

*Source:* IEG portfolio review based on World Bank data.
*Note:* n=the number of projects. AFR= Africa; EAP= East Asia and Pacific; ECA= Europe and Central Asia; LAC= Latin America and Caribbean; MENA= Middle East and North Africa; SAR= South Asia Region.

## Monitoring and Evaluation in Bank Projects

Bank projects on youth employment have weak results frameworks and few collect any labor market outcome data. Higher and middle-income countries describe their youth employment situations using data on: labor force participation and unemployment rates; levels of earnings; access to unemployment insurance; and the use of labor standards in the workplace. In low-income countries, youth employment is better described by a broader set of indicators: distribution of youth by primary activity; youth employment-to-population ratio; status of young workers in employment; youth employment by sector; mean earnings for wage and salaried workers; educational attainment of youth labor force; unpaid work; and working poverty (Fields 2007). However, Bank projects have weak results frameworks and few of the youth employment projects collect these indicators.

| Table D.13 | Frequently Used Youth Employment-Related Prior Actions in 15 DPOs, by Region (number of actions used by 15 DPOs) | | | | | |
|---|---|---|---|---|---|---|
| Prior actions supporting youth employment programs | AFR | ECA | LAC | MENA | SAR | Total |
| **Macroeconomic policies ("M")** | | | | | | |
| Economic growth | 14 | 10 | 3 | 11 | 14 | 52 |
| **Investment climate ("I")** | | | | | | |
| Improve the business environment and investment climate | 0 | 2 | 0 | 0 | 0 | 2 |
| Improve regulations to provide incentives to firms in hiring young people | 0 | 0 | 0 | 1 | 0 | 1 |
| Support to start up businesses | 0 | 0 | 0 | 1 | 0 | 1 |
| **Labor market institutions ("L")** | | | | | | |
| Improve information on the labor market | 0 | 0 | 1 | 4 | 0 | 5 |
| Counseling job search skills, matching and placement | 0 | 2 | 1 | 1 | 0 | 4 |
| Program for overseas employment for young people | 0 | 0 | 0 | 1 | 0 | 1 |
| **Education and skills ("E")** | | | | | | |
| Improve the quality of formal secondary and post-secondary vocational education and training | 21 | 6 | 3 | 0 | 0 | 30 |
| Provide information on training opportunities | 0 | 0 | 0 | 2 | 0 | 2 |
| Expand/improve work-based learning in post-secondary and secondary vocational education and training | 0 | 0 | 1 | 0 | 0 | 1 |
| Foster private sector participation in education and training (including governance, curricula and occupational standards) | 0 | 0 | 0 | 1 | 0 | 1 |
| **Social protection ("S")** | | | | | | |
| Social protection | 0 | 0 | 8 | 2 | 0 | 10 |
| Non-MILES | | | | | | |
| Healthcare | 1 | 2 | 1 | 0 | 1 | 5 |
| Total | 36 | 22 | 18 | 24 | 15 | 115 |

*Source:* IEG portfolio review based on World Bank data.
*Note:* AFR= Africa; DPO= Development Policy Operation; ECA= Europe and Central Asia; LAC= Latin America and Caribbean; MENA= Middle East and North Africa; SAR= South Asia Region.

Few impact evaluations were conducted and they cost considerably more than ESW. Only 6 of 90 projects in the portfolio include an impact evaluation. An impact evaluation costs between $640,000 in Uganda and $780,000 in Kenya, which is significantly above the average cost of economic and sector work. It involves additional local data collection and analysis for which teams tend to hire researchers from American universities. Also, impact evaluations tend to be financed by different sources, including the Bank's operational budget and various trust funds (including the Spanish Impact Evaluation Fund (SIEF), the Bank-Netherlands Partnership Program (BNPP), and so on). As a result, the costs of impact evaluations are hidden under several tasks and not transparently available on the Bank's project webpage.

| Figure D.3 | Skills Trained through Projects, by Intervention Category |

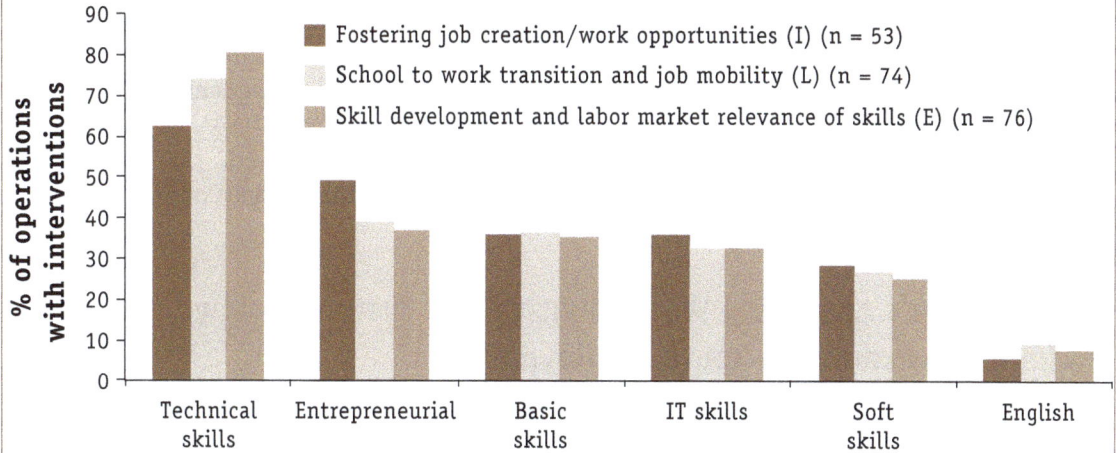

Legend:
- ■ Fostering job creation/work opportunities (I) (n = 53)
- ▢ School to work transition and job mobility (L) (n = 74)
- ▨ Skill development and labor market relevance of skills (E) (n = 76)

Y-axis: % of operations with interventions (0–90)

Categories: Technical skills, Entrepreneurial, Basic skills, IT skills, Soft skills, English

*Source:* IEG portfolio review based on World Bank data.
*Note:* IT= information technology.

## Economic and Sector Work on Youth Employment

The World Bank has undertaken analysis and promoted knowledge sharing to encourage youth employment and skills building. Between 2001 and 2011, World Bank teams prepared 34 pieces of economic and sector work and carried out 25 technical assistance activities related to "improving labor market outcomes." Most of this work (85 percent) was done after 2006. For the purpose of this evaluation, 21 ESW products with a youth employment focus were reviewed, all of them published since 2005.[3] (See appendix B for the list of 21 ESW products included). The Bank spent $4.4 million on 18 of these reports.[4] The average cost of these studies was about $245,000 each, and they took 12 to 24 months (depending on the need for additional surveys) to go from concept note to distribution to the government.

The ESW products were reviewed with respect to four dimensions:

- Strategic relevance comprising timeliness, government ownership and strategic coherence;

- Quality of contextual and diagnostic analysis including coverage of relevant factors, data, hypotheses testing, and clarity of presentation;

- Quality of conclusions and recommendations for youth employment with regard to macroeconomic conditions, the investment climate, labor market institutions, education, and social protection; and

- Dialogue and dissemination, including consultation with stakeholders, public availability of the report and national awareness, and the degree of follow-up.

In sum, this portfolio review chapter finds lending for youth employment has increased since the global crisis. Lending is mainly directed to countries that have introduced reforms, but not necessarily to those countries with the biggest youth employment problems. Bank operations mainly support skill development and smoothing the school-to-work transition. The most frequent interventions include labor market information and support for formal vocational training, with technical skills being most frequently supported. The results framework used by projects is weak and constrains the analysis of labor market outcomes for these projects.

## Did the Bank's Analytical Work Identify and Systematically Address Constraints to Youth Employment?

The IEG review of the Bank's analytical work finds good quality contextual and diagnostic analysis on countries' youth employment situation. Most of the 21 pieces of ESW reviewed made good use of the available data, organized additional surveys, and drew from regional and international experience. Almost all of the ESW provided satisfactory analytical underpinnings for conclusions on the link between economic growth and employment from a sector and historical perspective. Education, the supply of skills, and ALMPs were at the core of most studies. However, issues related to school-to-work transition and labor market regulations are mainly covered in labor market studies, and to a lesser extent in other types of reports. Reports examined gender difference in labor participation and youth employment rates.

Analytical work could become strategically more relevant by regularly monitoring the youth employment situation in higher risk countries, and proposing policy solutions. Although the Bank's response to government requests for analytical work was timely, ESW was not necessarily conducted in countries where youth employment is a pressing issue. In countries where youth employment is an important issue, the Bank could take the pulse at regular intervals to alert policymakers to the potential issues and policy interventions. It could also propose a programmatic approach with lending and nonlending activities.

Bank ownership for the report affects the dissemination process. Some reports, mainly those financed with trust funds, lack ownership by the Bank. As a result, the Bank did not pursue early dialogue with the government to establish the study priorities and build it into the government's own planning horizon. This was in sharp contrast to a number of cases where the study was clearly seen as a flagship, and in-country steering committees were established that provided feedback and advice through the preparatory and dissemination process.

Analytical work mainly suggests easing regulations for hiring youth, smoothing the school-to-work transition, and supporting low-wage public works programs in rural areas. Conclusions and recommendations on the macroeconomic conditions were rather general and not in-depth enough. Investment climate measures cover the promotion of small and medium enterprises, entrepreneurship development through training and microfinance programs, and raising the productivity and incomes in agriculture and informal sectors. Studies conclude and recommend easing the negative impact of public employment on youth, preventing discrimination of labor market regulations and taxes against youth, and improving school-to-work transition through career counseling, internships, and job search assistance.

Several pieces of Bank analytical work, among them the Serbia and Ghana labor market reports, analyze hiring and firing procedures and minimum wages in relation to their impact on youth informality. Instead of high-cost and poorly targeted ALMPs, various ESW products recommend self-targeted, low-wage public works programs—which are part of ALMPs—in rural areas. None of the ESW discusses how alternative regulations should be formulated.

The sociopolitical analysis could be strengthened and employment outcomes portrayed in different scenarios. Few reports have tested hypotheses on causality to be incorporated in youth employment programs. Most ESW did not evaluate the potential impact of alternative economic and demographic scenarios on youth employment outcomes. However, the ESW reviewed did provide relatively scant coverage of the sociopolitical context for youth employment, which consequently limited the policy design to maximize the chance of acceptance of the Bank's recommendations. Seven reports were of exceptionally high analytical quality.[5]

Rarely does an ESW report elaborate on how to identify constraints and implement its recommendations. Generally, ESW reports have too many recommendations, often not prioritized, and with no sequencing and identification of expected impact. Although some ESW with good analysis provided weak recommendations, six reports stand out as providing high quality recommendations.[6]

Reports could be strengthened by making recommendations in a country's governance and fiscal context, and in addressing the situation of minorities and women. Education interventions were discussed in detail, and recommendations focused on the governance of TVET to enhance quality of training, though often in countries with weak governance systems. Recommendations to expand unemployment insurance often lack analysis of the fiscal impact, but reports emphasize focusing on the poorest. Two reports (Serbia and Sri Lanka) mentioned minority groups, but lacked analysis of the specific constraints to their labor market participation. The reports also did not contain gender-specific recommendations, although poverty is concentrated among young unemployed women.

Dialogue and dissemination are important in enhancing the policy impact of analytical work. In some countries, consultations included continuous dialogue with stakeholders. For example, an advisory group with employers and government representatives was set up in Bangladesh. The participatory approach in Turkey and Sierra Leone brought together youth, workers, and the government, while in Argentina the Bank team worked closely with the government and academics. Dissemination of findings followed an established process. The Nigeria report was published in one of the leading Nigerian dailies.

Bank follow-up focused on skills development through TVET projects and a few DPLs. A programmatic approach to analytic work was used in Indonesia, Tunisia, and Turkey, where the ESW formed part of a comprehensive work program of youth, labor markets, employment, and education issues. Some ESW had a policy impact on the reform of several ALMP systems, on the National Youth Employment Program in Ghana, and in Sri Lanka. There was limited effort to disseminate and follow up on some high-quality ESW, including the Zambia report.

## Notes

1. IDA countries had a per capita income of less than $1,175 in 2010 and lacked the financial ability to borrow from IBRD. IDA loans are deeply concessional—interest-free loans and grants for programs aimed at boosting economic growth and improving living conditions. IBRD loans are non-concessional. Blend countries are eligible for IDA loans because of their low per capita incomes, but they are also eligible for IBRD loans because they are financially creditworthy.

2. A fragile situation is defined as having either: (i) a composite World Bank, African Development Bank, and Asian Development Bank Country Policy and Institutional Assessment rating of 3.2 or less; or (ii) the presence of a United Nations and/or regional peace-keeping or peace-building mission (for example, African Union, European Union, NATO), with the exclusion of border monitoring operations, during the past three years. Since 2000, IDA has provided over $5.9 billion in post-conflict reconstruction assistance to fragile and conflict-affected countries.

3. With the exception of one Tunisia report from 2004.

4. Data are not available for Sri Lanka, Tanzania, and Zambia.

5. Economic and Sector Work on Jordan, Mongolia, Serbia, Sierra Leone, Sri Lanka, Timor-Leste, and Zambia.

6. Serbia, Sierra Leone, Sri Lanka, Timor-Leste, Turkey, and Zambia.

## References

Fields, Gary. 2007. Labor Market Policy in Developing Countries: A Selective Review of the Literature and Needs for the Future. Cornell University and IZA.

World Bank. 2011. *World Development Report 2011: Conflict, Security, and Development.*

# Appendix E

The IFC Portfolio for Youth Employment

This appendix presents a detailed analysis of IFC projects that support or have the potential to support youth employment.

Job creation has been central to IFC's mission. The purpose of IFC is to create opportunity for people to escape poverty and improve their lives through: (i) mobilizing finance; (ii) promoting open and competitive markets in developing countries; (iii) supporting companies and other private sector partners where there is a gap; and (iv) helping to create jobs and deliver essential services to the poor and vulnerable (IFC 2011b).

As IFC is the largest developmental institution that supports the private sector, jobs and increasing job opportunities have been a natural focus. Since early 2000, IFC strategies have increasingly emphasized the role of the private sector, particularly small and medium enterprises, in job creation. Beginning in 2009, IFC corporate strategies explicitly stated that job creation is one means by which IFC helps people improve their lives. However, there is limited knowledge about the dynamics of job creation—which IFC interventions in which contexts are most likely to catalyze job creation—and the role that IFC plays in facilitating job creation. IFC is currently carrying out a study to examine these dynamics and the impacts of IFC investments and advisory interventions on job creation (IFC 2012a). IFC is also planning to work on achieving a better understanding of job creation effects through a pilot in the manufacturing, agribusiness, and services sectors.

IFC investment and advisory services do have the objective of job creation, based on the premise that projects result in private sector development, higher growth, and greater employment opportunities. These can be achieved through direct or indirect effects. Although this nexus between private sector development, growth, and job creation is a widely accepted view in the development community, there is evidence that growth is necessary, but not sufficient, for job creation of disadvantaged groups such as the poor and/or the youth (IFC 2009).

Although job creation is central to IFC's mission, youth employment has not been specifically targeted, except in the Middle East and North Africa region and a small number of other interventions. In addition, youth are the main beneficiaries in education sector projects.[1]

Youth unemployment in MENA has been recognized as a problem in IFC's regional strategies since the mid- 2000s. The Private Enterprise Partnership, a multi-donor facility for technical assistance to support private sector development in the region, had the mandate to "stimulate private sector growth and reduce the comparatively high unemployment, especially among the young and female entrants into the labor markets" (IFC 2006). IFC's recent MENA strategy (FY12–14) pays special attention to addressing the needs of youth by supporting: employment-generating real sector investments; access to finance for student borrowers; and improved quality of post-secondary education services (especially technical and vocational education) to meet the needs of the private sector and provide employment opportunities for youth.

## IFC's Portfolio Review

Youth has not been a specific target group in IFC projects, except in the education sector projects and a few advisory services with youth employment objectives. In IFC, employment data have not been categorized by age. Therefore, for IFC, this review focuses on projects with components focused on job creation and skills development. The portfolio review is based on the MILES conceptual framework used in this evaluation, focusing on I (investment climate) and E (education, skills, and training). On the investment side, the portfolio review is based on 853 clients (corresponding to 1,148 investment operations approved between FY01 and FY11) with jobs data. On the advisory services side, the portfolio includes 159 projects that were in the corporate system between FY06 and FY11 with either job creation objectives or employment indicators.

The review also included an in-depth analysis of 50 investment and 18 advisory services operations in the education sector.[2] IFC's education portfolio was included since the projects potentially improve the employability of the youth and most of the universities that IFC has invested in offer courses to current workers to upgrade skills, and/or have TVET courses. Ten projects specifically focused on operations that targeted youth as a beneficiary or tracked youth employment in the results indicators. Finally, the evaluation looked at special initiatives such as the 2011 e4e Initiative for Arab Youth that aims at narrowing the skills gap among young people in the Arab world.

There are other channels through which IFC creates employment opportunities, directly or indirectly, such as through investment climate reforms, and access to finance and infrastructure. Improving the investment climate for firms can create more and better jobs (World Bank 2005). In addition, IEG's review of countries analyzed as part of this evaluation demonstrates that poor investment climates, business, and labor regulations are common impediments to youth employment. Since FY06, IFC has supported 409 advisory services projects in 95 countries ($314 million) in areas including business entry, business operations, business taxation, doing business reform, investment policy and promotion, and special economic zones.[3]

Access to finance (A2F) is another key impediment to job creation and entrepreneurship (Enterprise surveys), as it is more difficult for young entrepreneurs to get access to finance. Financial market investment and advisory services interventions help address some of the access to finance problems for young entrepreneurs. There is some evidence that increased access to finance leads to increased employment creation (Bruhn 2008). However, there is little evidence that IFC interventions in access to finance have demonstrably led to direct job creation.

IFC has supported financial markets development with $37 billion worth of investments, nearly half of all IFC commitments since FY01. In the Access to Finance business line, over a six-year period between 2006 and 2011, approximately $343 million was spent on about 444 projects in SME banking, microfinance, and financial infrastructure (such as credit bureaus). In addition, the business line supports women entrepreneurs through the Gender Entrepreneurship Market (GEM) Women Business initiative, which works with groups of businesswomen both to build their capacity for presenting business plans to client banks and to assess their banking needs.

IEG also recognizes that improving access to infrastructure has economy-wide positive effects on job creation, but the predominant effects tend to be indirect. The impacts from infrastructure investments will be analyzed in a forthcoming IEG evaluation.

## INVESTMENT PROJECTS AND JOB CREATION

IFC clients provided 2.4 million direct jobs in 2010. Since FY05, IFC has been collecting employment data on its investment clients. Based on the internal Development Outcome Tracking System (DOTS), IFC clients in 2010 provided 2.4 million direct jobs, and the net job creation between 2009 and 2010 was approximately 70,000 jobs. It is difficult to assess the adequacy of these job creation figures, as there are no set benchmarks. Further, these figures do not include jobs created indirectly through IFC interventions. Currently, IFC is working on a study aimed at understanding the job creation impacts of IFC investments and advisory projects and private sector activities more broadly.

IFC's direct job creation was highest in the Latin America Region, whereas the direct jobs created in MENA countries was limited. However, IEG caveats that the number of clients that provide jobs data in MENA countries are limited, so the job creation is not presented at the country level, and the data presented does not include jobs created indirectly. Table E.1 indicates that Brazil, China, India, and Argentina, respectively, were the countries with the highest direct job creation supported by IFC. Although IFC has identified the issue of high unemployment rates (and high youth unemployment rates) in the MENA region in its strategies, direct employment by IFC clients in these countries has been limited. Indeed, direct jobs losses were higher than direct jobs created in MENA regions.

Youth are more likely to be employed in sectors such as agriculture, services, tourism, and information technology (OECD 2009; OECD 1998). Consistent with this evidence, the jobs created by IFC clients have been primarily in the agribusiness and forestry sector and the consumer and social services sectors (table E.2). This suggests that IFC investments, even in the absence of explicitly targeting youth, have likely helped improve opportunities for youth.

## ADVISORY SERVICES AND JOB CREATION

Between FY06 and FY11, of the 1,555 portfolio or completed advisory services projects, 159 projects had objectives and/or results indicators linked to job

| Table E.1 | Net Job Creation by IFC—the Top 4 Countries, MENA and South Africa | | | |
|---|---|---|---|---|
| Country | IFC direct net job creation 2006–2010 | Number of IFC clients that have tracked direct job creation | Youth unemployment (%) (2009,ILO) | Overall unemployment (%) |
| Brazil | 70,272 | 41 | 17.8 | 8.3 |
| Argentina | 31,273 | 16 | 21.2 | 8.6 |
| China | 47,802 | 61 | | 4.3 |
| India | 45,427 | 81 | 10.5 | 4.4 |
| MENA Region | -6,528 | 73 | | |
| South Africa | -509 | 9 | 48.2 | 23.8 |

Sources: IFC Employment Reach Data and ILO and WDR unemployment data.
Note: IFC= International Finance Corporation; ILO- International Labour Organization; MENA= Middle East and North Africa Region.

Direct Job creation data is based on the calendar year. The figures do not include indirect or induced jobs created by the clients. The data includes employment data of clients that had project approvals between FY01–FY11. Funds and the Financial Market Sector are excluded.

creation. Of the 110 projects with the objective of job creation, less than a third (32) had both a job creation objective and tracked corresponding employment indicators (figure E.2). However, the employment data have not been categorized by age group, and only a few advisory service projects have explicitly included youth as a beneficiary group. Projects with job creation objectives are mainly in the Sustainable Business Advisory (SBA) and Investment Climate business lines. In SBA, the projects were primarily focused on capacity building to improve the growth and competitiveness of small and medium enterprises, including linkages, value chains, and local

| Table E.2 | Net Direct Job Creation by Sector in IFC | | | | | |
|---|---|---|---|---|---|---|
| Net job creation | 2006 | 2007 | 2008 | 2009 | 2010 | Total |
| Agribusiness and forestry | 8,901 | 33,514 | 15,508 | 11,239 | 20,246 | 89,408 |
| Consumer and social services | 6,076 | 5,368 | 15,318 | 8,709 | 26,776 | 62,247 |
| Infrastructure | 0 | -60 | -227 | 3,344 | -943 | 2,114 |
| Manufacturing | 15,361 | -6,139 | 19,766 | 9,993 | 16,205 | 55,186 |
| Oil, gas, and mining | 2,142 | 4,614 | 12,879 | 6,298 | 5,895 | 31,828 |
| Telecom and information technology | 7,389 | 18,508 | -2,950 | 3,943 | 994 | 27,884 |
| Total | 39,869 | 55,805 | 60,294 | 43,526 | 69,173 | 26,8667 |

Source: IFC Employment Reach Data.
Note: Funds and Financial Market Sector are excluded.

Job creation data are based on the calendar year and include employment data of clients that had project approvals between FY01–FY11.

entrepreneurship projects. Investment Climate projects with objectives of job creation focused on business entry and operations, special economic zones, and investment and policy promotion.

IEG reviewed 30 of the completed projects with the objective and/or indicator of job creation. Of these, 23 could be rated for development effectiveness, and 57 percent of them were successful. Seventy percent of these successful projects (approximately 8 projects) tracked the number of jobs created.

With regard to education sector projects, very few IFC interventions explicitly targeted youth as a beneficiary. IFC supported 10 advisory services projects that had a youth employment objective. Six of these interventions were part of the Grassroots Business Initiative. These projects sought to: provide opportunities to youth through targeting and scaling up existing youth enterprise development initiatives; provide capacity building grants; and support loan guarantees and technical assistance to financial institutions and business development service providers who in turn offer business training and mentoring to informal/young rural micro- entrepreneurs. One example of this was the Angel program in Indonesia and Mali. The project concept was to encourage leading entrepreneurs and business people to invest and support start-up companies in their early stages of growth. These projects proved challenging to design and implement. Consequently, the program has since been spun-off. Similarly, in two other projects, IFC provided grants to a financial literacy education program for 15,000 youth or women in South Africa, and 420 internships or employment for Russian orphan students. IFC did not play an active role beyond providing grants in the financial literacy program, and the Russian program was spun–off into a stand-alone Russian NGO.

IFC supported equity type financing for young Indian entrepreneurs combined with structured mentoring. A fund has been established and five entrepreneurs have been financed who created 90 jobs through the project as

| Table E.3 | Advisory Services Projects that Included Job Creation in the Objective or Results Indicators | | | |
|---|---|---|---|---|
| Business line | Projects with both job creation objective and indicator (%) | Projects with job creation objective (%) | Projects with job creation indicator (%) | Projects with job creation objective and/or indicator (%) |
| Access to Finance | 0 | 11 | 4 | 9 |
| Investment Climate | 38 | 41 | 32 | 37 |
| Public-Private Partnerships Transaction Advisory | 3 | 5 | 5 | 6 |
| Sustainable Business Advisory | 59 | 43 | 59 | 48 |
| Total (Number) | 32 | 110 | 81 | 159 |
| *Source:* IFC Advisory Database, June 2011. | | | | |

of August 2010, while the targeted number is 50 entrepreneurs. The results of this project will be available by the end of FY12. IFC offered the Business Edge Program to build business skills for unemployed youth in Yemen. The IFC team partnered with the Yemen Education for Employment Foundation that provides training and job placement for recent graduates. The program has trained 715 young Yemenis and so far, 322 individuals—120 of them females—have been placed into jobs.

### Projects Improving Employability of Youth, Education Sector Portfolio, FY2001–11

The world's population has been growing, and economic growth and technological developments require a more educated/skilled labor force. Government supply of education services cannot meet the growing demand. There is wide recognition of the private sector's potential to meet this growing demand (IFC 2012a). Private institutions participate in each segment of the education system in most countries, and in some countries the private sector accounts for the majority of expenditures on education.

To support the private sector in education, IFC set up its education department in 2001. Since then, IFC's focus on private education has grown, with the addition of education as a strategic pillar in 2004 (table E.3). Between FY01 and FY11, IFC invested in 50 education sector projects, committing approximately $500 million through loan, equity, and guarantee facilities (figure E.1).[4] More than two-thirds (68 percent) were in tertiary education, and six of the tertiary projects included components for technical and vocational training (TVET). The remaining investments were at the primary/secondary level (26 percent), and in other types of education/training projects (6 percent).

**Figure E.1.** Growth in the IFC Education Portfolio

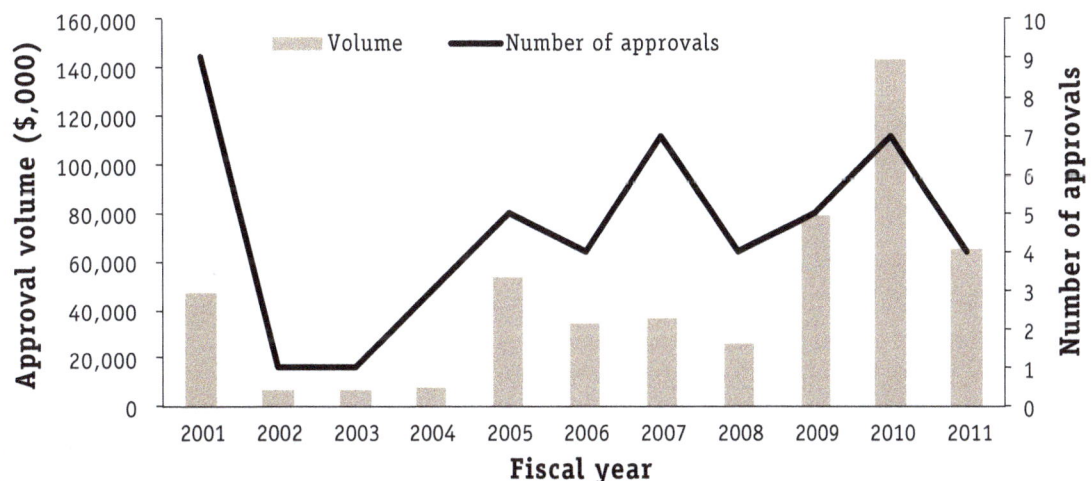

*Source:* IFC Internal data as of the end of June 2011.

IFC has three types of investments in the education sector: direct investments in educational institutions including construction of new buildings and expansion of existing facilities; student loan facilities and financing mechanisms that benefit low- and middle-income students; and school guarantee programs benefiting multiple schools. Traditionally, most of IFC's investments (70 percent) have concentrated on investments in educational institutions (figure E.2).

Thirty-eight percent of IFC's investments in education are concentrated in Latin America (59 percent by volume), followed by Sub-Saharan Africa (figure E.3). Although most (89 percent) of LAC investments have been in tertiary education, education investments in Africa were mainly in primary/secondary education (62 percent). Since 2007, IFC's investments in the MENA region have been increasing (19 percent of approved projects), with 80 percent of these investments in tertiary education.

IFC's education strategy is focused on providing access to education in underserved areas, and on providing employment opportunities to skilled professionals. In the early 2000s, IFC's focus was on supporting direct investments in educational institutions. For example, IFC supported a university in Argentina to expand in non-urban areas, as well as a university in Uruguay to expand its classroom facilities and libraries.

Over the years, IFC's education strategy has changed from focusing on investments in individual institutions to providing financing through financial intermediaries. Examples include a risk-sharing facility with IFC portfolio banks to provide loans to eligible private schools in Sub-Saharan Africa and a student loan program that will extend loans to

| Figure E.2 | IFC Education Investment Approvals, FY2001–2011 |

**A. By Education Level**

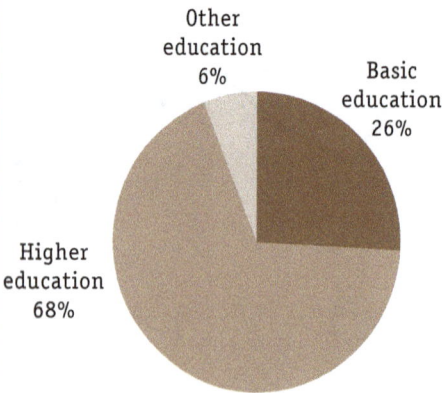

**B. By Type of Investment**

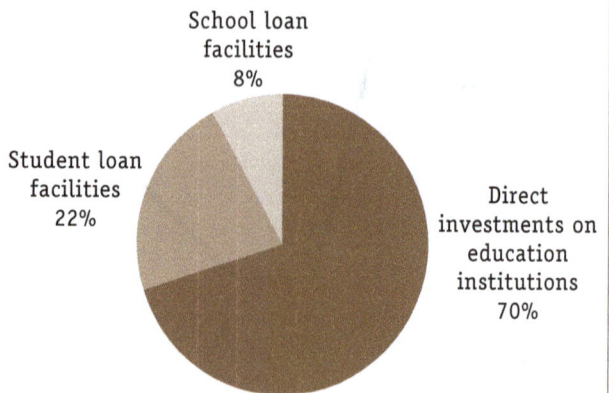

Other education 6%

Basic education 26%

Higher education 68%

School loan facilities 8%

Student loan facilities 22%

Direct investments on education institutions 70%

*Source:* IFC Internal data as end of June 2011.

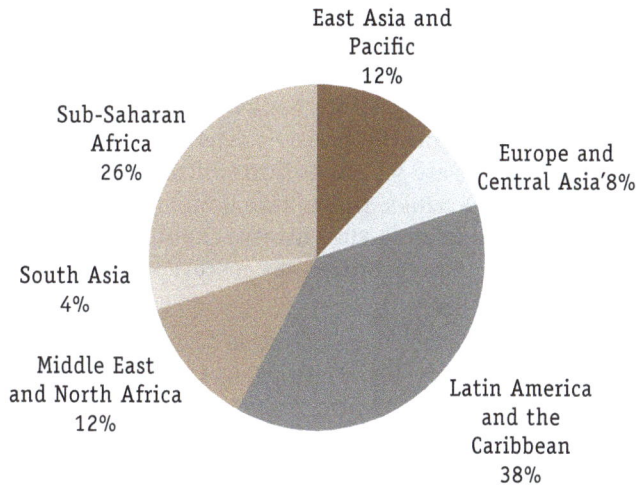

**Figure E.3    Regional Distribution of IFC Investments in Education, by number of approvals**

East Asia and Pacific
12%

Europe and Central Asia '8%

Latin America and the Caribbean
38%

Middle East and North Africa
12%

South Asia
4%

Sub-Saharan Africa
26%

*Source:* IFC Internal data as end of June 2011.

university students in the West Bank and Gaza (through the provision of wholesale finance to financial intermediaries for on-lending to educational institutions). Alternatively, support can go through direct lending to well-established institutions seeking to expand within their domestic or regional markets.

The move toward the wholesale approach was consistent with IFC's goal to broaden its reach to a larger number of educational institutions, SMEs, and students, thereby maximizing its development impact. However, IFC's experience with this approach has not yielded the expected outcomes. Therefore, IFC's recent global education strategy is focusing on investments in education providers who: (i) operate in multiple markets with the potential to increase access in underserved areas; (ii) move down-market to reach lower-income households; (iii) create centers of excellence in emerging markets; and (iv) provide employment opportunities for skilled professionals.

### ADVISORY SERVICES IN THE EDUCATION SECTOR

IFC has also supported educational institutions through capacity building, although the number of such interventions has been few. IFC has provided advisory services to improve the capacity of private educational institutions. IFC has provided assistance with the development of school management, curricula, and training capacity. It has also provided advice to governments on public and private partnerships. In addition, IFC has carried out market studies on education and training.

## Box E.1 — Africa Schools Program

IFC supports private primary and secondary schools in Africa through its Africa Schools Program. The overarching objective of the program is to help improve the educational quality and financial and managerial capacity of private K–12 schools in select Africa countries. IFC support combines investment and advisory services. The investment component of the program contains a risk-sharing facility with the banks. The risk sharing enables the bank(s) to develop a medium-term lending program for private schools. The accompanying technical assistance program is designed to prepare schools to borrow from the formal sector. Technical assistance also provides advice to the banks, which have limited experience in the education sector. It has also been designed to improve the business environment to support investments in private schools. The first of these facilities was approved in Ghana and then expanded to Kenya, Rwanda, Uganda, and Liberia.

The program has generally reached its objective of capacity building of schools. Thus far, the results of the parallel Advisory-Investment program in Ghana and Kenya have not met the access-to-finance targets, critical to the overall success of the program. The school facility in Ghana was expected to reach about 50 schools by 2009, However, the program reached only 25 beneficiary schools and the technical assistance program was closed in June 2011. Similarly, the facility in Kenya in 2010 reached 9 schools compared to a target of 100, and the number of nonperforming loans in the facility exceeds the target of five. Therefore, the current risk-sharing facility is on hold with the bank. The program is having difficulty in finding other partner banks that can extend loans to schools. In Rwanda, the program has been successful in reaching its target number of facilities, and it has fewer nonperforming loans than expected.

*Source:* IFC Africa School Projects Documents.

## Figure E.4 — Distribution of IFC Advisory Services Projects

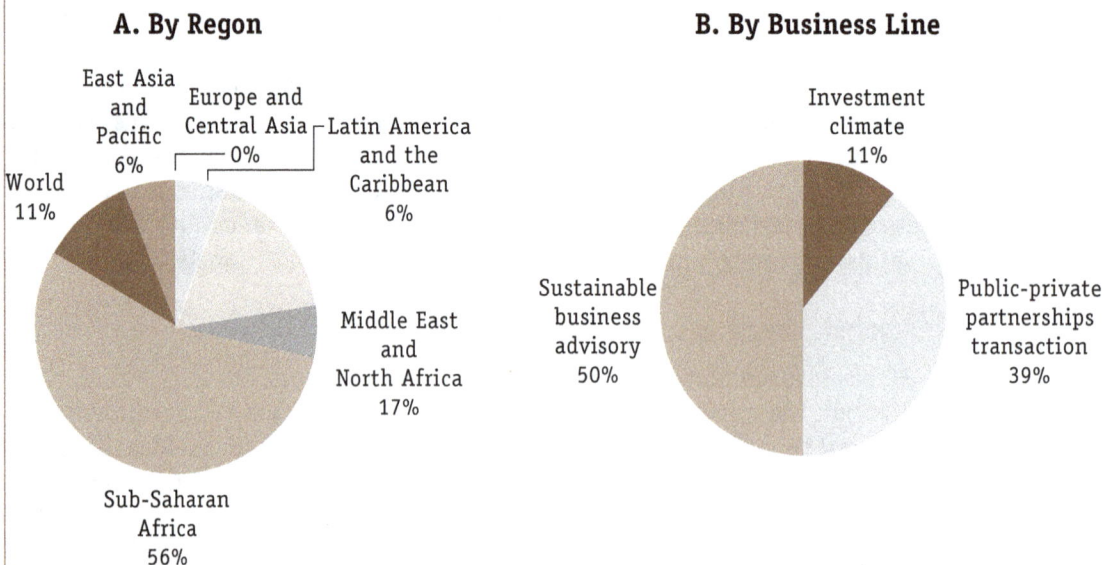

**A. By Regon**

East Asia and Pacific 6%; Europe and Central Asia 0%; Latin America and the Caribbean 6%; World 11%; Middle East and North Africa 17%; Sub-Saharan Africa 56%

**B. By Business Line**

Investment climate 11%; Public-private partnerships transaction 39%; Sustainable business advisory 50%

*Source:* IFC Internal Database as June 2011.

Between FY06 and FY11, IFC provided 18 advisory services projects totaling $12 million. More than half of these services were extended in Sub-Saharan Africa, mostly through the Sustainable Business Advisory business line (figure E.4). Five of these services were provided through the Africa Schools Program (box E.1). IFC helped develop MBA modules, implement a strategic and accreditation plan, and create a cooperative association/network among African business schools. The main objective was to build the capacity of African business schools, enterprise centers, and universities to provide relevant, practical SME management and entrepreneurship training on a sustainable basis. However, these types of activities are no longer a core strategic priority for IFC. The other projects included advice to governments through public-private partnerships, with the rest involving market studies.

IFC in collaboration with the Islamic Development Bank undertook a study to understand the reasons behind the gap between skills and labor market needs and possible approaches to improving Arab youth employability (IFC 2011a). The study identifies areas for action, including the need for greater private sector investment and the incentives needed for businesses to play a greater role in education and job creation. Based on these findings, IFC initiated the e4e Initiative for Arab Youth, a program based on a three-prong strategy of increased investment, an improved enabling environment, and changing mindsets to address the mismatch between employer needs and skills developed through the education system in the Arab World, including through an enhanced private sector role. The project focuses on the role that all stakeholders can play in addressing this problem and will guide the first joint Bank-IFC strategy in the region (box E.2).

## Training Programs

Training is an important component of advisory services projects. Approximately 35 percent of firms surveyed through the World Bank Enterprise Surveys identify an inadequately educated and trained workforce as a major constraint to productivity and growth (IFC 2011a, also see figure E.5). Yet, less than half the firms surveyed provide formal training to their workers.

IFC's advisory services focus on training and capacity building activities. Between FY07–FY11, around 70 percent of those services included a training component. The programs deliver a range of activities to different types of beneficiaries including: skills training to firms, SMEs, entrepreneurs, and farmers (39 percent); capacity building to financial institutions and their clients (34 percent); and institutional capacity building to government officials (25 percent). More recently, a few interventions have begun to focus on youth employment, such as the Business Edge in Yemen, which was provided to unemployed youth, young entrepreneurs, and young professionals seeking management skills.

In 2011, McKinsey undertook a study commissioned by IFC and the Islamic Development Bank to assess the growing skills gap among Arab youth in relation to labor market needs. According to one-third of the employers surveyed, graduates do not have the necessary work-relevant skills when hired, in large part because of the quality and relevance of education and training available to youth.

In June 2011, IFC developed the e4e Initiative for Arab Youth, with the objective of strengthening the link between education and employment opportunities. It focuses on reducing the mismatch between the skills that young people have and those demanded by the private sector.

The program has three pillars: (i) investments in Vocational Education and Training, universities, work readiness programs, and entrepreneurship training; (ii) improving the investment climate for private sector companies, including the regulatory framework for private education providers, setting up a qualifications framework, establishing independent standards and quality assurance bodies; and (iii) advocacy. These pillars require the collaboration of different stakeholders. IFC and the World Bank will work closely together to leverage the expertise and experience of the World Bank Group in the region. This initiative is in its very early stages. The conceptual framework and program components are consistent with the need for an integrated approach to address the issue of youth unemployment.

*Source:* e4e Initiative for Arab Youth documents.

IFC usually tracks the number of people trained and client satisfaction with the training to measure its development effectiveness. However, the translation of the knowledge gained through the training activities to performance has been seldom measured.[5]

The SME toolkit is one common tool that IFC uses to improve the skills of existing entrepreneurs and SMEs. The program uses information and communication technologies to help small and medium enterprises in emerging markets learn sustainable business management practices. So far, the SME toolkit has not been designed for new entrepreneurs, but it could be easily expanded to this group.

Business Edge, a program that delivers management training products and services, is specifically designed for SMEs and entrepreneurs. The product is a package of 36 different management workbooks in marketing, human resources, production and operations, finance and accounting, and productivity skills. It also includes trainer manuals, training of trainer sessions, and additional capacity-building tools for training firms. IFC delivers management, financial, and technical training to SMEs through the supply chain approach and targets managers and owners of SMEs. Since 2002, 60,000 people have been trained through the program. The Gender Entrepreneurship Markets Program targets women entrepreneurs with advisory assistance so that they

**Figure E.5  Skill Needs Versus Firm-Offered Training**

**A. Percent of Firms Identifying an Inadequately Educated Workforce as a Major Constraint**

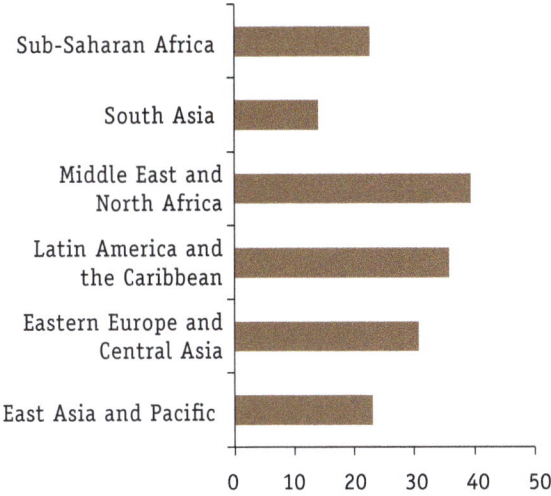

**B. Percent of Firms Offering Formal Training (average)**

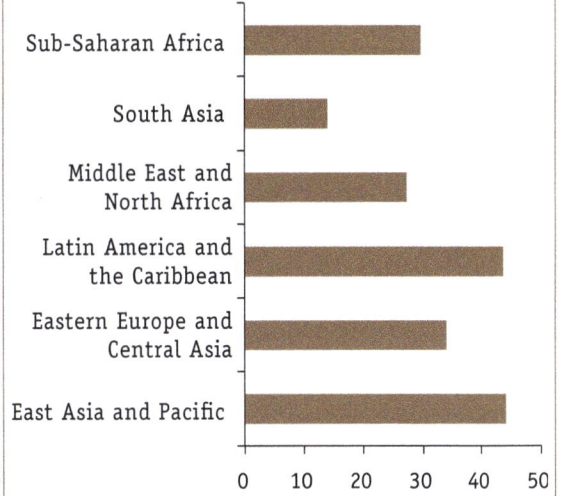

*Source:* www.enterprisesurveys.org, Workforce database.

can improve their financial literacy and be better positioned to approach the bank with loan applications, and to manage the loans they subsequently receive.

## Monitoring and Evaluation

On the investment side, IFC tracks direct jobs data for clients. Data were available for 45 percent of the active portfolio. On the advisory side, between FY06 and FY11, around 5 percent of the projects tracked employment data as part of measuring project outcomes/impacts. There are few evaluations to assess the effects of advisory interventions on outcomes such as productivity, jobs, and wages.

## Notes

1.  IFC's FY13-FY15 Education Investment Strategy (dated June 2012) will focus on expanding equitable access to quality education at affordable costs and leading to employment opportunities.

2.  Between FY01-FY11, 2741 investment operations were approved.

3. IFC's Advisory Services corporate roll out of projects took place in 2006. Therefore, IEG caveats the fact that the data entered into the system in the earlier years may not reflect the exact project approvals.

4. The information is based on approval Fiscal Year and Original Commitment volumes.

5. Business Edge projects track participants' reported performance improvement (productivity, accountability, valuation, and so on).

## References

Bruhn, Miriam. 2008. "License to Sell: The Effect of Business Registration Reform on Entrepreneurial Activity in Mexico." Policy Research Working Paper 4538. World Bank, Washington, DC.

International Finance Corporation. 2012. IFC Education Investment Strategy.

———. 2011a. "Education for Employment (e4e): Realizing Arab Youth Potential—Executive Summary." www.e4earabyouth.com

———. 2011b. IFC Road Map: FY12–14. Washington, DC: World Bank.

———. 2009. "What is Inclusive Growth?" http://siteresources. worldbank.org/INTDEBTDEPT/Resources/468980-1218567884549/ WhatIsInclusiveGrowth20081230.pdf

———. 2006. "PEP- MENA Annual Report." http://ifcnet.ifc.org/intranet/changemo. nsf/AttachmentsByTitle/OneIFCWeek_VirualFail_IFCDevelopmentImpactSourceSt udy/$FILE/IFC+source+study+fact+sheet.pdf

Organisation for Economic Co-operation and Development. 2009. Youth Employment. http://www.oecd.org/dataoecd/27/4/43280339.pdf

———. 1998. "Supporting youth pathways." Education Policy Analysis. Paris: Organisation for Economic Co-operation and Development.

World Bank. 2005. World Development Report: A Better Investment Climate for Everyone. Washington, DC.

# Appendix F

Lessons from Impact Evaluations and World Bank Group Operations

This appendix presents lessons for each intervention type (table 4.1) based on evidence from the systematic review of 38 impact evaluations, together with findings from impact evaluations of World Bank and IFC projects, completion reports for closed projects, and documentation of ongoing projects. It begins with a description of the bottlenecks that hinder youth employment in different contexts based on evidence of experience in 18 countries. It then shows how the Bank's analytical work program has identified and addressed such constraints.

## To What Extent Do Interventions Address Constraints to Youth Employment?

The following discussion of youth employment interventions tracks the outline found in table 4.1. It presents findings from the Independent Evaluation Group's (IEG) systematic review of impact evaluations and from World Bank Group projects. It examines the extent to which youth employment interventions have addressed the constraints identified. Evidence is presented by single interventions; however, these interventions generally form part of a youth employment program with several interventions.

### FOSTERING JOB CREATION AND WORK OPPORTUNITIES (I)

#### Business Environment Reforms

Business environment reforms may attract private sector investment in industries with high shares of youth employment. Innovation is associated with Doing Business indicators, such as access to credit, registering property, and contract enforcement. Using firm-level data from 71 countries covering OECD countries, transition, and developing countries, Dutz and others (2011) find that innovation is an important driver of employment growth for both large firms and small and medium enterprises (SMEs). Innovating firms report growth rates of 2 to 3 percent higher than non-innovators, as well as higher shares of unskilled and female workers.

The youth employment impact of business environment reforms has not been evaluated. Mexico greatly simplified registration procedures and introduced one-stop business registration in 2002. The impact evaluation (Bruhn 2008) found an increase in business registrations of 5 percent, employment increases of 3 percent, and improved business competition leading to price declines. The age impact is unknown.

The Bank-supported business environment reforms related to youth employment are relatively few, and little is known about their impact. The 15 youth employment-relevant Development Policy Operations (DPOs) identified in the portfolio include only four policy actions related to business climate reforms and job creation. In Mali, the Bank supported local artisans, mainly youth and women, by eliminating the 10 percent export tax and reducing the cost of import licenses for artisanal products; however, information on the sales and employment effect is not available. In Turkey, the share of private spending in total research and development increased slightly from 46.2 percent in 2007 to 47.3 percent in 2008 following investment climate reforms in export competitiveness and foreign direct investment. In Liberia and Sierra Leone, the Bank is supporting the youth-intensive fishing industry with an accredited sanitary authority to export fish to the European Union.

In Armenia, Bank-supported investment reforms and an enterprise incubator helped 18 local information technology companies attract foreign investors. Information technology exports increased by 30 percent annually, and the number of graduates employed in information technology rose by 15 percent annually. Bank support to Bhutan helped shorten the time (from 3 months to 9 days) involved in issuing approval for recruitment of foreign workers, though the effect on the employment situation of local workers is not known. It also helped reduce the time for setting up a new business from 62 to 43 days. These business reforms may have affected the income and employment situation for youth, although the extent is unknown.

Few IFC evaluations tracked job creation effects of reducing burdensome business registration and the cost of registration on firm entry. IFC has provided advice to many developing countries and governments on reform and simplification of business registration as a vehicle to foster economic development in business-friendly countries (Djankov and others 2006). IFC studies on the impact of five projects were conducted, including business simplification in Lima (Peru) and investment climate reform in Burkina Faso, Liberia, Rwanda, and Sierra Leone. The four Africa studies attempt to estimate private sector cost savings as well as private sector investment, business creation, job creation, and other economic benefits. Taken as a whole, the studies suggest that the projects have resulted in benefits to the private sector, including an estimated $14.5 million in private sector cost savings, 11,400–13,700 new businesses, $70–$232.5 million in private sector investment, and 52,700–64,300 jobs for all age groups. Although the results suggest positive job creation benefits for all age groups, findings are limited by the weakness in the methodology. Also, no information is available on the age, gender, and distributional effect of these new jobs.

A comprehensive approach to business environment reforms is needed for business to be sustainable. With IFC assistance, the city of Lima, Peru implemented reforms to simplify the complex, costly, and time-consuming business registration procedures, with positive initial impacts on increasing the number of business registrations (by over 260 percent). Reforms also reduced the cost of licensing (by 60 percent). However, tracking a cohort of unregistered businesses over time revealed that neither registration nor receipt of financial grants had any impact on subsequent business performance. This suggests that registration was not the key issue for small business, and that other investment climate constraints—such as taxes, mandatory benefit payments, access to finance, corruption, or infrastructure—may have been more binding (Alcazar and others 2011).

*Labor Market Regulations*

Labor market regulations mainly protect formal sector "insider" workers, and can make it more difficult for youth to enter the market. In developing countries with small formal sectors, most workers are outside of any labor market regulations. In middle-income countries, limited evidence exists on the impact of regulations on youth employment and earnings, such as increases in the minimum wage and tighter job security. Analysis of job security regulation in Latin America suggests that the unemployment effect of stricter regulations is almost two times larger for youth than for adult workers (Heckman and others 2000).

A minimum wage may lead to a flatter wage profile over time, and a possible unemployment effect on youth can be reduced by adopting a youth sub-minimum wage. Based on data from 17 OECD countries, Neumark and Wascher (2004) found that minimum wages reduce employment among youth; however, this negative employment effect can be reduced by a sub-minimum wage for youth. Portugal increased the youth minimum wage for teenagers in the late 1980s. Two wage effects were observed in the long run; first, a wage premium, consistent with an upgrading of the quality of jobs offered by the firm; and second, a flatter wage profile over time as firms would compensate a higher initial wage with a slower wage progression (Cardoso 2009).

A higher minimum wage does not necessarily increase poverty because it would lead to higher unemployment rates. The conditions for a minimum wage increase to affect poverty include the distance of the wage to the poverty line, the elasticity of labor demand, the extent of income sharing within and across households, and the sensitivity of the poverty measure to the depth of poverty (Fields and Kanbur 2007). These factors vary across countries.

A change in payroll taxes has different impacts on employment and wages. When Chile privatized social security, payroll taxes decreased but there was no employment effect because wages adjusted to the change in non-wage costs (Gruber 1997). Colombia introduced legislation in the 1990s to reduce severance payments for dismissal. The reform requires employers to deposit a monthly contribution to the formal sector employees' severance payment savings account, which is accessible upon separation. The severance payment reform in Colombia made the labor market more dynamic by increasing the exit rates into and out of unemployment, and younger workers were more affected. The increased flexibility led to higher unemployment during recessions and higher employment rates during expansion (Kugler 2005).

In middle-income countries, the Bank promoted reforms to make labor regulations more conducive to youth employment. In **Bulgaria**, the Bank supported legal amendments to increase the flexibility of working time and fixed-term and part-time contracts. It also supported a monthly bonus for unemployed recipients of social assistance who find employment on their own initiative. The employment rate of younger workers (ages 15–24) increased slightly from 21.6 percent in 2005 to 23 percent in 2009; but the overall youth unemployment rate remained persistently high.

In 2008, **Turkey,** with Bank support, reduced the social security contribution for employers in order to provide an incentive to hire youth and women. Turkey also lifted hiring quotas to allow flexibility, and financed social security contributions for employees with disabilities from the government budget. Yet, Turkey's labor regulations remain among the most rigid among the OECD countries, and the new changes do not appear to have had an effect on youth employment. The growth slow-down in 2007, the global economic crisis in 2008, and an increasing youth labor force participation rate from 31 percent in 2006 to 38 percent in 2008, contributed to an increase in the youth unemployment rate from 19 percent in 2006 to 25 percent in 2009 (for male youth, the rate went from 18.3 to 25.4 percent and for female youth, the rate went from 20.6 to 25 percent).

The 15 DPOs included in this review did not touch upon minimum wage issues. However, the Bank has offered technical advice on difficult policy reforms such as minimum wages (box F.3).

Bank-supported regulatory reforms have contributed to transparency and financial sustainability. In **Romania**, the Bank supported legislation to define unemployment benefits for adults at 75 percent of the minimum wage, and at 50 percent of the minimum wage for youth. The law brought transparency

---

**Box F.1**    Union Power and Youth Employment Issues in South Africa

The International Labor Organization (ILO) estimates the average minimum wage is considerably higher in South Africa ($390 in purchasing power parity) than in Mexico ($170) and Brazil ($286). The level of unionization is also much higher than average, and the bargaining power of the unions is evidenced by higher wage premiums for unionized labor. The unions have successfully bid up the wages of their members to levels that make recruiting of low-skilled manual workers unattractive in many industries exposed to international competition. Recently, Taiwanese garment investors in South Africa gave the unions an ultimatum of either accepting pay levels of 30 percent below the minimum wage or facing substantial job losses. The unions agreed to the pay cut for three years and negotiated an agreement that 5,000 additional jobs will be created. However, the unions successfully blocked a proposal for a youth sub-minimum wage, which could have promoted youth employment as evidenced in OECD countries. Despite various efforts by the Bank to provide technical advice on youth employment financed through trust funds, a/ the dialogue with the South African government focused on an electricity supply loan.

*Source:* IEG 2012c.

a. The Bank sponsored a conference on labor markets in May 2010. It used Spanish trust funds to elicit employers' opinions on youth wage subsidies, Australian trust funds to promote skills development, and started to use Dutch trust funds to write a series of technical briefs on skills shortages.

---

to the definition of unemployment benefits and contributed to a continuous budget surplus in the unemployment fund for three years.

IFC has supported the implementation of labor market regulations through the Better Work Program. Since 2005, IFC has been working in partnership with the International Labor Organization to improve both compliance with labor standards and competitiveness in global supply chains in various industries, such as garment/footwear, plantations, electronic equipment, and light manufacturing. IFC supported, with the partnership of multinational clothing retailer Gap Inc., the first supervisory skills training (SST) program—Better Factories Cambodia for garment industry supervisors.

Following the Cambodia experience, IFC launched the Better Work program in 2007 and replicated the program in Vietnam, Jordan, Haiti, and Indonesia. The program does not have a youth-specific target, but the demographic data in Haiti, Indonesia, and Jordan indicate that the main beneficiaries of the program are women (between 70 to 90 percent) and youth, aged 15–30 (around 60 percent). Results from a recent randomized evaluation show a 25 percent higher awareness of production targets, and a 10 percent increase in outputs based on training provided to supervisors in improving supervisor-worker relationships and compliance with standards.

### Youth Entrepreneurship Programs

Entrepreneurship training has demonstrated positive impacts for some groups, but limited effects on business performance. In the United States, the Growing America through Entrepreneurship (GATE) project provides training and business counseling. GATE increased the likelihood of starting a business by 3 to 5 percentage points, with significantly lower effects for women, but no impact on income and business performance (Fairlie and others 2012). In Bosnia, Bruhn and Zia (2011) found that while the business and financial literacy training program did not affect business survival or performance, it significantly improved business practices. Thus, the lack of business knowledge may not be the key constraint to new entrepreneurship; other much stronger constraints to business development and growth need to be addressed first, or as part of a more comprehensive support program.

Entrepreneurship training has unclear effects in Mexico. Mexico's training program "Probecat "provides a scholarship equivalent to the minimum salary to young beneficiaries to participate in a three-month training course for self-employment. An impact evaluation (Delajara and others 2006) finds no clear effect on employment or wages for the self-employed. However, on-the-job training in larger firms of unemployed youth leads to better employment and income outcomes than entrepreneurship training. Young women were found to have benefited most from the entrepreneurship program.

Comprehensive entrepreneurship programs comprising training, mentoring, networking, and microcredit are more likely to be effective. Karlan and Valdivia (2007) conducted a randomized study offering female clients of a microfinance institute in Peru entrepreneurship training in addition to weekly or monthly banking meetings. The group that got entrepreneurship training improved business practices and revenues and had greater repayment rates, suggesting that client outcomes can be improved by combining entrepreneurial training and coaching with access to credit.

The Bank supported entrepreneurship training in a number of countries. Early results from impact evaluations suggest negligible effects in Tunisia and positive effects for young entrepreneurs in rural areas in Uganda and Colombia. The Tunisia "Turning Thesis into Enterprise" program offers business training and coaching to undergraduate students who graduate with a business plan and submit their plan to a competition. Participants report a 3 percentage point increase in their probability to be self-employed (about 24 additional self-employed) from a low baseline of 4 percent. The result was stronger for men than for women. The training did not affect students' probability of finding a job or increasing their earnings (Premand and others 2012). In Colombia, the Social Development Policy Loan (DPL) (P106708) supported the Young Rural Entrepreneurs training programs (Jóvenes Rurales Emprendedores), which increased participants' employment rate by 13–14 percent (Castañeda and others 2010). In Uganda, the Bank NUSAF1 project used a $2.6 million Japanese Social Development Grant to do a pilot test of youth employment opportunities in collaboration with World Vision. Findings from an impact evaluation (box F.2 and table F.1) led to the scale-up of the Youth Opportunity Program and continuous support to young entrepreneurs under the follow-up Bank project, the Second Northern Uganda Social Action Fund (NUSAF2).

| Box F.2 | Midterm Evaluation of Uganda Youth Opportunities Program Finds Increased Earnings and Employment from an Unconditional Cash-Transfer to Finance Non-Formal Skills Training |

Uganda's Youth Opportunity Program provides unconditional cash grants to youth groups for investment in training or self-employment. Groups of 20 to 30 youth are asked to submit a proposal for purchasing skills training, tools, and other materials required to start an enterprise. Nearly 80 percent of participants enrolled in training (mainly tailoring and carpentry), and 13 percent re-enrolled in secondary school. Two years after the cash transfer, two-thirds of the participants are engaged in skilled work, mainly self-employed, compared to just one-third of the control group. The program doubled hours of employment and increased earnings and savings for youth by nearly 50 percent relative to the control group, with similar results for male and female youth. Participants rated the value of their business assets at $390—more than twice as high than that of the control group. The rate of return of project investment was 35 percent per year, which compares favorably with commercial lending rates to small firms. Findings suggest limited access to credit is a major constraint to participation in training and employment.

*Source:* Blattman and others 2011.

In post-conflict zones with small formal sectors, the Bank is supporting business training for young ex-combatants, thereby helping local business development. In Sierra Leone, the Bank is providing technical training, business development support, coaching, and other life skills training to 1,500 youth—among them ex-combatants—who already have a microenterprise or who are interested in self-employment. In Côte d'Ivoire, the Bank's self-employment program, which includes entrepreneurship development services, counseling, job placement service, training, start-up grants, and public works, has reached more than 16,700 youth-at-risk and ex-combatants during the first three years; however, no employment effect has been reported. In Eritrea, Bank support to a non-agriculture business training program trained 973 demobilized soldiers, 65 percent of them women; and provided business training and access to credit to 612 ex-soldiers. The economic participation rate of soldiers was high at 85 percent, and higher for males (91 percent) than for females (74 percent). About 80 percent of ex-soldiers earned enough income from one job to survive.

IFC's linkage and supply chain programs account for its most comprehensive effort to create jobs, develop SMEs, and support entrepreneurship through packages of interventions including training, finance, and supplier development. For instance, in 2006, IFC supported a linkage program in parallel to its investment in an energy company in India. The goal of the program was to use IFC investment in the client company as a catalyst to promote economic and social development of an economically backward region—Barmer District, (in Rajasthan, India). One of the components of the project was to provide skills and employment opportunities to rural communities, including youth. An entrepreneurship center was created, and youth were trained and matched with enterprises. In total, 4,174 jobs were created and $1,743,802 in sales revenue was generated.

IFC supported a few projects that sought to provide opportunities to youth entrepreneurs, mostly through the Grassroots Business Initiative, and more recently through Business Edge, Yemen. For example, a Grassroots business project sought to bring together leading business people in Indonesia and Mali to share their expertise, knowledge, networks, and financial resources to assist young, small-scale, social entrepreneurs in their communities. The project faced two challenges. First, in Indonesia large business partners made no investment in assisting SMEs run by youth. Second, the project was unable to develop a good pipeline of projects that could combine both business opportunities and grassroots benefits.

In a multi-country project, IFC supported a loan and technical assistance facility to provide the informal/young start-up micro-entrepreneurs with first-time access to financial markets. However, weak project design, loan product and selection criteria for the beneficiaries resulted in the project not meeting its objectives. Overall, these projects were not fully aligned with IFC's operational business model and the experience indicates that these types of projects are challenging to design and implement.

*Wage Subsidies to Provide Incentives for Hiring*

Temporary wage subsidies paid to employers to hire youth can have a positive impact on individual employment—mainly if work provides them with higher-level skills. The challenge is low take-up among employers. Kluve (2006), in a review of European countries, found these private sector incentive schemes to have a 30 to 50 percentage-points higher employment effect than skills-training programs offered under ALMPs. The Swedish Youth Practice Program subsidized wages of unemployed youth hired for six months in the private and public sector. However, subsidized participants were less likely to find employment compared to youth who received job search assistance, because there was insufficient planning and follow-up, as well as low-quality tasks without building any higher-level skills (Larsson 2003). Sri Lanka reports positive results from a wage subsidy paid to 22 percent of micro-entrepreneurs who were willing to hire low-skilled workers, mostly youth. The median firm reported a sales increase by 25 percent as a result of the hiring. After the subsidy expires, 86 percent of the firms plan to keep the worker (de Mel and others 2010). The U.K.'s New Deal wage subsidies program includes one day of training per week and positively affects youth employment, but it suffers from low uptake among employers (Van Reenen 2003).

Wage subsidies need to be high enough for employers to participate. The Bank supported wage subsidies in middle-income countries, including **Bulgaria, Turkey, Colombia,** and **Argentina**. In **Colombia**, the subsidy program benefited more than 100,000 workers, 40 percent of whom previously worked in the informal sector. However, because of low program uptake, the government stopped the subsidy and is now analyzing the pilot to identify lessons.

*Public Works Program*

Public sector employment programs are part of Active Labor Market Programs. ALMPs also include short-term skills training for jobseekers, private sector schemes to create job opportunities for youth, and job search assistance to help graduates and the unemployed find work. ALMPs can be targeted to youth or other population groups; however, their high costs to government require ALMPs to be well targeted and of limited duration. Public spending in OECD countries on ALMPs ranges from 0.2 percent of GDP in the United States and up to 2 percent of GDP in the Netherlands (Kluve 2010).

International evidence on direct employment in the public sector shows mixed results. In Europe, the post-program employment effect of public works programs is negative for youth, and scores below wage subsidies and skills training programs. There is little relationship between program effectiveness and other contextual factors, including in particular the macroeconomic environment and indicators for institutional features of the labor market (Kluve 2010). Van Reenen (2003) finds a positive post-program employment effect of the public works "environmental task force," which is part of the New Deal Program for youth in the United Kingdom.

Public works programs in Bank projects provide temporary work, but little is known about the post-program impact on employment. An impact evaluation (Jalan and Ravallion 2003) of the Bank-supported Trabajar program in Argentina, which provides short-term work to the poor unemployed at relatively low wages, finds the program has a positive income effect for youth during the program, but it does not report on post-program employment (table F.1). In Colombia, in the short run, unemployment decreased by 3.6 percentage points for youth in the public works program, and income increased by 15 percent for all participants. However, there is no post-program medium-term effect (table F.1). In Bulgaria, the public works program provided professional training to one-fourth of participants and helped reduce the number of social benefit recipients by 70 percent. In Turkey, 12,400 youth participated in temporary community employment programs, which include skills building on job search and entrepreneurship. In Kenya, the Kazi Kwa Vijana (KKV) work program provides income opportunities to participating youth and builds social and economic infrastructure. In El Salvador, about 8,000 youth participated in a six-month work program for skills building. These programs provide no information on medium- or longer-term employment.

Some countries are introducing internships for university graduates, among them Rwanda (IEG 2012b) and Tunisia (box F.3); the risk is that these publicly-funded internships for tertiary students mainly cater to the upper-income classes.

A previous IEG Evaluation of World Bank support to *Social Safety Nets 2000–2010* (IEG 2011c) and the Evaluation of the World Bank Group's response to the

| Table F.1 | Impact Evaluations of Bank Projects Promoting Work Opportunities | | | |
|---|---|---|---|---|
| Program to promote youth employment | Bank Project status | Intervention | Employment effect youth | Earnings effect youth |
| Tunisia Turning Thesis into Enterprises (Premand and others 2012) | Closed | Entrepreneurship training | Positive self-employment. None for employment | None |
| Uganda Youth Opportunities Program (Blattman 2011) | Active | Entrepreneurship training, grant to support business start-ups | Positive | Positive. None for females |
| Argentina Trabajar Program (Jalan and Ravallion 2003) | Closed 1999. Not included in portfolioa/ | Public works in local infrastructure | None | Positive income effect |
| Colombia Empleo en Acción: CO (CRL2) Technical Assistance Loan to support 2nd Private Sector Adjustment Loan (Sinergia 2007) | Closed | Public works program with temporary jobs of up to 5 months for the poorest unemployed, 18 and older | None | Positive income effect |

*Source:* IEG meta-review of Impact Evaluations. 2012.

a. Portfolio review includes World Bank Group projects approved in FY2001–2011. ^ Colombia Empleo en Accion Evaluation is in Spanish only and is not included in the systematic review. Colombia: Technical Assistance Loan to support the second Private Sector Adjustment Loan (Technical Assistance Loan to Support the Second Programmatic Labor Reform and Social Structural Adjustment Loan Project).

| Box F.3 | The Tunisia Internship Active Labor Market Program for University Graduates is Costly and Ineffective |
|---------|------------------------------------------------------------------------|

To tackle youth unemployment, Tunisia spends about $70 million annually on ALMPs, mainly consisting of paid internship programs targeted to university graduates. In 2010, the program had 138,670 participants. However, internships for first-time job seekers have not been very successful in helping beneficiaries transition into permanent employment, especially in disadvantaged regions where placement rates are below 15 percent, compared to the OECD benchmark placement rates for on-the-job training programs of above 80 percent.

Regional employment programs are not successful because they do not accommodate the region's needs and economic context. Data collected by the monitoring system are not being analyzed rigorously, and the impact of the ALMP programs on employment outcomes remains largely unknown. A reform of the ALMP portfolio in 2009 supported by the Bank Employment Development Policy Loan bundled over 20 ALMPs into six programs, thereby facilitating their management and financial control.

*Source:* World Bank 2010.

*Global Economic Crisis Phase II: Social Protection* (IEG 2012d) did not explicitly explore youth employment issues. However, both evaluations provided relevant insights for youth employment programs:

- Young workers were especially affected by the labor market contractions during the global economic crisis (World Bank 2011c). Automatic stabilizer programs, such as income support or public works programs have the potential to quickly employ people in a time of crisis and provide temporary income support.

- Public work programs need to be carefully designed and monitored to ensure that employment and income opportunities created reach the targeted groups (such as the poor and vulnerable, young people). Most of the public works programs reviewed by IEG did not track the effectiveness of targeting the intervention to the poor and the programs' impact on their welfare.

- More effort is needed to reform labor market policy and social insurance systems for the long term to protect both formal and informal workers—without distorting incentives for productive employment. Evidence shows that countries that built safety net systems during stable times were better prepared to protect themselves against the adverse impacts of global crises.

SMOOTHING TRANSITION FROM SCHOOL TO WORK AND JOB MOBILITY (L IN MILES)

### Counseling, Job Search Skills, Matching and Improving Information on the Labor Market

School-to-work transition interventions combine goals of skills development and labor market intermediation. Impact evaluations do not identify the marginal impact of school-to-work transition interventions. However, international evidence suggests adding school-to-work interventions to skills building interventions increases the employment effect of skills building. In the U.K.'s New Deal for Young People program, unemployed youth enter a four-month "gateway" with a personal advisor who assists in the job search. If still unemployed after the gateway period, youth either have to enroll in second-chance education or in subsidized job placement. The gateway program significantly raised the transition to employment (van Reenen 2003, Blundell and others 2004).

The U.S. Center for Employment Training (CET) keeps youth in training for employment-relevant skills until they find a position with the help of a counselor and active job placement assistance. Successes in California led to the scale up in other states (Miller and others 2003). The U.S. Job Corps is a multi-intervention program for disadvantaged youth with vocationally focused training in a residential setting and job placement assistance. Participation increases educational attainment, reduces criminal activity, and increases earnings over several post-program years. However, performance of the job placement service was weak and strengthening it could enhance program results (Schochet and others 2008, Lee 2009). A positive growth environment supported the success of these programs.

Job search assistance, better information, and on-the-job training helped reintegrate ex-soldiers in former Yugoslavia. In Bosnia and Herzegovina from 1996–1999, the Bank supported the re-integration of 300,000 ex-combatants—17 percent of them youth—into the workforce. The program included a municipal-level labor market information data system with job vacancies and job seeker registration, as well as education and retraining services with counseling and a job-finding service. The program had a positive impact on employment and earnings of demobilized soldiers. The likelihood of employment for youth increased by 28 percentage points and monthly income by 42 DM (Deutsch Mark); however, compared to other age groups, youth reported the smallest impacts from the program (Benus and others 2001).

The OECD recommends professional, proactive, and well-resourced career guidance for young people. Career guidance professionals need to have labor market experience, provide one-to-one advice to youth, be independent from teaching institutions, and have access to a wide range of information (OECD 2010).

Findings from the IEG systematic review of impact evaluations suggest that "counseling and job search assistance" is the only type of intervention that most often appears to provide positive labor outcomes. It also happens to be the least expensive intervention. However, its applicability to developing countries with a large informal sector is limited. More attention is also needed in measuring the long-term impact of reforms in vocational education and training systems and the impact of changes in labor market policies and regulations, as well as improving the quality of the formal technical and vocational education system.

Job search assistance is one part of a multi-service youth employment program in Bank projects, and little is known about its impact. In Bulgaria, the Bank helped reduce the social benefit payments made under the Guaranteed Minimum Income Program (GMI) to 18 months. GMI recipients had to participate in an employment activation program that included job search assistance. Within one year, the GMI program expenditures were reduced by 50 percent; however, this could have been due to benefits expiration or recipients finding work. In the Maldives, the Bank funded infrastructure for an employment service center to facilitate job search, but a qualified candidate to manage the center could not be identified, so the center did not become operational.

Job search assistance is common in youth employment programs in middle-income countries in a positive growth environment. These programs generally cater to all unemployed citizens. In Colombia, the public employment service to help individuals with job search and career guidance was expanded to 32 municipalities with Bank support. An additional 300 offices are to be created in the medium term. The Bank-supported Secondary Education Reform project in Turkey includes career guidance and counseling services and the introduction of the National Career Information System, which subsequently reported 1.2 million registered users within 2 years. Bank support in El Salvador helped strengthen 66 Bolsas de Empleo job search assistance offices. In Honduras, graduates of training and internship programs are registered in the National Employment System and receive counseling services, employment referrals, and follow up. About 33 percent of 4,800 disadvantaged youth found employment. Similarly, in Armenia, the Bank supported a job counseling service center for youth and for the disabled, which was widely used by the unemployed.

Three-quarters of the 90 Bank projects included in this review support improving information about the labor market (figure 2.2). While this information tends to be used by employment offices, little is known about how accessible job information is to job seekers in low-income countries. Two IEG Project Performance Assessment Reports on education in Yemen and Jordan found high unemployment rates among university graduates. They noted that more up-to-date labor market information was needed to inform job seekers, as well as more private sector representation in the governance of tertiary institutes (IEG 2011a).

The Bank-supported Serbia Employment Promotion Project undertook two impact evaluations to assess the effectiveness of "vacancy and job fairs" and "virtual enterprises." Findings show up to 10–15 percent of participants found a job immediately following the job fair, with low unit costs of job fairs (on average $200–$500 per 400–600 participants). The placement rates of beneficiaries of virtual enterprises were up to 30 percent after completion of the program. However, results for the virtual enterprise programs are inconclusive due to low participation. This evaluation is not included in the systematic review.

IFC has organized a few conferences bringing together private employers and the educational institutions in which it has invested. More recently, in Yemen, IFC offers the Business Edge Program to build business skills for unemployed youth. The IFC team partnered with the Yemen Education for Employment Foundation (YEFE) that provides training and job placement for recent graduates. YEFE works with employers to guarantee jobs to a percentage of the trainees, thus overcoming the skepticism many recent graduates have about additional training. YEFE includes 90 hours of Business Edge training in the six-month training course it provides free to youth. The total cost of the course is $270, covered by private donations. The program has trained 715 young Yemenis and so far, 322 individuals—120 of them females—have been placed into jobs.

### Overseas Employment

Migration affects the labor market in sending and receiving countries. Migration data are generally not collected by age group; however, youth are more mobile and thus are likely to represent a significant share of migrating workers. In Central Asia, a large share of the population emigrated, ranging from about 12 percent in Tajikistan to 25 percent in Kazakhstan in 2005. Emigration reduces unemployment in sending countries and can lead to a "brain drain" if the higher skilled are leaving. In the receiving country, migration increases the labor supply and can put downward pressure on wages, but it also contributes to aggregate demand. Remittances sent by emigrating workers are an important income source for their families back home, and, to take one example, amounted to 45.5 percent of GDP in Tajikistan in 2007 (Canagarjah and Kholmatov 2010).

Facilitating overseas employment requires job offers for migrants. In **Tunisia**, the Bank supported overseas employment of youth in France, where in 2009 Tunisians used only 1,546 (16 percent) of 9,000 work visas. An international employment service was created to establish contacts between employers in Europe to provide language and technical training to migrant workers. However, the impact was small, and the service facilitated only 69 foreign work contracts. However, it did lead to an increase in the migration quota from 16 percent to 31 percent by the end of 2010.

## Skills Development and Labor Market Relevance of Skills (E in MILES)

Globalization and technological advances are accelerating demand for skills in the labor market and for education reforms. Young workers in youth-intensive exporting sectors in Indonesia are disproportionately well educated—47 percent have completed secondary schooling, compared with 11 percent of other employed youth. Industries with high youth employment shares are concentrated in electronics and textile manufacturing (World Bank 2007).

These industrial changes in middle-income countries and increasingly also in low-income countries, require a labor force trained in mid-level technical, trade, and professional skills.

In addition, to supporting the general education system, World Bank Group projects support three main types of technical skills building: (i) formal technical education and vocational education training, also called apprenticeships, at the junior or secondary education level; (ii) short-term skills training; and (iii) remedial skills training targeted to disadvantaged youth. While the first is targeted to students to prepare them for the labor market, the second and third form part of active labor market programs and provide some short-term skills training to labor market participants to better prepare them for jobs. Each category addresses different skill training facets depending on the country context (table F.2).

Findings from low- and middle-income countries suggest that skills building projects (short-term training and formal TVET) are more effective when the following features are present (Fares and Puerto 2008, Betcherman and others 2007): (i) private sector involvement in training; (ii) classroom instruction combined with industry/employer attachment (internship, apprenticeship); and (iii) a comprehensive approach, combining training with other services, such as job counseling. Accordingly, several countries have started to reform or introduce new formal technical and vocational training, and short-term skills building courses targeted to the unemployed and disadvantaged groups.

The 2011 IEG Education Portfolio Note on all World Bank projects with education objectives (approved in FY2001–10) found that with regard to labor markets:

| Table F.2 | Three Types of Skill Building Supported by the World Bank Group | | |
|---|---|---|---|
| Characteristics | Formal Technical and Vocational Education | Short-term skills training | Remedial skills building |
| Target group | Post-primary students | Unemployed youth | Disadvantaged youth |
| Training duration | 1–3 years | 2–8 months | 2–8 months |
| Possible private sector involvement | Curriculum formulation and work-based practice | Classroom and work-based training | Classroom and work-based training |
| Type of skills learned | Vocation with or without degree | Any skills needed to find work | Reading, math, vocation |
| International examples | TVET in OECD countries | UK New Deal for Young People SENA Colombia | US Job Corps Jovenes en Accion in LAC |

Source: World Bank portfolio document review.
Note: OECD= Organisation for Economic Co-operation and Development; VET= technical and vocational education training.

- Weak results frameworks on the link between post-primary education and the labor force.

- Evidence that tertiary education and TVET investments have contributed to meeting labor market demands is thin.

- Objectives to improve learning outcomes and employment or other labor market outcomes have been more difficult to achieve than have objectives to increase access to education.

Based on these findings, the IEG Education Portfolio Note concluded that additional work needs to be done to: (i) strengthen the results frameworks of projects and monitoring and evaluation systems in countries; (ii) increase labor market relevance of post-primary education, and; (iii) improve targeting of the poor (IEG 2011c).

Promoting gender equality in education can lead to higher earnings for females. When women have control over household income (such as their own employment wages), more resources are devoted to children's education and health. A Country Gender Assessment (CGA) indicated that in Chile increasing female participation in the labor market leads to substantial poverty reduction and to increasing economic growth. Women's labor market participation also increases with the level of educational attainment. The *IEG Evaluation on Gender Development 2002–2007* found that Bank support for increasing women's labor force participation has generated only small or temporary results. Major efforts to influence labor markets did not particularly benefit women. However, Bank support to training appeared to have generated some improvements, particularly in countries where such access was previously limited for women (IEG 2010).

### Improving the Quality of Formal TVET

A recent OECD review "Learning for Jobs" finds that TVET has been neglected because of the strong emphasis on general and university education. In many countries, TVET is also perceived as having lower status. However, OECD countries are competing globally on the quality of their goods and services, which requires a professional workforce. For TVET to be successful, the review recommends a comprehensive approach including: (i) workplace training, because it provides learning opportunities for technical and soft skills and facilitates recruitment; (ii) professional career guidance; (iii) effective training of TVET teachers who work part-time to sustain their industrial know-how; (iv) incentives to employers to offer workplace learning; and (v) standardized assessments for TVET qualifications (OECD 2010).

TVET appears to generate better labor results than general education in middle-income countries. A study on the private returns to investment in education from 16 countries in East Asia and Latin America suggests that TVET seems to serve students better in entering wage employment compared with general secondary education. The highest returns were observed in Bolivia (72 percent of participation in wage employment compared to 40 percent for those with secondary education), China (86 compared to 70 percent), and Vietnam (57 compared to 36 percent) (Patrinos and others 2006).

The former socialist countries of Europe and Central Asia reformed their vocational training systems to respond to the needs of a market-based economy. The 1973 reforms in Romania added two years of general education and shortened vocational training accordingly. Malamud and Pop-Eleches (2010) find insignificant differences in unemployment, non-employment, and earnings for the cohorts before and after the reforms. However, the type of occupation changed and, after the reform, men were less likely to work as artisans and manual workers than their counterparts were.

Bank projects supported quality reforms in technical schools by seeking greater private sector involvement primarily in three ways: private sector representation on governance boards; private sector involvement in making curriculum more labor market relevant; and private sector provision of work-based training. The Bank is implementing this agenda in collaboration with other donors (box F.4) who generally have strong TVET systems in their own countries, including among them, Germany, Switzerland, and South Korea.

In many low-income areas, there is a limited formal private sector. In **India**, the Bank tried to encourage private sector involvement on the Board of Governors through the Technical Education/Engineering Quality Improvement Project I. This ensured industry involvement in matters such as curriculum revisions. At project closing, 96 percent of technical institutes had functioning Boards of Governors. However, the involvement of private sector employers is limited in areas without a thriving industry (IEG 2011b).

An IEG Project Performance Assessment Report in Zambia (IEG 2011e) found that weak management and financial obstacles affected the project's

| Box F.4 | Donor Coordination to Technical and Vocational Education and Training in Ghana |
| --- | --- |

The Ghana Skills Development Fund of the Council for Technical and Vocational Education and Training (COTVET) creates a coordinated approach in skills building among the World Bank, the African Development Bank (ADB), the Danish International Development Agency (DANIDA), and the Gesellschaft fuer Internationale Zusammenarbeit/Society for International Cooperation, Germany (GIZ). Donors co-finance the Ghana Skills Development Fund. Employers define the content and duration of the training and provide matching funds (larger formal sector employers are expected to pay 20–25 percent of the total training costs while informal sector employers or master craftspeople provide 10 percent in-kind contributions). The forthcoming ADB project and GIZ will both focus on master craftspeople and apprentice-based training in order to strengthen the capacity of the trade associations. TVET has targeted five job-creating sectors: garments, construction, auto mechanics, civil engineering, and hospitality and tourism. Scholarships will be provided for students who cannot afford to pay for training or apprenticeships.

*Source:* IEG 2012a.

sustainability. **Zambia's** TEVET project envisaged strengthening the influence of the private sector through local management boards of training institutions, and the channeling of government and private finance for training through the TEVET Fund. However, management boards had limited authority. The TEVET Fund was only briefly piloted with donor funding, and was not sustainable after funding closed without contributions from the government and private sector.

The TEVET Authority (TEVETA) Board, with nongovernment majority, has been chaired by a representative of the private sector. TEVETA used private sector representatives in developing the qualifications framework, occupational standards, and curricula. TEVETA helped develop linkages between individual training institutions and employers for trainee work experience, which was an important achievement that has proved difficult to secure in other similar projects.

Bank projects have supported: decentralizing financial and managerial control to training institutions; updating the curriculum, equipment, and facilities; and establishing quality assurance systems. In **Ghana**, the Bank is supporting TVET reforms, including: (i) a TVET management information system to better identify skill needs; (ii) guidelines for standards, qualification, and certification; (iii) the engagement of private training providers; (iv) the formation of national TVET policies and coordination; (v) competitive selection of training providers with private employers in the formal and informal sectors. In **Mauritania**, the Bank supported twinning programs with institutions in France, Morocco, and Canada to develop a new curriculum for the training of TVET instructors. Approximately 3,138 new instructors were trained, and training centers were equipped; 4,344 students have graduated from the centers, with 20 percent employed in the private sector. The outflow into employment increased from 60 percent to 80 percent during project time. The Bank supported **Turkey** in expanding vocational training to include half a million participants by 2010. It also organized a youth internship with a stipend for 1,285 graduates in vocational education in 2009. Related expenses were financed by the unemployment insurance fund.

IFC support was mainly to the tertiary level of vocational training. In June 2004, IFC provided a loan to build a new campus for the Institute of Business associated with the University of West Indies—a public sector institution, in Port of Spain, the Republic of **Trinidad and Tobago**. As of 2009, there have been 1,000 graduates (279 additional graduates since the project) with postgraduate degrees and diplomas and 19,000 executive trainees (4,432 additional trainees since the project) from the public and private sector benefiting from short-term management training programs. The project's business success is rated satisfactory. The economic rate of return calculations are 33.6 percent and 38.6 percent respectively, taking into account the net present value of the salary differential between incremental graduates and non-graduates of the Institute of Business and the opportunity

## IFC's Efforts to Provide Technical and Vocational Education and Training to Middle- and Low-Income Groups

Anhanguera Educacional Participacoes S.A. (AES), an IFC investee, provides tertiary education and technical and vocational training to young working adults from middle- and low-income backgrounds. AES is Brazil's largest private, for-profit post-secondary education company. AES delivers education services through its: (i) campus network (Anhanguera Educacional); (ii) vocational training centers (Microlins); and (iii) distance learning platform (Anhanguera/LFG). The TVET subsidiary currently enrolls 500,000 students per year across 657 franchises located in every Brazilian state. The TVET subsidiary's affordable fee structure (R$75–R$120 per month depending on the program and location) attracts a large number of low-income students (72 percent with family incomes below R$1,500 per month). Course offerings focus on high-demand and low-complexity skills that are professionally oriented and industry-relevant. The program guarantees a job interview following the completion of its courses. Student surveys suggest that AES graduates improve their earning potential by more than 50 percent. The average monthly wage of an incoming student is approximately $290, with income on graduation rising to approximately $450.

*Source:* IFC's inclusive business case study. 2011. http://www1.ifc.org/wps/wcm/connect/c70543804a7cce ba8c1efdf998895a12/IFC_2011 Case+Studies.pdf?MOD=AJPERES.

cost of study for incremental students. IFC is currently considering increasing its investments in TVETs and in institutions that help in transition from education to the workplace and provide more training in life skills.

### Expanding Work-Based Learning

Formal TVET programs are more effective when focused on providing skills closely matched with existing employment opportunities. Similarly, an updated meta-evaluation of 345 training programs in 90 countries by Fares and Puerto (2010) finds comprehensive training programs including workplace training and employment services to be more effective than pure institution-based training. Specifically, they find that: (i) training programs that combine in-classroom training with workplace training increase the likelihood of positive impact by 21–37 percentage points, while programs that offer this combination plus additional services increase the probability of positive outcomes by 44–55 percentage points; (ii) training programs targeting youth alone have a lower, but still positive and significant, likelihood of success; and (iii) results are improved under conditions of faster gross domestic product (GDP) growth.

Short-term work-based skills training improves labor market outcomes in Honduras. The **Honduras** EPEM (Entrenamiento para el Empleo) program (not supported by the Bank), provides workplace training for unemployed youth that is designed and delivered by employers. Developed by the government in collaboration with the association and chambers of commerce and industry, these associations play a crucial bridging role in promoting the program to member firms with vacancies and matching these jobs to the profiles of unemployed youth registered with the public job placement agency (which also provides stipends to program participants). Relative to a control group, an impact evaluation showed that participation in EPEM increased post-training wages, the probability of employment, and the likelihood of a formal sector job with social security and benefits (Rozada 2011).

Work-based training is offered in less than a third of the Bank's skills training projects. More than half of the Bank's projects with skills training have private sector participation in classroom education. However, considerably fewer projects include work-based learning, and only 13 projects use a comprehensive approach with the private sector (table F.3). In many low-income areas where the Bank is active, the small formal sector limits the number of work-based learning opportunities. In **Colombia**, Bank support to new legislation allowing employers to pay a sub-minimum wage in job training contracts increased the number of apprentices from 33,337 in 2002 to 220,000 in March 2005.

### Skills Recognition and Certification

Most OECD countries have established some sort of skills certification system to set skill standards for different occupations. Indeed, many developing countries have started following suit. The success of a skills certification system depends on its credibility with both potential trainees and employers. However, evidence on whether and how much skills certification has a signaling effect for prospective employers, thereby improving youth employment outcomes, is limited.

Accreditation is seen as a way of making the degree/diploma more valuable, especially if it involves a trusted private sector company. Most Bank-supported TVET projects with a quality assurance goal emphasized accreditation of programs. However, a constraint is the potential for manipulation of the accreditation process, thereby devaluing its credibility as an instrument for accountability. In India, Crisil India, a Standard & Poor's company with an established reputation for providing unbiased credit ratings of companies, has recently started rating Master of Business Administration

| Table F.3 | Private Sector Involvement in Skills Training | |
|---|---|---|
| | | Number of projects |
| Projects with skills training for young people | | 75 |
| with private sector participation in education | | 48 |
| with job counseling or job search support | | 34 |
| with work-based vocational training | | 29 |
| with private sector participation in education, counseling, and work-based vocational training | | 13 |
| *Source:* IEG portfolio review based on World Bank data. | | |

(MBA) institutes to ensure these institutes meet the needs of the market (IEG 2011b).

Chile has been experimenting with the certification of training programs within the Bank-supported Chilecalifica. The program has a positive impact, but the evaluation may overestimate the program's success due to sample selection bias. The role of skills certification in addressing information constraints is difficult to disentangle from the effects of other employment services.

IFC has not worked on developing skill certification systems.

### Remedial, Non-Formal Vocational Training

Non-formal, short-term skills training has a mixed effect around the world, with women often faring better than men. Latin America has several short training programs, which form part of ALMPs, and are not a part of the formal education system. These courses provide basic job readiness skills to increase the employability of disadvantaged youth. The Mexican Probecat offers short-term, on-the-job training complemented by internships in the private sector. Honduras and El Salvador have introduced similar programs. The Chile Joven program for at-risk youth has been replicated throughout Latin America. The Bank supports several of these programs.

Skill training for women leads to higher employment rates, better earnings, and shorter cost recovery times. The Procajoven project in Panama has an Insertion Modality for low-income jobless youth with 270 hours of classroom training on job readiness and technical training, followed by 172 hour-internship in a firm. The Transition Modality for secondary school graduate, first-time job seekers offers 120 hours in job readiness training and 344 hours in firm internships. Competitive public bidding led to the selection of training institutes, which had to submit letters from firms providing internships to ensure the market-relevance of courses. An evaluation finds no significant impact on the employment rate and monthly earnings of all participants, but significantly higher employment and earning impacts for young women. Participants of the Transition Modality are significantly more likely to find employment than those from the Insertion Modality program. The cost of training was recovered within a year for all participants and within only 3 months for women in the Transition Modality (Ibarraran and Rosas 2007).

About one-third of the Bank projects included in this portfolio review provide short courses in skill building to unemployed youth or disadvantaged groups, but little is known about the employment effect. In **Turkey**, the Bank supported 387 skills training (employability training) subprojects that trained 12,453 unemployed youth in public training centers. In 2006, about 12 percent of trainees dropped out, and about 43 percent of graduates were placed in jobs or started a business. However, no medium-term information is available. In **Indonesia**, private sector providers in the Life Skills Education for Employment and Entrepreneurship program train, certify, and match unemployed youth with domestic and overseas jobs in either the formal or informal sectors.

The four skills building projects with an impact evaluation show mixed results—although more so for females than males (table F.4). The Bank-supported **Kenya** Technical and Vocational Voucher Program (Hicks and others 2011) randomly awarded vouchers to youth for technical and vocational training. Among voucher winners, a random half were awarded a voucher that could only be used in public vocational institutions, while the other half were awarded a voucher that could be used in both private and public schools. The evaluation is ongoing.[1] The **Chile** Califica project evaluation did not identify program impacts on younger age groups. Positive monthly wage impacts were found for participants older than 40 years of age and individuals from metropolitan regions, as well as for trainees who received certification of job competencies but not for those without certification. There is no impact on employment; however, formalization of employment increased especially for individuals above the age of 40.

| Table F.4 | Impact Evaluations of Bank Projects Promoting School-to-Work Transition and/or Skills Building | | | |
|---|---|---|---|---|
| Program to promote Youth Employment and Source | Bank Project status | Intervention | Employment effect Youth | Earnings effect Youth |
| Bosnia and Herzegovina Emergency Demobilization and Reintegration Project (Benus 2001) | Closed 1999. Not included in portfolio review | Counseling, job search skills, matching, placement. Remedial education and vocational training | Positive | Positive |
| Kenya Technical and Vocational Vouchers Program (Hicks 2011) | Analytic and Advisory Activity | Training subsidies and vouchers for vocational training | Negative (still in training) | None |
| ChileCalifica Program Lifelong Learning and Training Project (Santiago Consultores 2009)b | Closed | Skills training with and without certification of job competencies. | None | None. Positive for age 40+ |
| Dominican Republic Juventud y Empleo (Tesliuc 2011; Card 2011) | Active | Remedial education/second chance /non-formal technical and vocational training. Vouchers and training subsidies | None | Positive |
| Colombia Jóvenes en Acción (Attanasio and others 2011). | Not applicable | Remedial education/second chance /non-formal technical and vocational training | Positive and Formality | Positive |

*Source:* IEG.

a. Portfolio review includes World Bank Group projects approved in FY2001–2011. Kenya: The TVET vouchers impact evaluation was a background report for the Skills Development for Youth in Kenya's Informal sector Analytic and Advisory Activity. Colombia: The Bank (P088857) supported the evaluation of the Jóvenes en Acción program.

b. ChileCalifica is a Life-long Learning and Training Project. Therefore, impact evaluation does not identify impact on youth; age break is 40 years in analysis.

The Juventud y Empleo program in the **Dominican Republic,** which is supported by the Inter-American Development Bank and the World Bank, features several weeks of basic skills and technical/vocational training by a private training provider, followed by an internship with fully-subsidized wages to ensure training responds to the needs of the local employers. During the internship, participants received limited follow-up with counseling and technical assistance. Nearly all interns were let go after the internship. The program had no effect on participants "employability" and employment, but a modest impact on earning (table F.4) (Card and others 2011). The **Colombia** Jovenes en Acción program, supported by the Inter-American Development Bank, has a significantly positive impact on formality of employment for both young men and women. For young women with skills training, earnings increased by 19.6 percent and their probability of paid employment by 6.8 percent when compared to women without training and to men (Attanasio and others 2011).

*Transport and Residential Change*

Many skills-building programs support the transport and residential expenses of trainees, which is helpful for youth from lower-income groups. In **Honduras**, participants receive a stipend during the training and internship to cover the costs of transportation and food for each day of attendance. In **St. Lucia**, trainees receive a stipend to pay for transportation, childcare, and other costs of participation. In **Burkina Faso**, Bank support financed residential boarding capacities for engineering students. In **Grenada**, trainees are paid a stipend during course work for transport and other costs; once they start their on-the-job apprenticeship, the stipend is paid by the employer. TVET trainees in Liberia receive a stipend to pay for transport and other expenses from the employer or the training institutions. The Bank is supporting transportation for girls to and from the training locations in Pakistan.

Summing up the experience from TVET and remedial skills building, two keys to success emerge, namely, a comprehensive approach and private sector involvement:

- First, comprehensive programs with a counseling and job search component in addition to the skills training perform stronger than programs that focused exclusively on skills training. The combination of labor-market relevance of skills training and career guidance are key.

- Second, private sector participation in skill development programs—including in the program design, the private provision of classroom and work-based training, the accreditation of training, as well as training of teachers—leads more often to success. Remedial education and non-formal technical and vocational training programs were especially sensitive to private sector participation.

## Note

1.  The Technical and Vocational Vouchers Program was launched in late 2008. Approximately 20 percent of participants chose courses that lasted a year or less, whereas close to 78 percent chose courses that were at least two years long. This means that the majority of voucher winners were still in school until December 2011 when the evaluations were done. Thus, the evaluated program impacts are not for the full sample, but rather form suggestive evidence of the short-run impacts of the program on the labor market outcomes, based on a representative subset of program participants.

## References

Alcazar, Lorena, Raul Andrade and Miguel Jaramillo. 2011. "Panel Tracer Study on the Impact of Business Facilitation Processes on Enterprises and Identification of Priorities for Future Business Enabling Environment Projects in Lima, Peru." Report 6. Impact Evaluation After the Fourth Round. Prepared for IFC.

Attanasio, Orazio, Adriana Kugler, and Costas Meghir. 2011. "Subsidizing Vocational Training for Disadvantaged Youth in Colombia: Evidence from a Randomized Trial." *American Economic Journal: Applied Economics* 3(3): 188–220.

Benus, Jacob, James Rude and Satyendra Patrabansh. 2001. "Impact of the Emergency Demobilization and Reintegration Project in Bosnia and Herzegovina." Department of Labor Bureau of International Affairs. Development Impact Evaluation (DIME).

Betcherman, Gordon, Martin Godfrey, Susana Puerto, Friederike Rother, and Antoneta Stavreska. 2007. "A Review of Interventions to Support Young Workers: Findings of the Youth Employment Inventory." Social Protection Discussion Paper No. 0715. Washington, DC: World Bank.

Blattman, Christopher, Nathan Fiala, and Sebastian Martinez. 2011. "Can Employment Programs Reduce Poverty and Social Instability Experimental Evidence from a Ugandan Aid Program." World Bank Policy Research Working Paper series.

Blundell, Richard, Monica Costa Dias, Costas Meghir, and John Van Reenen. 2004. "Evaluating the Employment Impact of a Mandatory Job Search Assistance Program." *Journal of the European Economic Association* 2(4): 569–606.

Bruhn, Miriam. 2008. "License to Sell: The Effect of Business Registration Reform on Entrepreneurial Activity in Mexico." Policy Research Working Paper 4538. World Bank, Washington, DC.

Bruhn, Miriam and Bilal Zia. 2011. "Stimulating Managerial Capital in Emerging Markets – The Impact of Business and Financial Literacy for Young Entrepreneurs," World Bank Policy Research Working Paper No. 5642.

Canagarajah, Sudharshan, and Matin Kholmatov. 2010. "Migration and Remittances in CIS Countries during the Global Economic Crisis." World Bank ECA Knowledge Brief. Volume 16.

Card, David, Pablo Ibarrarán, Ferdinando Regalia, David Rosas, and Yuri Soares. 2011. "The Labor Market Impacts of Youth Training in the Dominican Republic." *Journal of Labor Economics* 29(2): 267–300.

Cardoso, Ana Rute. (2009). "Long-Term Impact of Youth Minimum Wages: Evidence from Two Decades of Individual Longitudinal Data." IZA Discussion Paper No. 4236.

Castañeda, Carlos, José González, and Norberto Rojas. 2010. "Evaluación de Impacto del Programa Jóvenes Rurales Emprendedores del SENA." Fedesarrollo Working Paper No. 53 de 2012–2, Bogotá, Colombia.

de Mel, Suresh, David McKenzie, and Christopher Woodruff. (2010). "Wage Subsidies for Microenterprises." *American Economic Review: Papers & Procee*dings 100 (2): 614-18.

Delajara, Marcelo, Samuel Freije, and Isidro Soloaga. 2006. "An Evaluation of Training for the Unemployed in Mexico." Working Paper: OVE/WP-09/06. Inter-American Development Bank, Office of Evaluation and Oversight.

Dutz, Mark, Ioannis Kessides, Stephen O'Connell and Robert Willig. 2011. "Competition and Innovation-Driven Inclusive Growth." World Bank Policy Research Working Paper 5852.

Fairlie, Robert W., Dean Karlan, and Jonathan Zinman. 2012. "Behind the GATE Experiment: Evidence on Effects of and Rationales for Subsidized Entrepreneurship Training." NBER Working Paper No. 17804.

Fares, Jean, and Susana Puerto. 2009. "Towards Comprehensive Training." Social Protection Discussion Papers 52188. World Bank.

Fields, Gary, and Ravi Kanbur. 2007. "Minimum Wage and Poverty with Income-Sharing." *Articles & Chapters*. Paper 116.

Gruber, Jonathan. 1997. "The Incidence of Payroll Taxation: Evidence from Chile," *Journal of Labor Economics* 15(3) S72–101.

Heckman, James and Carmen Pagés-Serra. (2000). "The Cost of Job Security Regulation: Evidence from Latin American Labor Markets." *Economia* 1(1) 109-144.

Hicks, Joan Hamory, Michael Kremer, Isaac Mbiti, and Edward Miguel. 2011. "Vocational Education Voucher Delivery and Labor Market Returns: A Randomized Evaluation among Kenyan Youth, Report for Spanish Impact Evaluation Fund (SIEF) Phase II." Policy Note Human Development Network. World Bank.

Ibarraran, Pablo, and David Rosas. 2007. "Impact Evaluation of a Labor Training Program in Panama." OVE Inter-American Development Bank, Washington DC.

Independent Evaluation Group. 2012a. "World Bank and IFC Support for Youth Employment Programs." Background Paper. Country Case Study: Ghana. Forthcoming.

———. 2012b. "World Bank and IFC Support for Youth Employment Programs." Background Paper. Country Case Study: Rwanda. Forthcoming.

———. 2012c. "World Bank and IFC Support for Youth Employment Programs." Background Paper. Country Case Study: South Africa. Forthcoming.

———. 2012d. *The World Bank Group's Response to the Global Economic Crisis—Phase II.* Washington, D.C.: Independent Evaluation Group, the World Bank Group.

———. 2011a. "Project Performance Assessment Report on Higher Education Enhancement Project (HEEP) in Egypt, Higher Education Learning and Innovation Project (HELIP) in Yemen, and Higher Education Project in the Hashemite Kingdom of Jordan." Report No. 62651. Washington, DC: World Bank.

———. 2011b. "Project Performance Assessment Report on India's Third Technician Education Project (TTEP) and Technical/Engineering Education Quality Improvement Project I (TEQIP I)." Report No. 66056. Washington, DC: World Bank.

———. 2011c. "Social Safety Nets: An Evaluation of World Bank Support, 2000-2010." Washington, DC: World Bank.

———. 2011d. "World Bank Support to Education since 2001: A Portfolio Note." Washington, DC: World Bank.

———. 2011e. "Project Performance Assessment Report on Technical Education Vocational and Entrepreneurship Training Development Support Program (TEVET) in Zambia." Report No. 62585. Washington, DC: World Bank.

———. 2010. "Gender and Development." An Evaluation of World Bank Support, 2002–2008. The Washington DC: World Bank.

Jalan, Jyotsna and Martin Ravallion. 2003. Estimating the Benefit Incidence of an Antipoverty Program by Propensity-Score Matching. *Journal of Business and Economic Statistics, American Statistical Association* 21(1) 19–30.

Karlan and Valdivia. 2006. "Teaching Entrepreneurship: Impact of Business Training on Microfinance Clients and Institutions." Yale University.

Kluve, Jochen. 2010. "The effectiveness of European active labor market programs." *Labour Economics* 17: 904–918.

———. 2006. "The Effectiveness of European Active Labor Market Policy." Discussion Paper No. 2018. Institute for the Study of Labor.

Kugler, Adriana D. 2005. "The Effect of Job Security Regulations on Labor Market Flexibility. Evidence from Colombia Labor Market Reform." In *Law and Employment: Lessons from Latin American and the Caribbean*, eds. James J. Heckman and Carmen Pagés. Chicago: University of Chicago Press.

Larsson, Laura. 2003. "Evaluation of Swedish Youth Labor Market Programs." *The Journal of Human Resources* 38(4): 891–927.

Lee, David S. 2009. "Training, Wages, and Sample Selection: Estimating Sharp Bounds on Treatment Effects." *Review of Economic Studies* 76(3): 1071–1102.

Malamud, Ofer, and Cristian Pop-Eleches. 2010. "General Education versus Vocational Training: Evidence from an Economy in Transition." *Review of Economics and Statistics* 92(1): 43–60.

Miller, Cynthia, Johannes M. Bos, Kristin E. Porter, Fannie M. Tseng, Fred C. Doolittle, Deana N. Tanguay, and Mary P. Vencill. 2003. "Working with Disadvantaged Youth Thirty-Month Findings from the Evaluation of the Center for Employment Training Replication Sites." Manpower Demonstration Research Corporation Working Paper.

Neumark, David and William Wascher. (2004). "Minimum Wages, Labor Market Institutions, and Youth Employment: A Cross-National Analysis." *Industrial and Labor Relations Review* 57( 2): 223–248.

Organisation for Economic Co-operation and Development (OECD). 2010. Education at a Glance 2010. OECD Indicators.

———. 1998. "Supporting youth pathways." *Education Policy Analysis*. Paris: Organisation for Economic Co-operation and Development.

Patrinos, Harry Anthony, Cris Ridao-Cano, and Chris Sakellariou. 2006. "Estimating the Returns to Education: Accounting for Heterogeneity in Ability." Unpublished report.

Premand Patrick, Stefanie Brodmann, Rita Almeida, Rebekka Grun, and Mahdi Barouni. 2012. "Entrepreneurship training and self-employment among university graduates: Evidence from a randomized trial in Tunisia." World Bank Impact Evaluation Report. Washington, DC: World Bank.

Rozada, Martin-Gonzalez. 2011. "Evaluación de impacto del programa EPEM y Análisis Costo-Beneficio." Draft paper. Inter-American Development Bank.

Schochet, Peter, John Burghardt, and Sheena McConnell. 2008. "Does Job Corps Work? Impact Findings from the National Job Corps Study." *American Economic Review* 98(5): 1864–1886.

Van Reenen, John. 2003. "Active Labour Market Policies and the British New Deal for the Young Unemployed in Context." NBER Working Paper Series. Working Paper 9576.

World Bank. 2012a. "World Bank and IFC Support for Youth Employment Programs."
Background Paper. Country Case Study: South Africa. Forthcoming.

———. 2011a: Governance and Opportunity Development Policy Loan. Program
Document. May 26.

———. 2011b. "How Did the Great Recession Affect Different Types of Workers?
Evidence from 17 Middle-Income Countries." World Bank Policy Research Working
Paper 5636. Washington, DC: World Bank.

———. 2010. Tunisia Employment Development Policy Loan Project. Report Number
54341. Washington, DC: World Bank.

———. 2007. *World Development Report 2007: Development and the next generation.*
Washington, DC.

# Appendix G

Social Media Outreach Goals,
Methodology, and Results

IEG's Youth Employment Evaluation Team, in collaboration with IEG's Online Communications team, used social media to reach out to beneficiaries and stakeholders to complement its data collection activities and conduct public outreach to youth across the globe. The engagement plan aimed to gather additional information in the form of *qualitative data* that could: (i) be triangulated with other sources used in the evaluation; (ii) make the evaluation process transparent by posting study questions and updates online for public use; and (iii) create a group of interested stakeholders to champion the recommendations and findings of the completed evaluation.

## Methodology for Social Media Outreach

IEG used its existing Facebook and Twitter accounts to reach out to target groups with key messages and questions. Through these channels, IEG solicited comments from users worldwide. Specific questions were asked sequentially and in multiple formats. Each question was posted for a week. Some questions were posted both as open-ended queries to solicit descriptive comments and as polls to obtain quantitative data. Additionally, the evaluation team responded to questions posted by users on Facebook and Twitter, serving as a valuable source of information exchange.

IEG set up a dedicated tab/sub-page on Facebook for users to interact on youth employment issues. IEG also posted all of the questions on the Facebook Wall. Main topics covered included government strategies to address youth employment, gender differences in accessing labor market, access to credit and banking, and adequacy of skills and training among youth.

Each question was posted along with a descriptive picture to attract the interest of the users. According to Google Analytics, between December 20, 2011 and March 28, 2012, the page generated 300 visits. The top 10 countries from which users accessed the sub-page were the United States, Pakistan, United Kingdom, Armenia, Uganda, Egypt, Argentina, Switzerland, Chile, and Canada. IEG also ran advertising campaigns on Facebook for some questions targeting youth in particular countries and users with specific interests in youth and youth employment. Additionally, some questions were cross-posted on other organizations' Facebook profiles to make their users aware of the evaluation and to prompt their reactions.

On Twitter, IEG used a distinct hashtag[1]—#Youth&Jobs—to group content and people following the discussion. IEG researched and connected with the most influential Tweeters on youth and youth employment issues, such as the U.K.'s Youth Parliament, the World Bank's YouThink, UNICEF's Voices of the Youth, and so on. The outreach team also followed certain youth-related topics to stay updated on main events and developments.

IEG also supplemented its online outreach efforts with face-to-face presentations to youth groups. IEG presented the study and social media outreach plan at the World Bank Speaker's Bureau presentations to groups of students and interns visiting the World Bank and to interns from the Organization of American States and the Washington Center for Internships and Academic Seminars. The presentations focused on encouraging youth to participate in discussions and share their experiences.

## Responses from Social Media Outreach

During the three-month outreach campaign, IEG's posts on the Facebook Wall reached over 600,000 people, according to Facebook Insights.[2] IEG also received over 50 comments, which were synthesized into the "I, L and E" categories examined by the study. In addition, three polls garnered around 750 votes. Comments came from users in Afghanistan, Canada, Colombia, Egypt, Ghana, India, Kenya, Nepal, Pakistan, Sri Lanka, Zambia, Uganda, and the United States.

Although IEG reached out to youth groups and organizations working with youth, it is not possible to confirm the age or nationality of people responding to the outreach efforts unless it is stated in their social media profiles. However, the general demographic on IEG's Facebook page between January 1 and March 26, 2012 was predominantly comprised of people 18–34 years old. Males were the majority. Most users came from Pakistan, Egypt, India, Indonesia, the Philippines, Afghanistan, and the United States.

The outreach methodology and tools reached only literate individuals with Internet access and those who speak English. Nevertheless, it was a useful way to gather the opinions and experiences of youth. It also made the evaluation process more transparent and accessible and created interest in the evaluation before completion. Overall, the responses were in line with the finding that youth unemployment is a big issue across the world.

Data gathered from social media were analyzed, triangulated with other sources of data, and incorporated into this report to illustrate the findings.

Below is a summary of some of the comments received by question and topic posed on social media sites.

### SKILLS AND TRAINING

*Question*: Do you think most youth lack the business skills and connections to become successful entrepreneurs?

*Summary of responses*: Most youth have the business skills to become successful entrepreneurs but lack connections and financial empowerment. At the same time, more needs to be done to create better training opportunities targeting marketable skills for youth.

IEG also conducted a poll asking whether youth lack business skills and connections to be successful entrepreneurs. This poll generated 185 responses of which 209 said "Yes," and 76 said "No" (figure G.2).

## Figure G.1 — Facebook Demographics Based on Likes, July 1, 2012–March 26, 2012

Likes by Gender and Age?

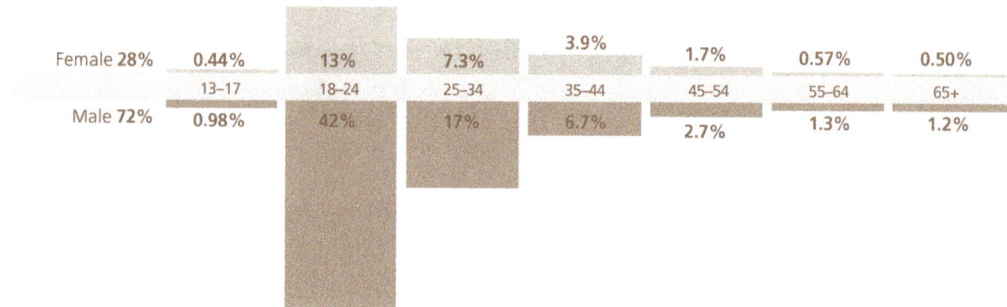

| | 13–17 | 18–24 | 25–34 | 35–44 | 45–54 | 55–64 | 65+ |
|---|---|---|---|---|---|---|---|
| Female 28% | 0.44% | 13% | 7.3% | 3.9% | 1.7% | 0.57% | 0.50% |
| Male 72% | 0.98% | 42% | 17% | 6.7% | 2.7% | 1.3% | 1.2% |

| Likes by Country? | Likes by City? | Likes by Language? |
|---|---|---|
| 2,098 Pakistan | 726 Cairo, Al Qahirah, Egypt | 5,752 English (US) |
| 1,451 Eygpt | 515 Karachi, Sindh, Pakistan | 918 English (UK) |
| 838 India | 503 Lahore, Punjab, Pakistan | 827 Arabic |
| 586 Indonesia | 348 Kabul, Kabol, Afghanistan | 476 Indonesian |
| 571 Philippines | 230 Alexandria, Al Iskandariyay, Egypt | 265 Spanish |
| 442 Afghanistan | 204 Dhaka, Bangladesh | 139 Portuguese (Brazil) |
| 402 United States | 203 Islamabad, Pakistan | 107 French (France) |
| More | More | More |

Source: Facebook Insights.

## GENDER DIFFERENCES

Question: Do females entering the labor force in your country face more social and labor market entry barriers than men?

Summary of responses: A majority of respondents agreed that women face more barriers entering the labor force than men.

## GOVERNMENT POLICIES TO GENERATE YOUTH EMPLOYMENT

Question: Is your government using any strategy to promote youth employment? Is it working?

Summary of responses: Responses varied but most said that there are no adequate government policies to address youth employment issues and provide necessary training. For example, a user from Egypt commented:

"The government does not offer such programs systematically. They keep talking about development of education at the college level to meet market needs, but nothing is done."

### Employment in Rural Areas

*Question*: If more employment opportunities in rural areas were accessible to young people, would they migrate less to urban areas?

This question was conducted on Facebook as a poll and received 180 responses of which 140 said "Yes," and 39 said "No." (figure G.3).

### Barriers in Accessing Credit

*Question*: In many countries, young people are excluded from the formal credit market and cannot get credit from state banks. What has been your experience in requesting loans or opening a bank account? Did you face any challenges because of your age or work history?

This question was conducted on Facebook as a poll, with a series of open-ended questions. It was cross-posted on IEG's Twitter account. As a poll question, "Do young people experience barriers in requesting loans or opening bank accounts in your country?" It generated 279 responses. Of all respondents, 184 responded "Yes" to the question, 37 responded "No," and 58 responded, "I do not know" (figure G.4).

| Figure G.2 | Results for Skills and Training Survey |
| --- | --- |

Do you think most youth lack the business skills and connections to become successful entrepreneurs? If yes, what do you think could be done/is done to help the youth to cope with these issues? (Take a poll and leave your opinion in the comment section to contribute to our study).

◉ Yes ••• 209 people

◉ No •••

**Asked By** 285 Votes • 7 Followers

**IEG**
Independent Evaluation Group (IEG)
about a week ago • 🔧 • Share • Delete

🚩 Ask Friends  +1 Follow

*Source:* IEG Facebook page.

## Figure G.3     Results on Rural Employment Survey

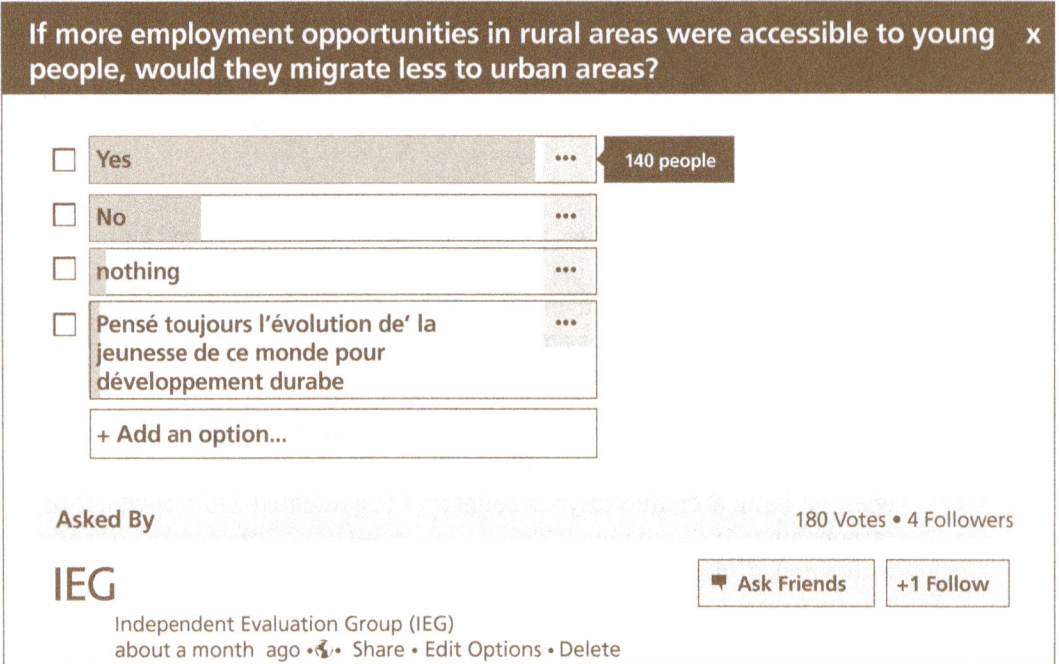

**If more employment opportunities in rural areas were accessible to young people, would they migrate less to urban areas?**   x

- ☐ Yes  •••  140 people
- ☐ No  •••
- ☐ nothing  •••
- ☐ Pensé toujours l'évolution de' la jeunesse de ce monde pour développement durabe  •••
- + Add an option...

**Asked By**        180 Votes • 4 Followers

**IEG**

⚑ Ask Friends    +1 Follow

Independent Evaluation Group (IEG)
about a month ago •⚘• Share • Edit Options • Delete

*Source:* IEG Facebook page.

---

## Figure G.4     Results on Access to Credit Survey

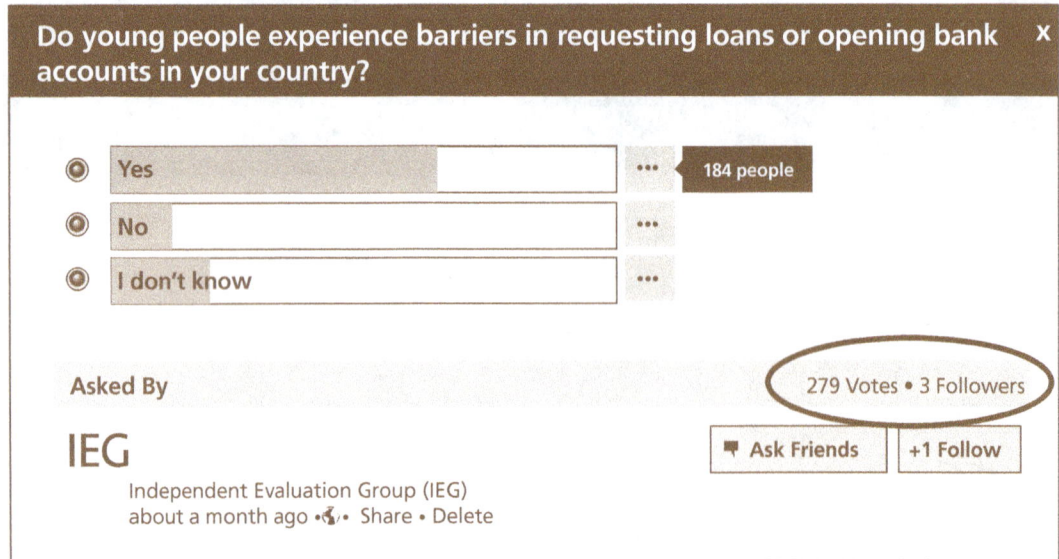

**Do young people experience barriers in requesting loans or opening bank accounts in your country?**   x

- ◉ Yes  •••  184 people
- ◉ No  •••
- ◉ I don't know  •••

**Asked By**        279 Votes • 3 Followers

**IEG**

⚑ Ask Friends    +1 Follow

Independent Evaluation Group (IEG)
about a month ago •⚘• Share • Delete

*Source:* IEG Facebook page.

## Notes

1. The # symbol, called a hashtag, is used to mark keywords or topics in a Tweet. It was created organically by Twitter users as a way to categorize messages.

2. This number is calculated by adding the numbers associated with People Reached for each posting. Facebook describes the People Reached metric as a number of unique people that have seen a post.

# Bibliography

Barrera, Felipe, Paul Gertler, and Ancieto Orbeta. 2009. "Youth and ICT in classrooms in Colombia." DIME.

Blom, Andreas, and Hiroshi Saeki. 2010. "Employability and Skill Set of Newly Graduated Engineers in India." Human Development Sector, South Asia Region. Washington DC: World Bank.

Breen, Richard. 2005. "Explaining Cross-National Variation in Youth Unemployment. Market and Institutional Factors." *European Sociology Review* 21(2): 125–134.

Cunningham, Wendy, Maria Laura Sanchez-Puerta and Alice Wuermli. 2010. "Active Labor Market Programs for Youth: A Framework to Guide Youth Employment Interventions." World Bank Employment Policy Primer. No. 16.

Djankov, S., C. Mcliesh and R.M. Ramalho. 2006. "Regulation and Growth," *Economic Letters* 92 (3): 395–401.

Godfrey, Martin. 2003. "Youth Employment Policy in Developing and Transition Countries – Prevention as Well as Cure." SP Discussion Paper Series No. 0320. The World Bank.

Greenberg, D.H., C. Michalopoulos, and P.K. Robins. 2003. "A meta-analysis of government-sponsored training programs." *Industrial and Labor Relations Review* 57(1):31–53.

Groenqvist, Hans. 2011. "Youth Unemployment and Crime: New Lessons Exploring Longitudinal Register Data." Working Paper 7/2011. Swedish Institute for Social Research (SOFI).

Independent Evaluation Group (IEG). 2012a. "Project Performance Assessment Report on Colombia Higher Education Improving Access Project (HEIAP) and Chile Lifelong Learning and Training Project (LLTP) and Chile Science for the Knowledge Economy Project (SKEP)." Report No. 68251. Washington, DC: World Bank.

———. 2012b. "World Bank and IFC Support for Youth Employment Programs." Background Paper. Country Case Study: South Africa. Forthcoming.

———. 2012c. "Review of the World Bank's Economic and Sector Work on Youth Employment." Unpublished paper. Basil Kavalsky.

———. 2012d. "The Matrix System at Work: An Evaluation of the World Bank's Organizational Effectiveness." Washington, DC: World Bank.

———. 2011a. "Assessing IFC's Poverty Focus and Results." Washington, DC: World Bank.

———. 2011b. "Project Performance Assessment Report on Jordan Higher Education Development Project (HEDF) and Education Reform for Knowledge Economy Program (ERKEP)." Report No. 62732. Washington, DC: World Bank.

———. 2011c. "Project Performance Assessment Report on Technical Education Vocational and Entrepreneurship Training Development Support Program (TEVET) in Zambia." Report No. 62585. Washington, DC: World Bank.

———. 2011d. "Social Safety Nets: An Evaluation of World Bank Support, 2000-2010." Washington, DC: World Bank.

———. 2009. "Project Performance Assessment Report on Burkina Faso Post-primary Education Project." Report No. 49142. Washington, DC: World Bank.

———. 2006. "From Schooling Access to Learning Outcomes: An Unfinished Agenda. An Evaluation of World Bank Support to Primary Education." Washington DC: World Bank.

———. 2005. "Project Performance Assessment Report on Yemen Vocational Training Project (VTP)." Report No. 32593. Washington, DC: World Bank.

International Finance Corporation (IFC). 2012b. IFC Open Source Study.

International Labour Organization. (ILO). 2012. Global Employment Trends for Youth. 2011b. Update.

Middleton, John, and Terry Demsky. 1989. "Vocational Education and Training: A Review of World Bank Investment." World Bank Discussion Paper 51. Washington, DC: World Bank.

National Institute of Statistics on Rwanda, Ministry of Health, Rwanda, and ICF International. 2012. *Rwanda Demographic and Health Survey 2010.*

Organisation for Economic Co-operation and Development (OECD). 2008. Employment Outlook, Paris. France.

Verspoor, Adriaan. 2008. At the crossroads: choices for secondary education in Sub-Saharan Africa. Africa Region Human Development Department. Washington DC.:World Bank.

World Bank Operations Evaluation Department (OED). 2004a. "Primary Education Portfolio Review." OED Working Paper Series.

———. 2004b. "Rationales and Results in Secondary Education Investments: A Review of the World Bank's Portfolio 1990–2001." OED Working Paper Series.

———. 2002. "Tertiary Education: Lessons from a Decade of Lending, FY1990–2000." OED Working Paper Series.

World Bank. 2011a. "The Job Crisis. Household and Government Responses to the Great Recession in Eastern Europe and Central Asia." Human Development ECA. Washington, DC.

————. 2011b. *Migration and Remittances Factbook 2011*. Washington, DC.

————. 2009. "Morocco: Country Partnership Strategy for the Kingdom of Morocco for the Period FY10–13." Report No. 50316-MA. Washington, D.C.: World Bank.

————. 2008a. Czech Republic Improving Employment Chances of the Roma. Human Development Sector Unit Europe and Central Asia. Washington, D.C.

————. 2008b. "Governance, Management, and Accountability in Secondary Education in Sub-Saharan Africa." Policy Research Working Paper No. 4721. Poverty Reduction and Economic Management Department, Africa Region. Washington, D.C.

————. 2008c. Institutions and Labor Market Outcomes in Sub-Saharan Africa. World Bank Working Paper No. 127. Human Development, Africa Region. Washington, D.C

————. 2006. Meeting the Challenges of Secondary Education in Latin America and East Asia: Improving Efficiency and Resource Mobilization. Washington, DC.

Xu, B. 2000. "Multinational enterprises, technology diffusion, and host country productivity growth." *Journal of Development Economics* 62: 477–493.

www.ingramcontent.com/pod-product-compliance
Lightning Source LLC
Chambersburg PA
CBHW080610270326
41928CB00016B/2997